AMERICAN WOMEN

images and realities

AMERICAN WOMEN
Images and Realities

Advisory Editors
ANNETTE K. BAXTER
LEON STEIN

A Note About This Volume

Eliza Leslie's (1787-1858) youthful literary ambitions found varied fulfillment. But in 1828 she produced a bestseller—a book of 75 recipes she had learned at Mrs. Goodfellow's Philadelphia cooking school. While her juvenile stories, game books and magazine sketches met with regular success, she achieved her greatest readership with cook books—*The Domestic Cookery Book* reaching 38 editions by 1851. She quickly expanded into the fields of domestic economy and personal etiquette. Generations of American women not only cooked as she said they should, they also behaved as this grand dame told them to behave.

MISS LESLIE'S

BEHAVIOUR BOOK

A GUIDE AND MANUAL FOR LADIES

[Eliza] Leslie

ARNO PRESS

A New York Times Company
New York • 1972

Reprint Edition 1972 by Arno Press Inc.

American Women: Images and Realities
ISBN for complete set: 0-405-04445-3
See last pages of this volume for titles.

Manufactured in the United States of America

- - - - - - - - - - - - -

Library of Congress Cataloging in Publication Data

Leslie, Eliza, 1787-1858.
  Miss Leslie's behaviour book.

  (American women: images and realities)
  Reprint of the 1859 ed.
  1. Etiquette for women. I. Title. II. Series.
BJ1856.L47 1972   395'.1'233   72-2611
ISBN 0-405-04465-8

MISS LESLIE'S

BEHAVIOUR BOOK.

A GUIDE AND MANUAL FOR LADIES

AS REGARDS THEIR

CONVERSATION; MANNERS; DRESS; INTRODUCTIONS; ENTREE TO SOCIETY;
SHOPPING; CONDUCT IN THE STREET; AT PLACES OF AMUSEMENT; IN
TRAVELING; AT THE TABLE, EITHER AT HOME, IN COMPANY, OR
AT HOTELS; DEPORTMENT IN GENTLEMEN'S SOCIETY; LIPS;
COMPLEXION; TEETH; HANDS; THE HAIR; ETC., ETC.

WITH FULL INSTRUCTIONS AND ADVICE IN

LETTER WRITTING; RECEIVING PRESENTS; INCORRECT WORDS; BORROWING;
OBLIGATIONS TO GENTLEMEN; OFFENCES; CHILDREN; DECORUM IN CHURCH;
AT EVENING PARTIES; AND FULL SUGGESTIONS IN BAD PRACTICES
AND HABITS EASILY CONTRACTED, WHICH NO YOUNG
LADY SHOULD BE GUILTY OF, ETC., ETC.

BY MISS LESLIE

AUTHORESS OF "MISS LESLIE'S CELEBRATED NEW COOKERY BOOK,"
"MISS LESLIE'S NEW RECEIPTS FOR COOKING," ETC.

Philadelphia:
T. B. PETERSON AND BROTHERS,
306 CHESTNUT STREET.

PREFACE.

It is said that soon after the publication of Nicholas Nickleby, not fewer than six Yorkshire schoolmasters (or rather six principals of Yorkshire institutes) took journeys to London, with the express purpose of prosecuting Dickens for libels—"each one and severally" considering himself shown up to the world as Mr. Squeers of Dotheboys Hall.

Now, if Dickens had drawn as graphic a picture of Dothe*girls* Hall, we firmly believe that none of the lady principals of similar institutes would have committed themselves by evincing so little tact, and adopting such impolitic proceedings. They would wisely have held back from all appropriation of the obnoxious character, and passed it over unnoticed; as if it could not possibly have the slightest reference to *them.*

5

Therefore we wish that those of our fair readers whom certain hints in the following pages may awaken to the consciousness of a few habitual misbehavements, (of which they were not previously aware,) should pause, and reflect, before they allow themselves to " take umbrage too much." Let them keep in mind that the purpose of the writer is to amend, and not to offend; to improve her young country-women, and not to annoy them. It is with this view only that she has been induced to " set down in a note-book" such lapses from *les bienséances* as she has remarked during a long course of observation, and on a very diversified field.

She trusts that her readers will peruse this book in as friendly a spirit as it was written.

ELIZA LESLIE.

CONTENTS.

MISS LESLIE'S

BEHAVIOUR BOOK.

CHAPTER I.

SUGGESTIONS TO VISITERS.

An amusing writer of the last century, justly complains of the want of definite words to express, distinctly and unmistakably, the different degrees of visits, with reference to their length. Whether the stay of the guest comprises ten minutes, an hour, an evening, a day, a week, or a month, still it goes under the vague and general term of a visit.

We propose, humourously, that if the stay of the guest exceeds a week, it should be called "a visitation." If it includes a dining, or a tea-drinking, or evening-spending, it may be termed "a visit;" while a mere call can be mentioned as "a vis."

The idea is a very convenient one, and we should like to see it carried out by general adoption. Meanwhile, we must, for the present, be contented with the old uncertain practice of saying only "visit" and "visiter." We think it our duty to explain that this chapter is designed for the benefit of such inexperienced females as may be about to engage in what we should like to call "a visitation."

To begin at the beginning:—

Do not *volunteer* a visit to a friend in the country, or in another town, unless you have had what is called "a standing invitation," with every reason to believe that it was sincerely and cordially given. Many invitations are mere "words of course," without meaning or motive, designed only to make a show of politeness, and not intended to be taken literally, or ever acted upon. Even when convinced that your friend is really your friend, that she truly loves you, has invited you in all sincerity, and will be happy in your society, still, it is best to apprize her, duly, of the exact day and hour when she may expect you; always with the proviso that it is convenient to herself to receive you at that time, and desiring her to let you know, candidly, if it is not. However close your intimacy, an unexpected arrival may possibly produce inconvenience to your hostess; particularly if her family is numerous, or her bedchambers few. The case is somewhat different, where the house is large, and where there is no scarcity of apartments for guests, of servants to wait on them, or of money to furnish the means of entertaining them liberally. But even then, the time of arrival should be previously intimated, and observed as punctually as possible. Such are now the facilities of travelling, and the rapidity of transmitting intelligence, that there is no excuse for unexpected or ill-timed visits; and when unexpected, they are too frequently ill-timed. When attempted as "agreeable surprises," they are seldom

very agreeable to the surprised. Also the improvement in manners has rendered these incursions old-
fashioned and ungenteel. Above all, never volunteer
visits to families whose circumstances are so narrow
that they can ill afford the expense of a guest.

Having received an invitation, reply to it immediately; and do not keep your friends waiting, day
after day, in uncertainty whether you mean to accept
or decline it; causing them, perhaps, to delay asking
other visiters till they have ascertained if you are to
be expected or not.

Excuse yourself from accepting invitations from
persons whom you do not like, and whose dispositions,
habits, feelings, and opinions are in most things the
reverse of your own. There can be no pleasure in
daily and familiar intercourse where there is no congeniality. Such visits never end well; and they sometimes produce irreconcilable quarrels, or at least a
lasting and ill-concealed coolness. Though for years
you may have always met on decent terms, you may
become positive enemies from living a short time under
the same roof; and there is something dishonourable
in laying yourself under obligations and receiving
civilities from persons whom you secretly dislike, and
in whose society you can have little or no enjoyment.

When you arrive, take occasion to mention how
long you intend to stay; that your hostess may plan
her arrangements accordingly. It is rude and inconsiderate to keep her in ignorance of the probable
duration of your visit. And when the allotted time
has expired, do not be persuaded to extend it farther,

unless you are earnestly, and with undoubted sincerity invited to do so. It is much better that your friends should part with you reluctantly, than you should give them reason to wish your visit shorter. Even if it *has* been very pleasant on both sides, it may not continue so if prolonged too far. Take care of wearing out your welcome. Besides, your room may be wanted for another guest.

On your first evening, enquire the hours of the house, that you may always be ready to comply with them. Rise early enough to be washed and dressed in time for breakfast; but if you are ready too early, remain in your own apartment, or walk about the garden, or go to the library till the cleaning and arranging of the sitting-room has been completed. Meanwhile, you can occupy yourself with a book, if you stay in your own room.

As soon as you quit your bed, take off the bed-clothes, (each article separately,) and spread them widely over the chairs, turning the mattrass or bed as far down as it will go. This will give the bedding time to air; and in all houses it should be done every morning, the whole year round. Before you leave the room, raise the windows as high as they will go, (unless it should be raining, or snowing,) that the apartment may be well ventilated. Fortunate are those who have been accustomed to sleeping always with the sash more or less open, according to the weather, or the season. Their health will be much the better for the excellent practice of constantly admitting fresh air into their sleeping-room. See Dr.

Franklin's essay on the "Art of Sleeping well." Mr. Combe, who has written copiously on this subject, says it not only improves the health, but the complexion; and that ladies who follow this practice continue to look young long after those who sleep in close rooms have faded and shrivelled. Except in a very unhealthy climate, or in the neighbourhood of marshes, no external air can be so unwholesome, or productive of such baneful effects on the constitution, as the same air breathed over and over again in a close room, and returning continually to the lungs, till before morning it becomes unfit to be breathed at all. Sleeping with the windows closed in a room newly painted has produced fatal diseases. To some lungs the vapour of white lead is poisonous. To none is it quite innoxious. Its dangerous properties may be neutralized by placing in newly-painted rooms, large tubs of water, into each of which has been mixed an ounce of vitriol. The tubs must be set near the walls, and the water and vitriol renewed every day. The introduction of zinc-paint promises to put that of white lead out of use; as zinc is quite as cheap, and not at all pernicious to health.

At sleeping hours the air of a bedroom should be perfectly free from all scents, either pleasant or otherwise. Many persons cannot sleep with flowers in their chamber, or with any sort of perfume. It is best not.

If when on a visit, you find that the chambermaid does not make your bed so that you can sleep comfortably, show her how to do it, (privately,) but say nothing to your hostess. There is but one way of making a bed properly; and yet it is surprising how little that way is known or remembered. First, shake up the bed high and evenly; turning it over, and see that the foot is not higher than the head. If there is a mattrass above the bed, turn the mattrass half up, and then half down, till you have shaken up the bed beneath. Next spread on the under-sheet, laying it well over the bolster to secure it from dragging down and getting under the shoulders. However, to most beds now, there is a bolster-case. Then tuck in the under-sheet, well, at both sides, to prevent its getting loose and disordered in the night. For the same reason tuck in the upper-sheet, well, at the foot, leaving the sides loose. Tuck in the blankets at bottom, but not at the sides. Lay the counterpane smoothly over the whole. Turn it down at the top; and turn down the upper-sheet above it, so as to conceal the blankets entirely.

Should the chambermaid neglect your room, or be remiss in filling your pitchers, or in furnishing you with clean towels, speak to her on the subject when alone. She will hardly, for her own sake, inform her mistress that you have had occasion to find fault with her; unless she is very insolent or sulky, she will say she is sorry, and will promise to do better in future. Complaining to her mistress of these neglects will probably give offence to the lady, who may be of that wayward (though too common) disposition which will allow no one except herself, to find any deficiency in *her* servants. As mistresses are frequently very touchy on these points, your hostess may hint that your statement is incredible, and that "no one ever complained before." Above all things, avoid letting her know that you have found or felt insects in your bed; a circumstance that may chance sometimes to happen even in the best kept houses. In a warm climate, or in an old house, the utmost care and the most vigilant neatness cannot always prevent it. It may be caused by the bringing of baggage from boats, or ships, and by servants neglecting their own beds; a too common practice with them, unless the mistress or her housekeeper compels them to be cleanly, and sees that they are so.

If you have proof positive that your bed is not free from these intolerable nuisances, confide this fact to the chambermaid only, and desire her to attend to it speedily. She will do so the more readily, if you promise her a reward in case of complete success. Enjoining her to manage this as quietly as possible, and to say nothing about it to any one, may spare you a scene with your hostess; who, though you have always regarded her as your warm friend, may, notwithstanding, become your enemy for life, in consequence of your having presumed to be incommoded in *her* house, where "nobody ever complained before." A well-bred, sensible, good-tempered woman will not, of course, take offence for such a cause; and will believe that there must have been good reason for the complaint, rather than suppose that her guest and her friend would mention so delicate a subject even to a servant, unless there was positive proof. And she will rightly think it was well to make it known, and have it immediately remedied. But all women who invite friends to visit them, are not sensible and good-tempered. Therefore, take care.

For similar reasons, should a servant purloin any article belonging to you, (and servants, considered quite honest, will sometimes pilfer from a visiter when they would not dare to do so from their mistress,) it is safest to pass it over, unless the article stolen is of consequence. You may find your hostess very un-willing to believe that a servant of *hers* could possibly be dishonest; and much may be said, or evidently *thought*, that will be very painful to you, her guest.

Notwithstanding all that may be said to you about "feeling yourself perfectly at home," and "considering your friend's house as your own," be very careful not literally to do so. In fact, it is impossible you *should* with any propriety—particularly, if it is your first visit. You cannot possibly know the real character and disposition of any acquaintance, till after you have had some experience in living under the same roof. If you find your hostess all that you can desire, and that she is making your visit every way agreeable, be very grateful to her, and let her understand that you are exceedingly happy at her house; but avoid staying too long, or taxing her kindness too highly.

Avoid encroaching unreasonably upon her time. Expect her not to devote an undue portion of it to you. She will probably be engaged in the superin-tendence of household affairs, or in the care of her young children, for two or three hours after breakfast. So at these hours do not intrude upon her,—but amuse yourself with some occupation of your own, till you see that it is convenient to the family for you to join them in the sitting-room. In summer afternoons, retire for an hour or more, soon after dinner, to your own apartment, that you may give your friends an opportunity of taking their naps, and that you may do the same yourself. You will be brighter in the evening, from indulging in this practice; and less likely to feel sleepy, when you ought to be wide awake, and ready to assist in entertaining your entertainers. A silent visiter, whether silent from dulness or indolence, or a habit of taciturnity, is never an agreeable one.

Yet, however pleasant the conversation, have sufficient self-denial to break off in seasonable time, so as not to keep the family up by continuing in the parlour till a late hour. Some of them may be tired and sleepy, though you are not. And between ten and eleven o'clock it is well to retire.

If you have shopping to do, and are acquainted with the town, you can be under no necessity of imposing on any lady of the family the task of accompanying you. To shop *for* others, or *with* others, is a most irksome fatigue. Even when a stranger in the place, you can easily, by enquiring of the family, learn where the best stores are to be found, and go to them by yourself.

While you are a guest at the house of a friend, do not pass too much of your time in visiting at *other* houses, unless she is with you. You have no right to avail yourself of the conveniences of eating and sleeping at her mansion, without giving her and her family the largest portion of your company.

While a guest yourself, it is taking an unwarrantable liberty to invite any of your friends or relatives to come there and spend a day or days.*

Refrain from visiting any person with whom your hostess is at enmity, even if that person has been one of your own intimate friends. You will in all probability be regarded as "a spy in the camp." There is nothing so difficult as to observe a strict neutrality; and on hearing both sides, it is scarcely possible not to lean more to the one than to the other. The friend whose hospitality you are enjoying will soon begin to look coldly upon you, if she finds you seeking the society of her enemy; and she may evince that coldness whenever you come home from these visits. However unjust her suspicions, it is too probable she may begin to think that you are drawn in to make her, and her house, and family, subjects of conversation when visiting her adversary; therefore, she will cease to feel kindly toward you. If you understand, soon after your arrival, that there is no probability of a reconciliation, send at once a concise note to the lady with whom your hostess is at variance; express your regret at the circumstance, and excuse yourself from visiting her while you remain in your present residence. This note should be polite, short, and decisive, and so worded as to give no offence to either side; for, before

* So it is to order the carriage without first asking permission of your hostess.

sending, it is proper for you to show it, while yet unsealed, to the friend with whom you are staying And then let the correspondence be carried no further The lady to whom it is addressed, will, of course, return a polite answer; such as you may show to your hostess.

It is to be presumed, she will not be so lost to all delicacy and propriety, as to intrude herself into the house of her enemy for the purpose of visiting you. But, if she does, it is your place civilly to decline seeing her. A slight coolness, a mere offence on a point of etiquette, which, if let alone, would die out like a tinder-spark, has been fanned, and blown into a flame by the go-betweening of a so-called *mutual friend*. We repeat, while you are a visiter at a house, hold no intercourse with any foe of that house. It is unkind and disrespectful to the family with whom you are staying, and very unsafe for yourself.

If you know that your friends are hurried with their sewing, or with preparations for company, offer to assist them, as far as you can. But if you are conscious of an incapacity to do such things well, it is better to excuse yourself by candidly saying so, than to attempt them and spoil them. At the same time, express your willingness to learn, if permitted. And you *may* learn, while staying at the house of a clever, notable friend, many things that you have hitherto had no opportunity of acquiring.

When called on by any of your own acquaintances, they will not expect you to ask them to stay to tea,

2

or to dinner. That is the business of your hostess—
not yours.

If you are a young lady that has beaux, remember
that you have no right to encourage the over-fre-
quency of their visits in any house that is not your
home, or to devote much of your time and attention
to flirtation with them. Above all, avoid introducing
to the family of your entertainers, young men whom
they are likely in any respect to disapprove. No
stranger who has the feelings of a gentleman, will
make a *second* visit to any house unless he is invited
by the head of the family, and he will take care that
his visits shall not begin too early, or continue too
late. However delightful he may find the society of
his lady-fair, he has no right to incommode the family
with whom she is staying, by prolonging his visits to
an unseasonable hour. If he seems inclined to do so,
there is nothing amiss in his fair-one herself hinting
to him that it is past ten o'clock. Also, there should
be "a temperance" even in his morning calls. It is
rude in a young lady and gentleman to monopolize
one of the parlours nearly all the forenoon—even if
they are *really* courting—still more if they are only
pretending to court; for instance, sitting close to each
other, and whispering on subjects that might be dis-
cussed aloud before the whole house, and talked of
across the room.

Young ladies noted for abounding in beaux, are
generally rather inconvenient visiters; except in very
spacious houses, and in gay, idle families. They
should not take the liberty of inviting the said beaux

to stay to dinner or to tea. Leave that civility to the head of the house,—without whose invitation no *gentleman* ought to remain.

It is proper for visiters to put out and pay for their own washing, ironing, &c. Therefore, carry among your baggage two clothes-bags; one to be taken away by the laundress, the other to receive your clothes in the interval. You may always hear of a washerwoman, by enquiring of the servants of the house.

On no consideration question the servants, or talk to them about the family, particularly if they are slaves.

Take with you a small writing-case, containing whatever stationery you may be likely to want during your visit; including post-office stamps. Thus you will spare yourself, and spare the family, the inconvenience of applying to them whenever you have occasion for pen, ink, paper, &c. If you have no ink with you, the first time you go out, stop in at a stationer's store, and buy a small sixpenny bottle that will stand steadily alone, and answer the purpose of an inkstand. Also, take care to be well supplied with all sorts of sewing articles. There are young ladies who go from home on long visits, quite unprovided with even thimbles and scissors; depending all the time on borrowing. Many visiters, though very agreeable in great things, are exceedingly troublesome in little ones.

Take care not to slop your washing-stand, or to lay a piece of wet soap upon it. Spread your wet towels carefully on the towel-rail. See that your trunks are not placed so near the wall as to injure the paper or paint when the lid is thrown back.

If, when travelling, you are to stop but one night at the house of a friend, it is not necessary, for that one night, to have *all* your baggage carried up-stairs, particularly if your trunks are large or heavy. Before leaving home, put into your carpet-bag all the things you will require for that night; and then no other article of your baggage need be taken up to your chamber. They can be left down-stairs, in some safe and convenient place, which your hostess will designate. This will save much trouble, and preclude all the injury that may otherwise accrue to the banisters and staircase-wall, by the corners of trunks knocking against them. It is possible to put into a carpet-satchel (that can be carried in your own hand) a night-gown and night-cap, (tightly rolled,) with hair-brush, combs, tooth-brush, &c. It is surprising how much these hand-satchels may be made to contain, when packed closely. No lady or gentleman should travel without one. In going from home for one night only, a satchel is, frequently, all that is requisite.

On concluding your visit, tell your entertainers that it has been pleasant, and express your gratitude for the kindness you have received from them, and your hope that they will give you an opportunity of returning their civilities. Give a parting gratuity to each of the servants—the sum being according to your means, and to the length of your visit.

Give this to each servant *with your own hands*, going to them for the purpose. Do not tempt their integrity, by intrusting (for instance) to the chambermaid the fee intended for the cook. She may dishonestly keep it to herself, and make the cook believe that you were "so mean as to go away without leaving any thing at all for her." Such things have happened, as we know. Therefore, give all your fees in person.

After you get home, write very soon (within two or three days) to the friend at whose house you have been staying, tell her of your journey, &c., and allude to your visit as having been very agreeable.

The visit over, be of all things careful not to repeat any thing that has come to your knowledge in consequence, and which your entertainers would wish to remain unknown. While inmates of their house, you may have unavoidably become acquainted with some particulars of their way of living not generally known, and which, perhaps, would not raise them in public estimation, if disclosed. Having been their guest, and partaken of their hospitality, you are bound in honour to keep silent on every topic that would injure them in the smallest degree, if repeated. Unhappily, there are ladies so lost to shame, as, after making a long visit, to retail for the amusement of their cronies, all sorts of invidious anecdotes concerning the family at whose house they have been staying; adding by way of corroboration—"I assure you this is all true, for I stayed five or six weeks at their house, and had a good chance of knowing." More shame then to tell it!

Whatever painful discoveries are made during a visit, should be kept as closely secret as if secrecy was enjoined by oath. It is not sufficient to refrain from "mentioning names." No clue should be given that could possibly enable the hearers even to hazard a guess.

CHAPTER II.

THE VISITED.

HAVING invited a friend to pass a few days or weeks at your house, and expecting her at a certain time, send a carriage to meet her at the rail-road depôt or the steam-boat wharf, and if her host or hostess goes in it, so much the better; but do not take the children along, crowding the vehicle, for the sake of giving them a ride. Arriving at your house, have her baggage taken at once to the apartment prepared for her, and when she goes up-stairs, send a servant with her to unstrap her trunks. Then let her be left *alone* to arrange her dress. It is to be supposed that before her arrival, the mistress of the house has inspected the chamber of her guest, to see that all is right—that there are *two* pitchers full of fresh water on the stand, and three towels on the rail, (two fine and one coarse,) with a china mug for teeth-cleaning, and a tumbler to drink from; a slop jar of course, and a foot-bath. We conclude that in all

genteel and well-furnished houses, none of these articles are wanting in every bedroom. On the mantel-
piece a candle or lamp, with a box of lucifer matches
beside it — the candle to be replaced by a new one
every morning when the chambermaid arranges the
room—or the lamp to be trimmed daily; so that the
visiter may have a light at hand whenever she pleases,
without ringing the bell and waiting till a servant
brings one up.

By-the-bye, when a guest is expected, see previously
that the bells and locks of her room are in order; and
if they are not, have them repaired.

If it is cold weather, let her find a good fire in her
room; and the shutters open, that she may have sufficient light. Also an extra blanket, folded, and laid
on the foot of the bed. If summer, let the sashes be
raised, and the shutters bowed. The room should
have an easy chair with a heavy foot-cushion before
it,—a low chair also, to sit on when shoes and stockings are to be changed, and feet washed. In a spare
chamber there should be both a mattrass and a
feather-bed, that your visiters may choose which
they will have uppermost. Though you and all your
own family may like to sleep hard, your guests may
find it difficult to sleep at all on a mattrass with a
paillasse under it. To many constitutions hard sleeping is not only intolerable, but pernicious to health.

Let the centre-table be furnished with a writing-
case well supplied with all that is necessary, the inkstand filled, and with *good black ink;* and some sneets
of letter-paper and note-paper laid near it. Also,

some books, such as you think your friend will like. Let her find, at least, one bureau vacant; *all* the drawers empty, so that she may be able to unpack her muslins, &c., and arrange them at once. The same with the wardrobe or commode, so that she may have space to hang up her dresses—the press-closet, likewise, should be for her use while she stays.

By giving up the spare bedroom *entirely* to your visiter you will very much oblige her, and preclude the necessity of disturbing or interrupting her by coming in to get something out of drawers, closets, &c.

Every morning, after the chambermaid has done her duty, (the room of the visiter is the first to be put in order,) the hostess should go in to see that all is right. This done, no further inspection is necessary for that day. There are ladies who, when a friend is staying with them, are continually slipping into her chamber when she is out of it, to see if the guest has done nothing amiss—such as moving a chair to suit her own convenience, or opening a shutter to let in more light, at the possible risk of hastening imperceptibly the fading of the carpet. There are families who condemn themselves to a perpetual twilight, by living in the dimness of closed shutters, to the great injury of their eyes. And this is endured to retard awhile the fading of furniture too showy for comfort. We have seen staircase-windows kept always shut and bolted, (so that visiters had to grope their way in darkness,) lest the small portion of stair-carpet just beneath the window should fade before the rest.

It is not pleasant to be a guest in a house where

you perceive that your hostess is continually and fretfully on the watch, lest some almost imperceptible injury should accrue to the furniture. We have known ladies who were always uneasy when their visiters sat down on a sofa or an ottoman, and could not forbear inviting them to change their seats and take chairs. We suppose the fear was that the more the damask-covered seats were used, the sooner they would wear out. Let no visiter be so rash as to sit on a pier-divan with her back near a mirror. The danger is imminent—not only of breaking the glass by inadvertently leaning against it, but of certainly fretting its owner, with uneasiness, all the time. Children should be positively interdicted taking these precarious seats.

It is very kind and considerate to enquire of your guest if there is any d.sh, or article of food that she particularly likes, so that you may have it on the table while she stays; and also, if there is any thing peculiarly disagreeable to her, so that you may refrain from having it during her visit. A well-bred and sensible woman will not encroach upon your kindness, or take an undue advantage of it, in this respect or any other.

For such deficiencies as may be avoided or remedied, refrain from making the foolish apology that you consider her "no stranger"—and that you regard her "just as one of the family." If you invite her at all, it is your duty, for your own sake as well as hers, to treat her well in every thing. You will lose nothing by doing so.

If she desires to assist you in sewing, and has brought no work of her own, you may avail yourself of her offer, and employ her in moderation—but let it be in moderation only, and when sitting in the family circle. When alone in her own room, she, of course, would much rather read, write, or occupy herself in some way for her own benefit, or amusement. There are ladies who seem to expect that their guests should perform as much work as hired seamstresses.

Let the children be strictly forbidden to run into the apartments of visiters. Interdict them from going thither, unless sent with a message; and then let them be made to understand that they are always to knock at the door, and not go in till desired to do so. Also, that they are not to play and make a noise in the neighbourhood of her room. And when she comes into the parlour, that they are not to jump on her lap, put their hands into her pockets, or rummage her work-basket, or rumple and soil her dress by clinging to it with their hands. Neither should they be permitted to amuse themselves by rattling on the lower keys when she is playing on the piano, or interrupt her by teazing her all the time to play "for them to dance." All this we have seen, and the mothers have never checked it. To permit children to ask visiters for pennies or sixpences is mean and contemptible. And, if money *is* given them by a guest, they should be made to return it immediately.

Enquire on the first evening, if your visiter is accustomed to taking any refreshment before she retires for the night. If she is, have something sent up to her room every night, unless your own family are in the same habit. Then let sufficient for all be brought into the parlour. These little repasts are very pleasant, especially at the close of a long winter evening, and after coming home from a place of public amusement.

To "welcome the coming — speed the parting guest"— is a good maxim. So when your visiter is about to leave you, make all smooth and convenient for her departure. Let her be called up at an early hour, if she is to set out in the morning. Send a servant up to strap and bring down her trunks, as soon as she has announced that they are ready ; and see that an early breakfast is prepared for her, and some of the family up and dressed to share it with her. Slip some cakes into her satchel for her to eat on the road, in case, by some chance, she should not reach the end of her journey at the usual hour. Have a carriage at the door in due time, and let some male member of the family accompany her to the starting-place and see her off, attending to her baggage and procuring her tickets.

CHAPTER III.

TEA VISITERS.

WHEN you have invited a friend to take tea with you, endeavour to render her visit as agreeable as you can; and try by all means *to make her comfortable.* See that your lamps are lighted at an early hour, particularly those of the entry and stair-case, those parts of the house always becoming dark as soon as the sun is down; and to persons coming in directly from the light of the open air, they always seem darker than they really are. Have the parlours lighted rather earlier than usual, that your guest, on her entrance, may be in no danger of running against the tables, or stumbling over chairs. In rooms heated by a furnace, or by any other invisible fire, it is still more necessary to have the lamps lighted early.

If there is a coal-grate, see that the fire is burning clear and brightly, that the bottom has been well-raked of cinders and ashes, and the hearth swept clean. A dull fire, half-choked with dead cinders, and an ashy hearth, give a slovenly and dreary aspect to the most elegantly furnished parlour. A sufficiently large grate (if the fire is well made up, and plenty of fresh coal put on about six o'clock) will generally require no further replenishing during the evening,

unless the weather is unusually cold; and then more
fuel should be added at eight or nine o'clock, so as to
make the room comfortable.

In summer evenings, let the window-sashes be kept
up, or the slats of the venitian blinds turned open, so
that your guest may find the atmosphere of the rooms
cool and pleasant. There should always be fans
(feather or palm-leaf) on the centre-tables.

The domestic that attends the door should be
instructed to show the guest up-stairs, as soon as she
arrives; conducting her to an unoccupied apartment,
where she may take off her bonnet, and arrange her
hair, or any part of her dress that may require change
or improvement. The lady should then be left to
herself. Nothing is polite that can possibly incommode or embarrass—therefore, it is a mistaken civility
for the hostess, or some female member of the family
to follow the visiter up-stairs, and remain with her all
the time she is preparing for her appearance in the
parlour. We have seen an inquisitive little girl permitted by her mother to accompany a guest to the
dressing-table, and watch her all the while she was at
the glass; even following her to the corner in which
she changed her shoes; the child talking, and asking
questions incessantly. This should not be. Let both
mothers and children understand that, on all occasions,
over-officiousness is not politeness, and that nothing
troublesome and inconvenient is ever agreeable.

The toilet-table should be always furnished with a
clean hair-brush, and a nice comb. We recommend
those hair-brushes that have a mirror on the back, so

as to afford the lady a glimpse of the back of her head and neck. Better still, as an appendage to a dressing-table, is a regular hand-mirror, of sufficient size to allow a really *satisfactory* view. These hand-mirrors are very convenient, to be used in conjunction with the large dressing-glass. Their cost is but trifling. The toilet-pincushion should always have pins in it. A small work-box properly furnished with needles, scissors, thimble, and cotton-spools, ought also to find a place on the dressing-table, in case the visiter may have occasion to repair any accident that may have happened to her dress.

For want of proper attention to such things, in an ill-ordered, though perhaps a very showy establishment, we have known an *expected* visiter ushered first into a dark entry, then shown into a dark parlour with an ashy hearth, and the fire nearly out: then, after groping her way to a seat, obliged to wait till a small hand-lamp could be procured to light her dimly up a steep, sharp-turning stair-case; and then, by the same lamp, finding on the neglected dressing-table a broken comb, an old brush, and an empty pincushion, —or (quite as probably) nothing at all—not to mention two or three children coming to watch and stare at her. On returning to the parlour, the visiter would probably find the fire just then making up, and the lamp still unlighted, because it had first to be trimmed. Meanwhile, the guest commences her visit with an uncomfortable feeling of self-reproach for coming too early; all things denoting that she was not expected so soon. In such houses everybody comes

too early. However late, there will be nothing in readiness.

The hostess should be in the parlour, prepared to receive her visiter, and to give her at once a seat in the corner of a sofa, or in a fauteuil, or large comfortable chair; if a rocking-chair, a footstool is an indispensable appendage. By-the-bye, the dizzy and ungraceful practice of rocking in a rocking-chair is now discontinued by all genteel people, except when entirely alone. A lady should never be seen to rock in a chair, and the rocking of a gentleman looks silly. Rocking is only fit for a nurse putting a baby to sleep. When children get into a large rocking-chair, they usually rock it over backward, and fall out. These chairs are now seldom seen in a parlour. Handsome, stuffed easy chairs, that are moved on castors, are substituted—and of these, half a dozen of various forms are not considered too many.

Give your visiter a fan to cool herself, if the room is warm, or to shade her eyes from the glare of the fire or the light—for the latter purpose, a broad hand-screen is generally used, but a palm-leaf fan will do for both. In buying these fans, choose those whose handle is the firm natural stem, left remaining on the leaf. They are far better than those with handles of bamboo, which in a short time become loose and rickety.

There are many persons who, professing never to use a fan themselves, seem to think that nobody can by any chance require one; and therefore they selfishly keep nothing of the sort in their rooms.

If, in consequence of dining very late, you are in the custom of also taking tea at a late hour—or making but slight preparations for that repast—waive that custom when you expect a friend whom you know to be in the practice of dining early, and who, perhaps, has walked far enough to feel fatigued, and to acquire an appetite. For her accommodation, order the tea earlier than usual, and let it be what is called "a *good* tea." If there is ample room at table, do not have the tea carried round,—particularly if you have but one servant to hand the whole. It is tedious, inconvenient, and unsatisfactory. There is no comfortable way of eating bread and butter, toast, or buttered cakes, except when seated at table. When handed round, there is always a risk of their greasing the dresses of the ladies—the greasing of fingers is inevitable—though that is of less consequence, now that the absurd practice of eating in gloves is wisely abolished among genteel people.

Still, if the company is too numerous for all to be commodiously seated at the usual family table, and if the table cannot be enlarged—it is better to have tea carried round by *two* servants, even if an extra one is hired for the occasion, than to crowd your guests uncomfortably. One person too many will cause inconvenience to all the rest, however the hostess may try to .pass it off, by assuring the company that there is quite room enough, and that she has seen a still larger number seated round that very table. Everybody knows that "what's impossible a'n't true."

In setting a tea-table, see that there is not only

enough, but *more than enough* of cups and saucers, plates, knives and forks, spoons, napkins, &c. Let the *extra* articles be placed near the lady of the house,—to be distributed, if wanted. We have known families who had the means and the inclination to be hospitable, that never sat down to table without several spare *covers*, as the French call them, ready for accidental guests.

Unless you have domestics on whom you can implicitly rely, it is well to go into the eating-room about ten minutes before the announcement of tea, and to see that all is right; that the tea is strong and properly made, and the pot (which should be scalded twice) is not filled nearly to overflowing with a superabundance of water. The practice of drowning away all the flavour of the tea is strangely prevalent with servants; who are also very apt to neglect scalding the tea-pot; and who do not, or will not, remember that the kettle should be boiling hard at the moment the water is poured on the tea—otherwise the infusion will be insipid and tasteless, no matter how liberally the Chinese plant has been afforded.

If your cook is not *habitually* a good coffee-maker, the coffee will most probably be sent in cold, thick, and weak—for want of some previous supervision. Let it have that supervision.

We have heard of tea-tables (even in splendid establishments) being left entirely to the *mis*management of incompetent or negligent servants; so that when the company sat down, there was found a deficiency in some of the indispensable appendages;

3

such as spoons, and even forks, and napkins—butter-knives forgotten, and (worse than all) *cooking-butter* served in mistake for the better sort. By-the-bye, the use of cooking-butter should be abolished in all genteel-houses. If the butter is not good enough to eat on the surface of cold bread or on warm cakes, it is not good enough to eat in the inside of sweet cakes, or in pastry, or in any thing else; and is totally unfit to be mixed with vegetables or sauces. The use of butter is to make things taste well; if it makes them taste ill, let it be entirely omitted: for bad butter is not only unpalatable, but unwholesome. There are houses in which the money wasted on one useless bauble for the drawing-room would furnish the family with excellent fresh butter for a whole year—enough for all purposes.

We know, *by experience*, that it is possible to make very fine butter even in the State of New York, and to have it fresh in winter as in summer, though not so rich and yellow. Let the cows be well fed, well sheltered, and *kept fat* and clean—the dairy utensils always in perfect order—churning done twice or thrice every week—all the milk worked well out—and the butter will surely be good.

If cakes for tea have been made at home, and they have turned out failures, (as is often the case with home-made cakes where there is not much practice in baking them,) do not have them brought to table at all, but send to a shop and get others. It is rude to set before your guests what you know is unfit for them to eat. And heavy, tough, ill-baked things are discreditable to any house where the means of obtaining better are practicable.

In sending for cakes to a confectioner, do not *a second time* allow him to put you off with stale ones. This many confectioners are in the practice of doing, if it is passed over without notice. Stale cakes should at once be sent back, (with a proper reproof,) and fresh ones required. ·Let the confectioner with whom you deal, understand that he is *not* to palm off his stale cakes upon *you*, and that you will not keep them when sent. You will then find that fresh ones will generally be forthcoming. It is always well to send for cakes in the early part of the afternoon.

Have a pitcher of ice-water on the side-table, and a tumbler beside every plate—as most persons like to finish with a glass of water.

Do not, on sitting down to table, inform your guest that "you make no stranger of her," or that you fear she will not be able to "make out" at your plain table. These apologies are ungenteel and foolish. If your circumstances will not allow you *on any consideration* to make a little improvement in your usual family-fare, your friend is, in all probability, aware of the fact, and will not wish or expect you to incur any inconvenient expense on her account. But if you are known to possess the means of living well, you ought to do so; and to consider a good, though not an extravagantly luxurious table as a necessary part of your expenditure. There is a vast difference between laudable economy and mean economy. The latter (whether it shows itself in bad food, bad fires, bad lights, bad servants) is never excused in persons who dress extravagantly, and live surrounded by costly furniture, and who are universally known to be wealthy, and fully able to afford comfort, as well as show.

If you invite a friend to tea, in whose own family there is no gentlemen, or no man-servant, it is your duty previously to ascertain that you can provide her on that evening with an escort home; and in giving the invitation, you should tell her so, that she may know on what to depend. If you keep a carriage, it will be most kind to send her home in it.

Even if it is your rule to have the entry-lamp extinguished at a certain hour, let your servants understand that this rule must be dispensed with, as long as an evening-visiter remains in the house. Also, do not have the linen covers put on the furniture, and the house audibly shut up for the night, before she has gone. To do this is rude, because she cannot but receive it as a hint that she has staid too long.

If your visiter is obliged to go home with no other escort than your servant-man, apprize him, in time, that this duty will be expected of him; desiring that he takes care to be at hand before ten o'clock.

A lady that has no escort whose services she can command, ought not to make unexpected tea-visits. In many cases these visits produce more inconvenience than pleasure. If you wish to "take tea sociably" with a friend, inform her previously of your intention. She will then let you know if she is disengaged on that evening, or if it is in any way inconvenient to receive you; and she will herself appoint another time. Generally, it is best not to volunteer a tea-visit, but to wait till invited.

If you are engaged to take tea with an intimate friend, who assures you that you will see none but the family; and you afterward receive an invitation to join a party to a place of public amusement, which you have long been desirous of visiting, you may retract your first engagement, provided you send an apology in due time, telling the exact truth, and telling it in polite terms. Your intimate friend will then take no offence, considering it perfectly natural that you should prefer the concert, the play, or the exhibition, to a quiet evening passed at her house with no other guests. But take care to let her know as early as possible.* And be careful not to disappoint her again in a similar manner.

If you are accustomed to taking coffee in the evening, and have an insuperable dislike to tea, it is best not to make an *unexpected* visit—or at least, if you go at all, go early—so as to allow ample time for the making of coffee—a much slower process than that of tea; particularly as there may chance to be no roasted coffee in the house. Much inconvenience has been caused by the "sociable visiting" of determined coffee-drinkers. It is very easy to make green or black tea at a short notice—but not coffee.

---

* Where the city-post is to be depended on, a note can always be sent in that way.

In inviting "a few friends," which means a small select company, endeavour to assort them suitably, so as not to bring together people who have no community of tastes, feelings, and ideas. If you mix the dull and stupid with the bright and animated, the cold and formal with the frank and lively, the professedly serious with the gay and cheerful, the light with the heavy, and above all, those who pride them--selves on high birth (high birth in America?) with those who boast of "'belonging to the people," none of these "few friends" will enjoy each other's society; the evening will *not* go off agreeably, and you and the other members of your family will have the worst of it. The pleasantest people in the room will naturally congregate together, and the task of entertaining the unentertainable will devolve on yourself and your own people.

Still, it is difficult always to assort your company to your satisfaction and theirs. A very charming lady may have very dull or very silly sisters. An intelligent and refined daughter may be unfortunate in a coarse, ignorant mother, or a prosing, tiresome, purse-proud father. Some of the most delighted persons you may wish to invite, may be encumbered with relations totally incapable of adding any thing to the pleasure of the evening;—for instance, the numerous automatons, whom we must charitably believe are speechless merely from diffidence, and of whom we are told, that "if we only knew them," we should discover them, on intimate acquaintance, to be "quite intelligent people." Perhaps so. But we cannot help thinking that when a head is full of ideas, some of them will involuntarily ooze out and be manifest. Diffidence is very becoming to young people, and to those who are new to the world. But it is hardly credible that it should produce a painful taciturnity in persons who have passed from youth into maturity; and who have enjoyed the advantages of education and of living in good society. Still those who, as the French say, have "a great talent for silence," may redeem themselves from suspicion of stupidity, by listening attentively and understandingly. A good talker is never displeased with a good hearer.

We have often met with young ladies from whom it was scarcely possible for one of their own sex to extract more than a few monosyllables at long intervals; those intervals being passed in dozing, rather than in hearing. And yet, if any thing in the shape of a beau presented itself, the tongues of these "dumb belles" were immediately loosened, and the wells of their minds commenced running as glibly as possible. To be sure, the talk amounted to nothing definite; but still they *did* talk, and often became quite lively in a few minutes. Great is the power of beaux!

To return to the tea-table.—Unless you are positively sure, when you have a visiter, that she drinks the same tea that is used in your own family, you should have both black and green on the table. Either sort is often extremely disagreeable to persons who take the other. Drinkers of green tea, for instance, have generally an unconquerable aversion to black, as tasting like hay, herbs, &c., and they find in it no refreshing or exhilarating property. In some, it produces nausea. Few, on the other hand, dislike the taste of *good* green tea, but they assign as a reason for not drinking it, that it is supposed from its enlivening qualities to affect the nerves. Judge Bushrod Washington, who always drank green, and avoided black, said that, "he took tea as a beverage, not as a medicine." And there are a vast number of sensible people in the same category. If your guest is a votary of green tea, have it made for her, in time for the essence of the leaves to be well drawn forth. It is no compliment to give her green tea that is weak and washy. And do not, at your own table, be so rude as to lecture her upon the superior wholesomeness of black tea. For more than a century, green tea was universally drunk in every house, and there was then less talk of nervous diseases than during the reign of Souchong,—which, by-the-bye, is nearly exploded in the best European society.

In pouring out, do not fill the cups to the brim. Always send the cream and sugar round, that each person may use those articles according to their own taste. Also, send round a small pot of hot water, that those who like their tea weak may conveniently dilute it. If tea is handed, a servant should, at the last, carry round a water-pitcher and glasses.

Whether at dinner or tea, if yourself and family are in the habit of eating fast, (which, by the way, is a very bad and unwholesome one, and justly cited

against us by our English cousins,) and you see that
your visiter takes her food deliberately, endeavour
(for that time at least) to check the rapidity of your
own mastication, so as not to finish before she has
done, and thus compel her to hurry herself uncomfortably, or be left alone while every one round her
is sitting unoccupied and impatient. Or rather, let
the family eat a little more than usual, or seem to do
so, out of politeness to their guest.

When refreshments are brought in after tea, let
them be placed on the centre-table, and handed round
from thence by the gentlemen to the ladies. If there
are only four or five persons present, it may be more
convenient for all to sit round the table—which should
not be cleared till after all the visiters have gone,
that the things may again be offered before the departure of the guests.

If a friend makes an afternoon call, and you wish
her to stay and take tea, invite her to do so at once,
as soon as she has sat down; and do not wait till she
has risen to depart. If she consents to stay, there
will then be ample time to make any additional pre-
paration for tea that may be expedient; and she will
also know, at once, that you have no engagement for
the evening, and that she is not intruding on your
time, or preventing you from going out. If you are
intimate friends, and your guest is disposed to have a
long chat, she will do well to ask you, at the beginning, if you are disengaged, or design going out that
afternoon.

We knew a very sensible and agreeable lady in

Philadelphia, who liking better to have company at home than to go out herself, made a rule of inviting every day, half a dozen friends (not more) to take tea with her—just as many as could sit round the table, "with ample room and verge enough." These friends she assorted judiciously. And therefore she never asked a whole family at once; those who were left out understanding that they would be invited another time. For instance, she would send a note for the father and mother only—to meet another father and mother or two. A few weeks after, a billet would come for the young people only. But if there were *several* young people, some were delayed—thus—"I wish James and Eliza to take tea with me this evening, to meet so-and-so. Another time I promise myself the pleasure of Edward's company, and Mary's."

This distribution of invitations never gave offence.

Those who were honoured with the acquaintance of such a lady were not likely to be displeased at so sensible a mode of receiving them. These little tea-drinkings were always pleasant, and often delightful. The hostess was well qualified to make them so.

Though the refreshments were of the best kind, and in sufficient abundance, and the fires, lights, &c. all as they should be, there was no ostentatious display, and the ladies were dressed no more than if they were spending a quiet evening at home—party-finery being interdicted—also, such needle-work as required constant attention to every stitch.

If you have a friend who is in somewhat precarious health, and who is afraid of being out in the night air, or who lives in a distant part of the town. invite her to dinner, or to pass the day, rather than to tea. She will then be able to get home before twilight.

There is in Boston a very fashionable and very distinguished lady, who, since her return from Europe, has relinquished the custom of giving large parties; and now entertains her friends by, almost every day, having two or three to dine with her,—by invitation. These dinners are charming. The hour is according to the season—earlier in winter, later in summer—the guests departing before dark, and the lady always having the evening to herself.

We know a gentleman in Philadelphia, who every Monday has a family-dinner at his house, for all his children and grandchildren, who there meet and enjoy themselves before the eyes of the father and mother —a friend or two being also invited. Nothing can be more pleasant than to see them all there together, none staying away,—for parents, children, sons-in-law, daughters-in-law, sisters-in-law, brothers-in-law, are all at peace, and all meeting in friendship—un-happily, a rare case, where there is a large connection, and considerable wealth.

We wish that social intercourse was more frequently conducted on the plan of the few examples above cited.

Should chance-visiters come in before the family have gone to tea, let them at once be invited to partake of that repast; which they will of course decline, if they have had tea already. In a well-provided house, there can be no difficulty in adding something to the family tea-table, which, in genteel life, should never be discreditably parsimonious.

It is a very mean practice, for the members of the family to slip out of the parlour, one by one at a time, and steal away into the eating-room, to avoid inviting their visiter to accompany them. The truth is always suspected by these separate exits, and the length of absence from the parlour—and is frequently betrayed by the rattle of china, and the pervading fumes of hot cakes. How much better to meet the inconvenience (and it cannot be a great one) by decently conducting your accidental guest to the table, unless he says he has already taken tea, and will amuse himself with a book while the family are at theirs.

Casual evening visiters should avoid staying too late. Ten o'clock, in our country, is the usual time to depart, or at least to begin departing. If the visit is unduly prolonged, there may be evident signs of irrepressible drowsiness in the heads of the family, which, when perceived, will annoy the guest, who must then feel that he has stayed too long—and without being able to excuse himself with any approach to the elegance of William Spencer's apology to the charming Lady Anne Hamilton.

> Too late I stay'd—forgive the crime;
>   Unheeded flew the hours,
> For noiseless falls the foot of Time
>   That only treads on flowers.
> Ah! who with clear account remarks
>   The ebbing of the glass,
> When all its sands are diamond sparks,
>   That dazzle as they pass!

CHAPTER IV.

THE ENTRÉE.

A LADY is said to have the *entrée* of her friend's room, when she is allowed or assumes the privilege of entering it familiarly at all times, and without any previous intimation—a privilege too often abused. In many cases, the visited person has never really granted this privilege, (and after growing wise by experience, she rarely will;) but the visiter, assuming that she herself must, under all circumstances, be welcome, carries her sociability so far as to become troublesome and inconvenient. Consequently, their friendship begins to abate in its warmth. No one likes to be annoyed, or be intruded on at all hours. So the visited begins to think of the adage, "My room is my castle," and the visiter finds that seeing a friend under all circumstances somewhat diminishes respect, and that "familiarity brings contempt."

There are few occasions on which it is well, on entering a house, to run directly to the chamber of your friend, and to bolt into her room without knocking; or the very instant *after* knocking, before she has time to desire you to enter, or to make the slightest arrangement for your reception. You may find her washing, or dressing, or in bed, or even engaged in repairing clothes,—or the room may be in great disorder, or the chambermaid in the act of cleaning it. No one likes unseasonable interruptions, even from a very dear friend. That friend would be dearer still, if she had sufficient tact and consideration to refrain from causing these annoyances. Also, friendships are not always lasting—particularly those that become inordinately violent, and where both parties, by their excessive intimacy, put themselves too much into each other's power. Very mortifying disclosures are sometimes made after a quarrel, between two Hermias and Helenas, when recrimination begins to come, and mutual enmity takes the place of mutual kindness.

A familiar visit will always begin more pleasantly, if the visiter enquires of the servant at the door if the lady she wishes to see is at home, and then goes into the parlour, and stays there till she has sent her name, and ascertained that she can be received up-stairs.* Then (and not till then) let her go to her friend's room, and still remember to knock at the door before she enters. Let her have patience till her friend bids her come in, or has time to rise, cross the room, and come to open the door, if it is fastened.

It is extremely rude, on being admitted to a private apartment, to look curiously about, as if taking an inventory of all that is to be seen. We have known ladies whose eyes were all the time gazing round, and

---

* If the visiter has been properly announced, a well-trained servant will, in all probability, run up before her, and open the room-door.

even slily peering under tables, sofas, &c.; turning their heads to look after every person who chanced to be moving about the room, and giving particular attention to whatever seemed to be in disorder or out of place. Nay, we have known one who prided herself upon the gentility of her forefathers and foremothers, rise from her seat when her hostess opened a bureau-drawer, or a closet-door, and cross the room, to stand by and inspect the contents of said bureau or closet, while open—a practice very common with ill-taught *children*, but which certainly should be rebuked out of them long before they are grown up.

Make no remark upon the work in which you find your friend engaged. If she lays it aside, desire her not to quit it because of your presence; but propound no questions concerning it. Do not look over her books, and ask to borrow them. In short, meddle with nothing.

Some ladies never enter the room of an intimate friend without immediately exclaiming against its heat or its cold—seldom the latter, but very frequently the former, as it is rather fashionable to be always too warm; perhaps because it makes them seem younger. If they really are uncomfortably warm on a very cold day, we think it can only be from the glow produced by the exercise of walking. This glow must naturally subside in a few minutes, if they would sit down and wait with a little patience, or else avail themselves of the fan which ought to be at hand in every room. We have known ladies of this warm temperament, who had sufficient consideration always to carry a pocket·

fan in winter as well as summer. This ·is far better than to break out instantly with a complaint of the heat of the room, or to run and throw up a window-sash, or fling open the door, at the risk of giving cold to others. No intimacy can authorize these freedoms in a cold day, unless permission has first been asked, and sincerely granted.

If you are perfectly certain that you have· really the entrée of your friend's room, and even if she has the same of yours, you have no right ever to extend that privilege to any other person who may chance to be with you when you go to see her. It is taking an unjustifiable liberty to intrude a stranger· upon the privacy of her chamber. If another lady is with you, waive your privilege of entrée for that time, take your companion into the parlour, and send up the names of both, and do not say, "Oh! come up, come up—I am on no eeremony with her, and I am sure she will not *mind you.*" And how can you be sure? Perhaps in reality, she *will* mind her very much, and be greatly discomfited, though too polite to appear so.

There are certain unoccupied females so over-friendly as to take the entreé of the whole house. These are, generally, ultra-neighbourly neighbours, who run in at all hours of the day and evening; ferret out the ladies of the family, wherever they may be—up-stairs or down; watch all their proceedings when engaged, like good housewives, in inspecting the attics, the store-rooms, the cellars, or the kitchens. Never for a moment do they seem to suppose that their hourly visits may perhaps be inconvenient or

unseasonable; or too selfish to abate their frequency,
even when they suspect them to be so, these inveterate
sociablists make their incursions at all avenues. If
they find that the front-door is kept locked, they glide
down the area-steps, and get in through the basement.
Or else, they discover some back-entrance, by which
they can slip in at "the postern-gate"—that is, alley-
wise:—sociablists are not proud. At first, the sociablist will say, on making her third or fourth appearance for the day, "Who comes to see you oftener
than I?" But after awhile even this faint shadow of
an apology is omitted—or changed to "Nobody minds
me." She is quite domesticated in your house—an
absolute *habitué*. She sees all, hears all, knows all
your concerns. Of course she does. Her talk *to* you
is chiefly gossip, and therefore her talk *about* you is
chiefly the same. She is *au-fait* of every thing concerning your table, for after she has had her dinner
at her own home, she comes bolting into your dining-
room and "sits by," and sees you eat yours. It is
well if she does not begin with "a look in" upon you
before breakfast. She finds out everybody that
comes to your house; knows all your plans for going
to this place or that; is well acquainted with every
article that you wear; is present at the visits of all
your friends, and hears all their conversation. Her
own is usually "an infinite deal of nothing."

A sociablist is commonly what is called good-
natured, or else you would not endure her at all—and
you believe, for a time, that she really has an extraordinary liking for you. After awhile, you are unde-

4

ceived. A coolness ensues, if not a quarrel, and you are glad to find that she carries her sociability to another market, and that a new friend is now suffering all that you have experienced. To avoid the danger of being overwhelmed by the sociability of an idle neighbour, discourage the first indications of undue intimacy, by making your own visits rather few, and rather far between. A young lady of good sense, and of proper self-respect, will never be too lavish of her society; and if she has pleasant neighbours, will visit them always in moderation. And their friendship will last the longer.

CHAPTER V.

INTRODUCTIONS.

Fashion, in its various unmeaning freaks, sometimes decrees that it is not "stylish to introduce strangers." But this is a whim that, whenever attempted, has neither become general nor lasted long. It has seldom been adopted by persons of good sense and good manners—and very rarely by that fortunate class whose elevated standing in society enables them to act as they please, in throwing aside the fetters of absurd conventionalities, and who can afford to do so.

Non-introduction has been found, in many instances, to produce both inconvenience and vexation. Persons who had long known each other by reputation, and who would have rejoiced in an opportunity of becoming personally acquainted, have met in society, without being aware of it till afterward; and the opportunity has never recurred. One of our most distinguished literary Americans was seated at a dinner-party next to an European lady equally distinguished in literature; but as there were no introductions, he was not aware of her presence till the party was over and the lady gone. The lady knew who the gentleman was, and would gladly have conversed with him; but as he did not speak, because he was not introduced, she had not courage to commence—though she might have done so with perfect propriety, considering who *he* was, and who *she* was.

Still worse—from not knowing who are present, you may inadvertently fall upon a subject of conversation that, for private reasons, may be extremely irksome or painful to some of the company; for instance, in discussing a public character. Severe or mortifying remarks may unintentionally be made on the near relative, or on the intimate companion, of one whom you would on no account desire to offend. And in this way you may make enemies, where, under other circumstances, you would have made friends. In such cases, it is the duty of the hostess, or of any mutual acquaintance, immediately to introduce both parties, and thus prevent any further animadversions that may be *mal-a-propos*, or in any way annoying. It is safest, when among strangers, to refrain from bitter animadversions on anybody.

In introducing a gentleman to a lady, address *her*

first, as for instance—"Miss Smith, permit me to make you acquainted with Mr. Jones"—or, "Mrs. Farley, allow me to present Mr. Wilson"—that is, you must introduce the gentleman to the lady, rather than the lady to the gentleman. Also, if one lady is married and the other single, present the single lady to the matron, as—"Miss Thomson, let me introduce you to Mrs. Williams."*

In introducing a foreigner, it is proper to present him as "Mr. Howard from England"—"Mr. Dupont from France"—"Mr. Wenzel from Germany." If you know of what European city he is a resident, it is better still, to say that he is "from London,"— "Paris,"—"Hamburg." Likewise, in introducing one of your own countrymen very recently returned from a distant part of the world, make him known as "Mr. Davis, just from China"—"Mr. Edwards, lately from Spain"—"Mr. Gordon, recently from South America." These slight specifications are easily made; and they afford, at once, an opening for conversation between the two strangers, as it will be perfectly natural to ask "the late arrived" something about the country he has last visited, or at least about his voyage.

When presenting a member of Congress, mention the State to which he belongs, as, "Mr. Hunter of Virginia"—"Mr. Chase of Ohio," &c. Recollect that both senators and gentlemen of the house of repre-

---

* It is well to present a lady or gentleman from another city, as "Miss Ford of New York"—"Mrs. Stephens of Boston"— "Mr. Warren of New Orleans."

sentatives are members of Congress—Congress including the two legislative bodies. In introducing a
governor, designate the state he governs—as, "Governor Penington of New Jersey." For the chief
magistrate of the republic, say simply—"The President."

In introducing an officer, tell always to which service he belongs—as "Captain Turner of the Navy"—
"Captain Anderson of the Army."

We regret the custom of continuing to give military
titles to militia officers. Foreigners are justly diverted
at finding *soi-disant* generals and colonels among men
who fill very subordinate stations in civil life—men
that, however respectable in their characters, may be
deficient in the appearance, manners, or education
that should belong to a regular officer. This foolish
practice can only be done away by the militia officers
themselves (those that really are gentlemen—and
there are many) magnanimously declining to be called
generals, colonels, &c. except on parade occasions;
and when actually engaged in militia duty. Let them
omit these titles on their cards, and request that no
letters be directed to them with such superscriptions;
and that in introductions or in conversation they may
be only addressed as plain Mr. It is still more absurd
to continue these military titles long after they have
ceased to hold the office,—and above all, to persist in
them when travelling in foreign countries, tacitly
permitting it to be supposed that they own commissions
in the regular service.

English tourists (even when they know better)

make this practice a handle for pretending, in their books, that the officers of the American army are so badly paid, or so eager to make additional money, that they exercise all sorts of trades, and engage in the humblest occupations to help themselves along. They tell of seeing a captain stitching coats, a major making shoes, a colonel driving a stage, and a general selling butter in market—sneeringly representing them as regular officers of the United States army.   Is it true that we republicans have such a hankering after titles?   If so, "reform it altogether."   And let one of the first steps be to omit the "Esq." in directing a letter to an American citizen, for whom the title can have no meaning.   In England it signifies the possessor of an estate in the country, including the office of justice of peace.   In America, it means a magistrate only; who may live in a city, and own not an inch of ground anywhere.   But why should all manner of men, of all trades, and professions, expect to see an "Esq." after their name, when with reference to *them*, it can have no rational application?

An introduction should always be given in a distinct and audible voice, so that the name may be clearly understood.   The purpose is defeated, if it is murmured over in so low a tone as to be unintelligible And yet how often is this the case; for what reason it is difficult to divine.   It is usual for the introducee to repeat the name of the introduced.   This will prove that it has really been heard.   For instance, if Mrs. Smith presents Miss Brook to Miss Miles, Miss Miles immediately says, "Miss Brook"—or better still—

"Miss Brook, I am glad to meet you," or something similar. Miss Miles then begins a talk.

If you introduce yourself to a lady whom you wish to know, but who does not know *you*, address her by her name, express your desire to make her acquaintance, and then give her your card. Replying that it affords her pleasure to meet you, she will give you her hand, and commence a conversation, so as to put you quite at ease after your self-introduction.

In introducing members of your own family, always mention, audibly, the name. It is not sufficient to say "my father," or "my mother"—"my son," "my daughter"—"my brother," or "my sister." There may be more than one surname in the same family. But say, "my father, Mr. Warton,"—"my daughter, Miss Wood"—or "my daughter-in-law, Mrs. Wood"—"my sister, Miss Mary Ramsay"—"my brother, Mr. James Ramsay," &c. It is best in all these things to be explicit. The eldest daughter is usually introduced by her surname only—as "Miss Bradford" —her younger sisters, as "Miss Maria Bradford"— "Miss Harriet Bradford."

In presenting a clergyman, put the word "Reverend" before his name—unless he is a bishop, and then, of course, the word "Bishop" suffices. The head of a college-department introduce as "Professor"—and it is to them only that the title properly belongs, though arrogated by all sorts of public exhibitors, mesmerists and jugglers included.

Where the company is large, the ladies of the house should have tact enough to avoid introducing and

placing together persons who cannot possibly assimi-
late, or take pleasure in each other's society. The
dull, and the silly, will be far happier with their com-
peers. To a woman of talent, and a good conversationist, it is a cruelty to put her unnecessarily in
contact with stupid, or unmeaning people. She is
wasted and thrown away upon such as are neither
amusing nor amusable. Neither is it well to bring
together a gay, lively woman of the world, and a
solemn, serious, repulsive dame, who is a contemner
of the world and all its enjoyments. There can be no
conversation that is mutually agreeable, between a
real lady of true delicacy and refinement, and a so-
called lady whose behaviour and talk are coarse and
vulgar,—or between a woman of highly cultivated
mind, and one who is grossly ignorant of every thing
connected with books, and who boasts of that ignorance. We have heard a lady of fashion say, "Thank
God, I never read." The answer might well have
have been, "You need not tell us that."

In inviting but a small company, it is indispensable
to the pleasure of all, that you ask none who are
strikingly unsuitable to the rest—or whose presence
will throw a damp on conversation. Especially avoid
bringing into the same room, persons who are at
notorious enmity with each other, even if, unhappily,
they should be members of the same family. Those
who are known as adversaries should be invited on
different evenings.

Avoid giving invitations to bores. They will come
without.

The word "bore" has an unpleasant and an inelegant sound. Still, we have not, as yet, found any substitute that so well expresses the meaning,—which, we opine, is a dull, tiresome man, or "a weariful woman," either inveterately silent, or inordinately talkative, but never saying any thing worth hearing, or worth remembering—people whom you receive unwillingly, and whom you take leave of with joy; and who, not having perception enough to know that their visits are always unwelcome, are the most sociable visiters imaginable, and the longest stayers.

In a conversation at Abbotsford, there chanced to be something said in reference to bores—those beings in whom "man delights not, nor woman neither." Sir Walter Scott asserted, humourously, that bores were always "good respectable people." "Otherwise," said he "there could be no bores. For if they were also scoundrels or brutes, we would keep no measures with them, but at once kick them out the house, and shut the door in their faces."

When you wish an introduction to a stranger lady, apply to your hostess, or to some of the family, or to one of the guests that is acquainted with that lady: you will then be led up and presented to her. Do not expect the stranger to be brought to you; it is your place to go to her.

If you are requested by a female friend to introduce her to a distinguished gentleman, a public character, be not so ungenerous as to go *immediately* and conspicuously to inform him of the fact. But spare her delicacy, by deferring the ceremony for a while; and then take an opportunity of saying to him, "I shall be glad to make you acquainted with my friend Miss Morris. Come with me, and I will introduce you." When the introduction has thus taken place, you may with propriety leave them together to entertain each other for awhile; particularly if both parties are capable of doing so. And then, after a quarter of an hour's conversation, let the lady release the gentleman from further attendance, by bowing to him, and turning to some other acquaintance who may not be far off. She can leave *him* much more easily than he can leave *her*, and it will be better to do so in proper time, than to detain him too long. It is generally in his power to return to her before the close of the evening, and if he is pleased with her society, he will probably make an opportunity of doing so.

If he is what is called a lion, consideration for the rest of the company should admonish her not to monopolize him. But lions usually know how to get away adroitly. By-the-bye, she must not talk to him of his professional celebrity, or ask him at once for his autograph.

We saw no less a person than Charles Dickens compelled, at a large party, to devote the whole evening to writing autographs for a multitude of young ladies—many of whom, not satisfied with obtaining one of his signatures for themselves, desired half a dozen others for "absent friends." All conversation ceased with the first requisition for an autograph He had no chance of saying any thing. We were a little ashamed of our fair townswomen

Should it fall to your lot to introduce any of the English nobility, take care (before hand) to inform yourself exactly what their titles really are. Americans are liable to make sad blunders in these things. It may be well to know that a duke is the highest title of British nobility, and that his wife is a duchess. His eldest son is a marquis as long as his father lives, on whose demise the marquis becomes a duke. The wife of a marquis is a marchioness. There are a few marquises whose fathers were not dukes. The younger sons are termed Lord Henry, Lord Charles, Lord John, &c. The daughters Lady Caroline, Lady Augusta, Lady Julia. The family name is generally quite different from the title. Thus, the name of the Duke of Richmond is Lenox—that of the Duke of Rutland, Manners. The family name of the Duke of Norfolk (who ranks first of the English nobility) is Howard. The present Duke of Northumberland's name is Algernon Percy. Arthur Wellesley was that of the great Duke of Wellington. His eldest son was Marquis of Douro, and his second son Lord Charles Wellesley. The children of a marquis are called Lord Frederick, or Lord Henry, and Lady Louisa, or Lady Harriet.

The next title is viscount, as Viscount Palmerston. The next is earl, whose wife is a countess, and the children may be Lord Georges and Lady Marys.

After the viscounts come the barons, whose children are denominated the Honourable Miss, or Mr. John Singleton Copley, (whose father was Copley, the celebrated American painter,) is now Baron

Lyndhurst. His eldest daughter is the Hon. Miss Copley. In common parlance, barons are always termed lords. Some few have two titles—as Lord Say and Sele—Lord Brougham and Vaux. After William the Fourth had suddenly dissolved the parliament that held out so long against passing the reform bill, and the king, appointing a new cabinet, had placed Lord Brougham at the head of the ministry, a ridiculous comic song came out at one of the minor theatres, implying that now his majesty has swept out the whole parliament, "he takes up his broom and valks," (Brougham and Vaux.)

When the widow of a nobleman marries a man who has no title, she always retains hers. Thus when the widow of the Earl of Mansfield married Colonel Greville, (a nephew of the Earl of Warwick,)—on their door-plate the names were—"The Countess Dowager of Mansfield, and the Hon. Colonel Greville,"—a rather long inscription. A nobleman's daughter marrying a commoner, retains her original title of Lady, but takes his surname—thus, Lady Charlotte Campbell, whose father was Duke of Argyle, became, on her marriage with Dr. Bury, a clergyman, Lady Charlotte Bury. It will be understood that if a nobleman's daughter marries a nobleman, her title merges in his—but if she marries a commoner, she retains what title she had originally—her husband, of course, obtaining no rank by his marriage.

The title of a baronet is Sir—as Sir Francis Burdett, Sir Walter Scott. His children are Mr. and Miss, without any "Hon." affixed to their names.

Baronets are a grade below barons, but the title is hereditary, descending to the eldest son or next male heir. In directing to a baronet, put "Bart." after his name. A knight is also called Sir, as Sir Thomas Lawrence, Sir Edwin Landseer, &c.; but his title being only for life, dies with him.* It is always conferred by the sovereign touching his shoulder with a sword, and saying, for instance, "Rise up, Sir Francis Chantry." In writing to a knight, put "Knt." The wives of both baronets and knights are called Lady. The wife of Sir John Franklin (who was knighted) is Lady Franklin—not Lady *Jane* Franklin, as has been erroneously supposed. She could not be Lady Jane unless her father was a nobleman.

A nobleman always signs his title only, without designating his exact rank—the Duke of Athol signing himself "Athol"—the Duke of Bedford, "Bedford" —the Marquis of Granby, "Granby"—the Earl of Chesterfield, "Chesterfield," &c. The wives of peers give their Christian name with their title—as Isabella Buccleuch—Margaret Northampton—Elizabeth Derby, &c.

The English bishops are addressed in letters as the Lord Bishop of Rochester, the Lord Bishop of Bath and Wells. The Archbishop of Canterbury, who is Primate of England,—(Head of the English Church,) is called His Grace, or Your Grace. The bishops are all (by virtue of their office) members of the

---

* Distinguished men of all professions, doctors, lawyers, artists, authors, and officers of the army and navy, frequently receive the honour of knighthood.

House of Peers or Lords. They sign their Christian
name with the title of their bishopric, as John Durham
—William Oxford.

All full noblemen have an hereditary seat in the
House of Peers, which they take on attaining the age
of twenty-one, and it continues while they live.
Their younger sons, the Lord Johns and Lord Frede-
ricks, can only have a seat in the House of Commons,
and to that they must be elected, like the other members. Baronets, not being peers, must also be elected
as commons.

Americans going to England would do well to look
over a book of the British Peerage, so as to save
themselves from making blunders, which are much
ridiculed in a country where little allowance is made
for republican habits and for republican ignorance of
what appertains to monarchical institutions.* It
would not be amiss even to know that a full coat of
arms, including shield, supporters, crest, and scroll
with a motto, belongs only to the chief of a noble
family; and that the younger branches are entitled
only to the crest, which is the head of the same animal
that stands erect on each side of the shield as if to support it, such as stags, foxes, bears, vultures, &c. A
baronet has a shield only, with a bloody or wounded
hand over the top.

Our countrymen abroad sometimes excite ill-concealed mirth, by the lavish use they make of titles
when they chance to find themselves among the no-

* It would be well if all the public offices at Washington were
furnished with copies of the British Peerage. Perhaps they are.

bility. They should learn that none but servants or
people of the lower classes make constant use of the
terms "my lord," and "my lady"—"your lordship,"
or "your ladyship"—"your grace," &c., in conversing
with persons of rank. Formerly it was the custom,
but it is long since obsolete, except, as we have
said, from domestics or dependants. Address them
simply as Lord Derby, or Lord Dunmore—Lady
Wilton, Lady Mornington, &c.

CHAPTER VI.

CONDUCT IN THE STREET.

When three ladies are walking together, it is better
for one to keep a little in advance of the other two,
than for all three to persist in maintaining one un-
broken line. They cannot all join in conversation
without talking across each other—a thing that, in-doors
or out-of-doors, is awkward, inconvenient, ungenteel,
and should always be avoided. Also, three ladies
walking abreast occupy too much of the pavement,
and therefore incommode the other passengers. Three
young *men* sometimes lounge along the pavement, arm
in arm. Three young *gentlemen* never do so.

If you meet a lady with whom you have become
but slightly acquainted, and had merely a little conversation, (for instance, at a party or a morning visit,) and
who moves in a circle somewhat higher or more

fashionable than your own, it is safest to wait till she recognises you. Let her not see in you a disposition to obtrude yourself on her notice.

It is not expected that all intimacies formed at watering-places shall continue after the parties have returned to their homes. A mutual bow when meeting in the street is sufficient. But there is no inter-changing of visits, unless both ladies have, before parting, testified a desire to continue the acquaintance. In this case, the lady who is eldest, or palpably highest in station, makes the first call. It is not customary for a young lady to make the first visit to a married lady.

When meeting them in the street, always speak first to your milliner, mantua-maker, seamstress, or to any one you have been in the practice of employing. To pass without notice any servant that you know, is rude and unfeeling, as they will attribute it to pride, not presuming to speak to you themselves, unless in reply. There are persons who having accepted, when in the country, much kindness from the country-people, are ashamed to recognise them when they come to town, on account of their rustic or unfashionable dress. This is a very vulgar, contemptible, and foolish pride; and is always seen through, and de-spised. There is no danger of plain country-people being mistaken for vulgar city-people. In our coun-try, there is no reason for keeping aloof from any who are respectable in character and appearance. Those to be avoided are such as wear tawdry finery, paint their faces, and leer out of the corners of their eyes, *looking* disreputably, even if they are not disreputable in reality.

When a gentleman meets a lady with whom his acquaintance is very slight, (perhaps nothing more than a few words of talk at a party,) he allows her the option of continuing the acquaintance or not, at her pleasure; therefore, he waits till she recognises him, and till she evinces it by a bow,—he looking at her to give the opportunity. Thus, if she has no objection to numbering him among her acquaintances, she denotes it by bowing first. American ladies never curtsey in the street. If she has any reason to disapprove of his character or habits, she is perfectly justifiable in "cutting" him, as it is termed. Let her bow very coldly the first time, and after that, not at all.

Young ladies should yield the wall to old ladies. Gentlemen do so to all ladies.

In some cities it is the custom for all gentlemen to give their arm to all ladies, when walking with them. In others, a gentleman's arm is neither offered nor taken, unless in the evening, on slippery pavements, or when the streets are very muddy. A lady only takes the arm of her husband, her affianced lover, or of her male relatives. In the country the custom is different. There, a gentleman, when walking with a lady, always gives her his arm; and is much offended when, on offering his arm, the lady refuses to take it. Still, if it is contrary to the custom of her place, she can explain it to him delicately, and he will at once see the propriety of her declining.

5

When a lady is walking between two gentlemen, she should divide her conversation as equally as practicable, or address most of it to him who is most of a stranger to her. He, with whom she is least on ceremony, will excuse her.

A gentleman on escorting a lady to her own home, must not leave her till he has rung the bell, and waited till the servant has come and opened the door, and till she is actually in the house. Men who know no better, think it sufficient to walk with her to the foot of the steps and there take their departure, leaving her to get in as she can. This we have seen— but not often, and the offenders were not Americans.

If you stop a few minutes in the street to talk to an acquaintance, draw to one side of the pavement near the wall, so as not to impede the passengers—or you may turn and walk with her as far as the next corner. And never stop to talk in the middle of a crossing. To speak loudly in the street is exceedingly ungenteel, and foolish, as what you say will be heard by all who pass by. To call across the way to an acquaintance, is very unlady-like. It is best to hasten over, and speak to her, if you have any thing of importance to say.

When a stranger offers to assist you across a brimming gutter, or over a puddle, or a glair of slippery ice, do not hesitate, or decline, as if you thought he was taking an unwarrantable liberty. He means nothing but civility. So accept it frankly, and thank him for it.

When you see persons slip down on the ice, do not

laugh at them. There is no fun in being hurt, or in being mortified by a fall in the public street; and we know not how a *lady* can see any thing diverting in so painful a circumstance. It is more feminine, on witnessing such a sight, to utter an involuntary scream than a shout of laughter. And still more so, to stop and ascertain if the person that fell has been hurt.

If, on stopping an omnibus, you find that a dozen people are already seated in it, draw back, and refuse to add to the number; giving no heed to the assertion of the driver, that "there is plenty of room." The *passengers* will not say so, and you have no right to crowd them all, even if you are willing to be crowded yourself—a thing that is extremely uncomfortable, and very injurious to your dress, which may, in consequence, be so squeezed and rumpled as never to look well again. None of the omnibuses are large enough to accommodate even twelve grown people *comfortably;* and that number is the utmost the law permits. A child occupies more than half the space of a grown person, yet children are brought into omnibuses *ad libitum.* Ten grown persons are as many as can be really well seated in an omnibus—twelve are too many; and a *lady* will always regret making the thirteenth—and her want of consideration in doing so will cause her to be regarded with unfavourable eyes by the other passengers. It is better for her to go into a shop, and wait for the next omnibus, or even to walk home, unless it is actually raining.

Have your sixpence ready in your fingers a few minutes before you are to get out; and you may request any gentleman near you to hand it up to the driver. So many accidents have happened from the driver setting off before a lady was entirely out of the vehicle and safely landed in the street, that it is well to desire the gentleman not to hand up the sixpence till after you are fairly clear of the steps.

When expecting to ride in an omnibus, take care to have sufficient small change in your purse—that is, sixpences. We have seen, when a quarter-dollar has been handed up, and the driver was handing down the change, that it has fallen, and been scattered among the straw. There was no stopping to search for it, and therefore the ride cost twenty-five cents instead of six: the driver, of course, finding the change himself, as soon as he got rid of all his passengers.

It is most imprudent to ride in an omnibus with much money in your purse. Pickpockets of genteel appearance are too frequently among the passengers. We know a gentleman who in this way lost a pocket-book containing eighty dollars; and various ladies have had their purses taken from them, by well-dressed passengers. If you are obliged to have money of any consequence about you, keep your hand all the time in that pocket.

If the driver allows a drunken man to come into an omnibus, the ladies will find it best to get out; at least those whose seats are near his. It is, however, the duty of the gentlemen to insist on such fellows being refused admittance where there are ladies.

No lady should venture to ride in an omnibus after dark, unless she is escorted by a gentleman whom she knows. She had better walk home, even under the protection of a servant. If alone in an omnibus at night, she is liable to meet with improper company, and perhaps be insulted.

CHAPTER VII.

SHOPPING.

WHEN you go out shopping, it is well to take with you some *written* cards, inscribed with your residence as well as your name. For this purpose to use engraved visiting-cards is an unnecessary expense. That there may be no mistake, let your shopping-cards contain not only your street and number, but the side of the way, and between what streets your house is situated. This minuteness is particularly useful in Philadelphia, where the plan and aspect of the streets is so similar. Much inconvenience, disappointment, and delay have resulted from parcels being left at wrong places. If you are staying at a hotel, give also the number of your chamber, otherwise the package may be carried in mistake to the apartment of some other lady; the servants always knowing the number of the rooms, but not always remembering the names of the occupants; usually speaking of the ladies and gentlemen as No. 25, No. 42, &c.

There is another advantage in having cards with you when you go out shopping: if you should chance to forget your reticule, or handkerchief, and leave it on the counter, the shopkeeper will know exactly by the card where to send it, or for whom to keep it till called for.

If you intend to purchase none but small articles, take but little money in your purse, so that if you chance to lose it, the loss may not be great.* When you buy articles of any consequence, they will always be sent home at your request—and (unless you keep a standing account at that store) desire the bill to be sent along; and sent at an hour when you will certainly be at hand to pay it. Be careful to take receipts for the payment; and keep the receipts on a file or wire. We have known instances when, from the clerk or storekeeper neglecting or delaying to cross out an account as soon as paid, the same bill was inadvertently sent twice over; and then by having the receipt to show, the necessity of *paying it twice over* was obviated. Look carefully at every item of the bill, and see that all is correct. Sometimes (though these oversights are of rare occurrence) the same article may accidentally be set down twice in the same bill. But this is easily rectified by taking the bill to the storekeeper, and showing it to him

In subscribing for a magazine or newspaper, and paying in advance, (as you always should,) be especially careful of the receipts given to you at paying. So many persons are in the habit of allowing these

---

* When circumstances render it expedient to carry much money out with you, divide it; putting half in one purse or pocket-book. and half in another, and put these portions into two pockets.

accounts to run on for years, that if you neglect preserving your receipts, and cannot produce them afterward, you may be unintentionally classed among the delinquents, and have no means of proving satisfactorily that you have really paid.

Many ladies keep a day-book, in which they set down, regularly, all the money they have expended on that day; adding up the whole every week. An excellent plan, and of great importance to every one who is mistress of a family.

In making purchases for other persons, have bills made out; and send the bills (receipted) with the articles purchased, as an evidence of the exact price of the things, and that they were paid for punctually. The friends that have commissioned you to buy them, should *immediately* repay you. Much inconvenience may be felt by a lady whose command of money is small, when a friend living in a distant place, and probably in opulent circumstances, neglects or postpones the payment of these sums. She should, at the beginning, send money amply sufficient to make these purchases. It is enough that you take the trouble of going to the stores, selecting the desired articles, and having them packed and sent off. She has no right to put you to the slightest pecuniary inconvenience. There have been instances, where articles thus bought for a lady in a far-off place, have not been paid for by that lady till after the lapse of many months. For such remissness there is no excuse. To go shopping for a friend is rarely a pleasant business. Besides its encroaching on your time, there is always a danger of the purchases proving unsatisfactory, or not suiting the taste of her for whom they are intended.   Also, circumstances may prevent the articles reaching her as soon as expected.   Whenever practicable, it is best to send all such packages by the Transportation Line—that charge to be paid by the owner, on delivery.

It is not well to trouble a gentleman with the care of a parcel, unless it is quite small, and he has to pass the door of the house at which it is to be delivered; or unless his residence is in the immediate neighbourhood.

When visiting the shops, if you do not intend to buy at that time, but are merely looking round to see varieties of articles before you determine on what to purchase, candidly say so to the persons standing at the counter.   They will (particularly if they know you) be perfectly willing to show you such things as you desire to see, in the hope that you may return to their store and buy of them afterward.   At the same time, avoid giving unnecessary trouble; and do not, from mere curiosity, desire such things to be brought to you as you have no intention of buying at all.

The practice that is called cheapening, or beating down the price, is now nearly obsolete.   Most tradesmen have a fixed price for every thing, and will not abate.

It is but rarely that you will meet with articles of really good quality on very low terms, unless near the close of the season, when the storekeepers, anxious to get rid of their old stock, generally put down the prices of the goods that are left on hand; knowing that by the return of next season, these will be super-

seded by things of a newer fashion. Economical
ladies, who are not resolutely determined on wearing
none but articles of the very latest fashion, may thus
supply themselves with excellent silks, lawns, &c. in
August and September, at prices far below what they
would have given in May or June. And then they
can lay them by till next summer. In the same way
they can purchase merinoes, mousselines de laine, &c.
in January, February, and March, much lower than in
November and December. It is best always to buy
rather too much than too little; and to have a piece
left, rather than to get a scanty pattern, such as will
barely hold out, leaving nothing for repairs or alterations. There is much advantage in getting an extra
yard and a half, or two yards, and keeping it back for
new sleeves. Unless you are small and slender, it is
not well to buy a dress embroidered with a border
pattern. They are always scanty in width, and have
that look when made up. The skirts are never quite
wide enough. A tall woman requires as full a skirt
as a fat one; else her height will make her look lanky
and narrow.

When bespeaking an article to be made purposely
for you, ascertain from the maker what will be the
cost, and then request him to write down the terms on
a card, or a slip of paper, or on a leaf of your tablet.
If he says he cannot tell how much it will be, or that
he knows not what price to fix on it, or that he cannot
decide till after it is finished, it will be safest and
wisest for you to decline engaging it, till he *has* calcu-
lated the amount, or something very near it. Persist

in this condition being a *sine qua non.* It is his place to know every thing connected with his business, and to be able to judge of his outlay, and his profits. If you do not insist on a satisfactory answer when making the bargain, you may in the end find yourself greatly overcharged, (as we know by experience;) the price in the bill, after the article is made, and sent home, proving infinitely higher than you would have been willing to give if previously aware of it. In dealing with foreigners whose language is not yours, take especial care that there is a correct understanding on both sides.

When on a visit to a city with which you are not familiar, enquire where the best shops are to be found, and make memorandums of them in your tablets. This will spare your friends the trouble of accompanying you on your shopping expeditions. And if you have a small pocket-map of the town, there will be no danger of losing your way. Except to ladies whose chief delight is in seeing things connected with dress, to go shopping with a stranger is usually very tiresome. Also, the stranger will feel less constraint by going alone; and more at liberty to be guided by her own taste in selecting, and to consult her pecuniary convenience in regard to the price. It is only when you feel that you have reason for distrusting your own judgment, as to the quality and gentility of the articles, that it is well to be accompanied by a person of more experience. And then you will, most probably, be unwilling to fatigue her by going to as many shops as you would like to visit. In most cases, it is best

to go shopping without any companion, except, perhaps, a member of your immediate family. Gentlemen consider it a very irksome task to go on shopping
expeditions, and their ill-concealed impatience becomes
equally irksome to you.

If you have given the salesman or saleswoman
unusual trouble in showing you articles which you
find not to suit, make some compensation, by at least
one or two small purchases before leaving the store;
for instance, linen to lay by as a body-lining for a
future dress, gloves, mits, a neck-ribbon, cotton spools,
pins, needles, tape, black sewing-silk, &c.,—things
that will always come into use.

Remember that in all American stores, the rule of
"first come, first served," is rigidly observed. Therefore, testify no impatience if a servant-girl, making a
sixpenny purchase, is served before you—which she
certainly will be, if her entrance has preceded yours.

There are still some ladies who think that one of
the great arts of shopping, is to disparage the articles
shown to them, to exclaim at the price, and to assert
that at other places they can get exactly such things
infinitely lower. When shopping, (as well as under
all other circumstances,) it is best to adhere to the
truth. If you really like the article, why not gratify
the salesman by saying so. If you know that the
price is in conformity to the usual rate, you need not
attempt to get it lower, for you will seldom succeed—
unless, indeed, on that day the tradesman is particularly anxious to sell, having a sum of money to make
up, and being somewhat at a loss. Perhaps then, he

may abate something; but if he does not himself propose the abatement, and if he is largely in business, and sure of plenty of custom, there will be little use in your urging it.

If you are a stranger in the city, (Philadelphia for instance,) do not always be exclaiming at the prices, and declaring that you can buy the same articles much lower and much handsomer in New York, Boston, or Baltimore. For certain reasons, prices are different in different places. If an article is shown to you in Philadelphia as "something quite new," refrain from saying that it has been out of fashion these two years in New York. This may injure its sale with bystanders, chancing to hear you. You need only say "that it is very pretty, but you do not want it now."

It is strange, but no less strange than true, that though the distance between New York and Philadelphia is reduced to less than half a day's travel, it takes a year or more, for the New York fashions to get to Philadelphia, and many of them never arrive at all. There are certain dress-makers and milliners in the latter city, who, if you show them any thing quite fresh from New York, will habitually reply, "Oh! we made that, here in Philadelphia, a year or two ago." You need not believe them. Our American ladies derive all their ideas of costume from France; and as New York rejoices in the most extensive and the most speedy intercourse with that land of taste and elegance, the French fashions always get there first. The wonder is that so long a time elapses before they prevail in the other cities. We must say, however, that whatever is fantastic and extreme, is generally modified and softened down in Philadelphia. In provincial towns, and in remote new settlements, we often see a disposition to carry to the utmost a fashion already too showy or gaudy.

When you see on another lady a new article of dress that you admire, it is *not* ill-manners, (but rather the contrary,) to tell her so. But unless you really desire to get one exactly like it for yourself, and are sincerely asking for information, it is considered very rude to enquire where she bought it, and what was the cost. And it is peculiarly vulgar to preface the enquiry by the foolish words—"If it is a fair question." The very doubt proves that you know the question to be a very unfair one. And so it is. We have never known that expression used except to introduce something rude and improper. Any lady who is asked an impertinent question, would be perfectly justifiable in saying, "Excuse me from answering"—and then immediately changing the conversation. Yet there are ladies who are always catechising others about their dress. You are not bound to give explicit answers to these, or any other questions concerning your personal affairs. Much mischief accrues in society, from some ladies being too inquisitive, and others too communicative.

It is really a great fatigue, both of body and mind, to go shopping with a very close economist, particularly if you know that she can well afford a sufficiently liberal expenditure. The length of time she will ponder over every thing before she can "make up her mind;" the ever-besetting fear that she may possibly have to give a few cents more in one store than in another; her long deliberation as to whether a smaller than the usual quantity may not be "made to do;" her predilection for bargain-seeking in streets far off, and ungenteel; the immense trouble she gives to the persons behind the counter,—all will induce you to forswear trying a second time the experiment of attending on the progress of a shopper who sets out with the vain expectation of obtaining good articles at paltry prices.

In what are called "cheap shops," you will rarely find more than two or three things that are really cheap. If of bad quality, they are not *cheap*, but dear. Low-priced ribbons, for instance, are generally flimsy, tawdry, of ugly figures, and vulgar colours,— soon fading, and soon "getting into a string." Yet there are ladies who will walk two miles to hustle in the crowd they find squeezing toward the counter of the last new emporium of cheap ribbons; and, while waiting their turn, have nothing to look at around them but lots of trash, that if they bought they would be ashamed to wear. Coarse finery is trumpery.

On the other hand, for ladies of small means, it is not indispensable to their standing in society, that they should deal only at stores noted for selling *higher* than the usual price. It is a very poor boast; particularly when they cannot afford it.

Whatever may be the caprices of fashion, a lady of good taste (and we may add, good sense,) will not, in buying dresses, select those of large figures, and high glaring colours. There is something peculiarly ungenteel and ungraceful in a white ground with large red flowers and green leaves wandering over it. Even if the fabric is brocade, it has a look of calico. Red and green is only beautiful in real flowers. In a lady's dress, it somehow looks unlady-like. A great variety of bright colours is only suited to a carpet. For a dress, two are quite sufficient. And then if one is blue, pink, scarlet, or orange, let it be contrasted with brown, gray, olive, or some chaste and quiet tint that will set it off. Few silks are more becoming than those in which the figure is formed by a darker shade of the same colour as the ground. Silks of one colour only, trim the best—variegated trimming looks confused and ineffective. No colours are more ungenteel, or in worse taste, than reddish lilacs, reddish purples, and reddish browns. The original tint of aronetta, or anatto, is the contempt of ladies; but by previously washing the article in strong, warm pot-ash water, before it is put into the solution of aronetta, you will obtain a beautiful bird-of-paradise colour, entirely free from all appearance of the unpopular powder.

Buy no silk that is stiff and hard, however thick and heavy it may seem. It will crack and split, and wear worse than a soft silk that appears much thinner. Venture on no satin that is not of excellent quality. A thin satin frays and ravels, and is not worth making up. For common wear, a soft, thick India silk is generally excellent. We have never seen a *good one* for less than a dollar a yard. The figured or embossed India silks are not worth buying,—wearing rough and fuzzy, and fraying all over. For a serviceable, long-lasting home dress, there is nothing equal to a very thick, soft, double-width India black satin, such as is called two yards wide, and sells at two dollars a yard. But they have become very scarce. Never use satin to cover cord. It ravels too much. Velvet and satin should be corded with substantial silk. If you cannot match the exact shade, let it be darker rather than lighter. A belt-ribbon should always be darker than the dress. Cord merino with itself. A cording of silk will not wash.

If you cannot get lace that is tolerably fine, wear none at all, rather than have it coarse. We have seen lace called Brussels, so coarse that it looked as if made of cotton, though in truth it was of thread. There was no real beauty in it. Genuine Brussels lace is exquisitely fine.

Large showy ornaments, by way of jewellery, are exceedingly ungenteel. They always tell their own story, of glass stones set in gilding, not gold. If you cannot obtain real jewels, never attempt sham ones. It requires no practised eye to detect them—particularly false diamonds.

Do not interfere with the shopping of other customers, (who may chance to stand near you at the counter,) by either praising or deprecating any of the articles they are looking at. Leave them to the exercise of their own judgment; unless they ask your opinion. And then give it in a low voice, and sincerely.

If you meet an acquaintance unexpectedly in a store, it is not well to engage in a long conversation with her, and thus detain persons behind the counter from waiting on other customers. Finish your purchase-making first, and then you will have leisure to step aside and converse. A store is not the place for social intercourse, and you may chance to say something there, that bystanders should not hear. "Greetings in the market-place" should always be short.

It is not admissible to try on kid gloves in a store. After buying a pair, ask for the glove-stretcher, (which they keep in all good shops, for the convenience of customers,) and then stretch the gloves upon it, unless you have a glove-stretcher at home. This will render them easy to put on when you take them into wear. Glove-stretchers are to be bought at the variety stores; or ought to be. They will save many a new glove from tearing.

In buying stockings, whether silk or cotton, you will find it cheapest in the end, to get those of the best *English* manufacture, particularly those of fine quality. For winter, and to wear with boots, English stockings of unbleached cotton are very comfortable, feeling warmer than those that are perfectly white. It is to be lamented that all black stockings (even of silk) are painful and injurious to the feet, the copperas dye being poisonous.

In buying black mits, see that they are *really of silk*, otherwise they will stain your hands, and look brown and foxy. Much cotton is now substituted for silk: a way having been discovered of carding silk

6

anu cotton together, before the thread is spun. Linen also, is shamefully adulterated with cotton, and it is difficult for purchasers to discover the cheat before the article is washed. Linen is frequently injured in the piece by bad bleaching-salts; so that after the first washing, it drops into holes, such as are caused by vitriol. Of this we have had sad experience in several instances, when the linen was supposed to be of the best quality.

Always object to a parcel being put up in newspaper—as the printing-ink will rub off, and soil the article inclosed. If it is a little thing that you are going to take home in your own hand, it will smear your gloves. All shopkeepers in good business can afford to buy proper wrapping-paper, and they generally do so. It is very cheap. See also that they do not wrap your purchase in so small a bit of paper as to squeeze and crush it.

If you go out with much money, (which is never advisable,) divide it into two portions, putting part in your pocket-book or porte-monnaie, and the remainder into your purse, so that if you lose it, or have your pocket picked, the loss may be less. Do not carry notes in your purse, but keep them in your pocket-book. Little gold dollars had best go into your porte-monnaie. If kept in your purse with small change, you will be very likely to lose them, or to mistake them for three-cent pieces if the light is bad.

Once, on embarking in a New York steamboat, we saw a gentleman having bought a penny paper, give the news-boy a gold eagle in mistake for a cent. The gentleman was instantly apprized of his error by a bystander, who had seen it; but the boy had already prung upon the wharf and was lost in the crowd.

We knew an instance of a lady in New York giving a hundred-dollar note to a strawberry woman, instead of a note of one dollar. Neither note nor woman were seen or heard of more.

In getting change see that three-cent pieces are not given to you for five cents.

And now a few words to saleswomen. They have always, when commencing that vocation, two important qualities to cultivate (exclusive of cleverness in business)—civility, and patience. In these two requisites, few of our American young women are deficient. Let them also learn activity in moving, and quickness in recollecting where all the articles called for are to be found, so as not to keep the customers waiting too long, while they, the sellers, are searching the shelves and boxes. Also, if a lady wishes to match something, (for instance, a piece of silk,) it is foolish and useless to bring her a piece that is not *exactly* like; trying to persuade her to take it, and calling it " as good a match as she is likely to get." Of course she will *not* take a piece that is only *tolerably* like, but not quite the same; for unless it matches exactly, it is no match at all. If a customer enquires for light blue ribbon it is absurd to bring her dark blue, saying "we have no light blue"—or to say "we have no pink, but we have scarlet—we have no lilac, but we have purple." Or still worse, to try to persuade the customer that deep crimson is · a beautiful shade of scarlet; or worse than all, that those very unbecoming tints, called improperly rose-white and pearl-white, are really a pure dead white; when you know very well that they are no such thing. Both white and black are very difficult to match *precisely*.

Let the yard-measure be visible to the customers. In some shops the measure is at the back of the counter, hidden behind a glass case. This practice of measuring out of sight, sometimes gives rise to a suspicion that the measure is not true, as it is so easy to deceive where the brass nails that mark it are con cealed from view of the customers.

Every female who keeps, or attends in a store, should discourage the visits of her friends at business hours. If she looks off to chat with her shop-visiters, she cannot attend properly to her customers; and those visiters may be inconsiderate and obtrusive enough to interfere, by putting in their word, and praising the beauty or cheapness of the articles, by way of promoting the interest of the seller, which it ultimately *will not*.

Show as much civility and attention to a customer plainly dressed, and walking on foot, or getting out of an omnibus, as you would to a lady elegantly attired, and coming in her own carriage. The former may prove the most profitable customer. Be careful to exhibit no temper, even if you have had the trouble of showing a variety of goods to one who goes away without buying any thing. Another time, perhaps, she may come and make large purchases: but if you offend her, she will assuredly never enter the store again. Recollect that no one feels under the least compulsion to buy what does not suit them. You would not yourself. Habitual courtesy is a valuable qualification, and always turns to good account.

CHAPTER VIII.

PLACES OF AMUSEMENT.

It would be well in *all* places of public amusement, if there could be an apartment appropriated to the ladies, in which they might deposit their cloaks, hoods, &c. in charge of a responsible attendant; her care to be rewarded by a small gratuity. Ladies would then be under no necessity of carrying warm outer-garments into a crowded and heated room; or of wearing their bonnets, and thereby intercepting the view of persons seated behind them; always a grievance where the benches are not sufficiently elevated, or where there is no difference at all in their respective elevation, as is sometimes the case. Also, the appearance of the female part of the company is always more elegant, when wearing bandeaus, caps, or other light head-dresses; young persons requiring their hair only, or the slight decoration of a flower or a ribbon. It is very painful and fatiguing to be for several hours continually dodging your head from side to side, and stretching your neck this way and that, and peeping wherever you can obtain a tantalizing glimpse between the bonnets of ladies seated immediately before you. This, in addition to the annoyance of being squeezed on a bench that is over-full, is enough to destroy nearly all the pleasure of the exhibition; and to make a large portion of the audience regret that they came.

If you wish to secure a good seat, go early. It is better to sit there an hour before the commencement of the performance, than to arrive after it has begun. The time of waiting will soon pass away, in conversation with the friends whom you have accompanied.

When invited to join a party to a place of amusement, begin to prepare in ample time; so as not to keep them waiting for you. When a *large* party is going to a place of amusement, (for instance, the theatre, or opera,) it is better that each family should go thither from their own home, (being provided with their own tickets,) than that they should all rendezvous at the house of one of the company; at the risk of keeping the whole party waiting, perhaps for the very youngest members of it. When a box has been taken, let the tickets be sent to all the persons who are to have seats in it, and not retained by the taker of the box till the whole party has assembled at the door of the theatre. If the tickets are thus distributed, the persons from each house can go when they please, without compelling any of the party to wait for them.

Still, to make an entrance after the performance has begun, is (or ought to be) very embarrassing to ladies. It excites the attention of all around, diverting that attention from the performance; and there is always, when the house is full, and the hour late, some delay and difficulty in reaching the seats, even when the seats have been secured.

If it is a concert, where places cannot be previously engaged, there are, of course, additional reasons for going in due time; and the most sensible and best-behaved part of the audience always endeavour to do so. But if you are unavoidably late, be satisfied to pay the penalty, by quietly taking back-seats, if no others are vacant. We have seen young ladies not arriving till after the entertainment had commenced, march boldly up to the front benches, and stand there looking steadfastly in the faces of gentlemen who with their parties had earned good seats by coming soon after the doors were opened. The ladies persevering in this determined stare, till they succeeded in dislodging these unfortunate gentlemen, and compelling them to quit their seats, to leave the ladies who belonged to them, and to stand for the remainder of the evening, perhaps in a distant part of the room American *men* are noted, everywhere, for their politeness to females. We wish we could say the same of the politeness of our fair countrywomen in return. Yet frequently they will avail themselves of these civilities from strangers, without rewarding them with a word of thanks, or even a bow of acknowledgment.

English tourists remark (and with truth) that there is no position in which American ladies appear to such disadvantage as when crowding the galleries of our legislative assemblies; ejecting gentlemen to whom it is of importance to hear the debates; and still worse, intruding upon the floor of the senate-chamber, and compelling the senators to relinquish their places, and find others where they can, or else to stand all the time. And among these ladies, there may be very few who are really capable of enjoying or appreciating the eloquence of our distinguished orators, or of entering understandingly into the merits of the question. Often these damsels are whispering half the time about some nonsense of their own; and often, as is surmised, the chief object of the ladies whose visits to the capitol are most frequent, is the chance of a few words of flirtation with some of the most gallant among the members; or the possibility of being escorted home by a congressman, who has but little to do, or at least who does but little. We think the English parliament is right in excluding ladies from their halls, except when the queen goes there in state, to open or prorogue the session. Let them be satisfied with reading the debates in the newspapers

We acknowledge that it is very interesting to see and hear the most eminent men of our country arranging the affairs of the nation; to become acquainted with their personal appearance, and to listen to their eloquence. But the privilege should not be abused as it is, by those who, after all, listen so badly, or comprehend so badly, that if questioned an hour afterward, they could scarcely repeat the purport of one single sentence,—nor perhaps even recollect the subject of debate. Such instances we have known— and not a few of them either.

To laugh deridingly, or to whisper unfavourable remarks during the performance of a concert or a play, is a rudeness of which few American ladies are guilty. Still, we occasionally see some of that few, who, much to the annoyance of those persons near them who really wish to enjoy what they came for, talk audibly in ridicule of the performers; the performers being, in all probability, near enough to hear these vexatious remarks, and to be disconcerted by them. We heard of a highly respectable actress who was so mortified by the unfeeling animadversions of some young ladies in a stage-box, that she forgot her part, was unable to utter a word, or to restrain her tears, and became so nervous that she played badly during the remainder of the piece, and was in consequence, severely handled next day by the newspaper critics. This was very hard.

Parents before taking their children to the theatre, should first ascertain whether the play is such as will amuse or interest them. Small children are invariably restless, troublesome, and finally sleepy at a performance that affords *them* no entertainment, and they will be better at home. Yet we have seen little girls brought to see the painful tragedy of the Gamester —or still worse, the dreary comedy of the Stranger. How is it that young ladies are frequently matronized to plays that even their mothers cannot witness without blushes?

CHAPTER IX.

TRAVELLING.

No lady should set out on a journey unprovided with an oiled-silk bag for the reception of tooth-brushes, soap, a hair-brush, and a towel. Let the bag be about half a quarter of a yard longer at the back than at the front; so as to leave a flap to turn over, and tie down, when all the articles are in. It should be square, (exclusive of the flap,) and about a quarter and half-quarter in length, and the same in breadth; stitched in compartments, something like an old-fashioned thread-case, only that the compartments differ much in size. The two smallest are for two tooth-brushes. Another should be broad enough to contain a hair-brush. For travelling, have a hair-brush with a mirror at the back, and if you can get one that has also a dressing-comb attached to it, so much the better. The largest compartment (which should occupy the centre) is for a towel, and a cake of soap. If you are obliged to start in haste, all these things can be put in while wet from recent use, the towel being rolled or folded into as small a compass as possible. The oiled silk will prevent the wet from oozing through. When all are in, turn over the flap at the top, (which should be furnished with two long strings of broad, white tape,) and tie it securely down. Carry this bag in the square satchel which all ladies now keep in their hands when travelling, and which contain such things as they may want during the day, precluding the necessity of opening their large carpet-bag, till they stop for the night.

In a carpet-bag pack nothing but white articles, or such as can be washed, and will not be spoiled by the bag chancing to get wet. Have your name engraved on the lock of your carpet-bag, and also on the brass plate of your trunks. Besides this, write your full direction on several cards, make a small hole in each, and runuing a string through the hole, tie a card to the handle of each trunk, and sew one on the side of your carpet-bag—the direction designating the place to which you are going. Your name in full should be painted in white letters on every trunk. This costs but a trifle, and secures the recognition of your baggage when missing. It is also an excellent plan to tie round the handle of each trunk or bag, a bit of ribbon—blue, red, or yellow—all the bits being off the same piece.*

Write on a large card, a list and description of each trunk, box, &c. and give the card to the gentleman who escorts you. It will greatly assist him in identifying all the articles that comprise your baggage.

Be quite ready at least a quarter of an hour before the time for starting. Nelson said he traced all the

---

* In a former work of the author's, *The House Book*, published by A. Hart, Philadelphia, will be found ample directions for packing trunks, &c.

most fortunate events of his life to his practice of being, on every occasion, quite prepared a quarter of an hour too early. It is a good rule.

Previous to departing, put into the hand of your escort rather more than a sufficient sum for the expenses of your journey, so as to provide for all possible contingencies. He will return you the balance when all is paid. Having done this, should any person belonging to the line come to you for your fare, refer them to the gentleman, (mentioning his name,) and take care to pay nothing more yourself.

Dress very plainly when travelling. Few ladies that *are* ladies wear finery in rail-cars, and steam-boats—still less in stages—stage-roads being usually very dusty. Showy silks, and what are called dress-bonnets are preposterous—so are jewellery ornaments, which, if real, you run a great risk of losing, and if false, are very ungenteel. Above all, do not travel in white kid gloves. Respectable women never do.

The best travelling-dresses are of merino, or alpaca; plain mousseline de laine; grey or brown linen; or strong India silk, senshaw for instance. In warm weather, gingham is better than printed lawn, which rumples and tumbles and "gets into a string" directly. The sleeves wide, for if tight to the arm, they will stain with perspiration. Your travelling-dress for summer should have a large cape or pelerine of the same. Beside which, carry on your arm a large shawl for chilly mornings and evenings. No lady should travel in cold weather, without a warm cloak, mantilla, or pelisse,—furs, &c. of course—and travelling-boots lined with fur or flannel; having also inner soles of lambs-wool, varnished on the leather side to make them water-proof. Take with you one of those very useful umbrellas, that are large enough to shelter one person from the rain, and can also be used as a parasol. Do not pack it away in a trunk, for you may want it in the transit from rail-car to steamboat. Keep it near you all the time, with your satchel and extra shawl. By all means wear a white collar.

If you are fortunately able to ride backward as well as forward, you will be less incommoded with flying sparks, by sitting with your back to the engine. A spark getting into the eye is very painful, and sometimes dangerous. It is possible to expel it by blowing your nose very hard, while with the other hand you wipe out the particle of cinder with a corner of your handkerchief, pulling down the lower eye-lid. We have seen this done successfully. Another way is to wrap the head of a pin in the corner of a fine, soft cambric handkerchief, and placing it beneath the lid, sweep all round the eye with it. If this does not succeed, get out at the first station-house where you can stop long enough, procure a bristle-hair from a sweeping-brush, tie it in a loop or bow with a bit of thread, and let some one insert it beneath your eye-lid, and move it slowly all round, so as to catch in it the offending particle of coal, and bring it out. Or if there is time, send to the nearest apothecary for an eye-stone, (in reality, a lobster's eye,) and soak it five minutes in a saucer of vinegar and water to give it activity, then, wiping it dry, and carefully inserting

it beneath the eye-lid, bind a handkerchief over it.
The eye-stone will go circling round the eye, and
most likely take up the mote in its course. When
the pain ceases, remove the handkerchief, and wash
the eye with cold water.

To read in a rail-car is very injurious to the eyes,
from the quivering, tremulous motion it seems to communicate to the letters of the page. It is best to abstain from your book till you are transferred to the
steamboat.

Many persons cannot talk in a rail-car without a
painful exertion of the voice. And it is not an easy
task, even to those whose lungs are strong. You can
easily excuse yourself from conversing with your escort,
by telling him that your voice is not loud enough to
be heard above the racket of the cars, and that though
you will gladly listen to *him*, he must allow you to
listen without replying, except in as few words as
possible. If he finds a gentleman with whom he is
acquainted, desire him to talk to his friend, and leave
you to hear their conversation as a silent auditor.

If you pass the night in a steamboat, and can afford
the additional expense of a *whole* state-room, by all
means engage one as soon as you go on board. The
chambermaid will give you the key and the number,
and you can retire to it whenever you please, and
enjoy the luxury of being alone, and of washing and
dressing without witnesses. If you are constrained to
take a berth in the ladies' sleeping-cabin, it is not the
least necessary to retire to it immediately after supper.
By doing so you will have a very long, tiresome night,

and be awake many hours before morning. And if you are awake, do not be continually calling upon the poor chambermaid, and disturbing her with inquiries, such as "Where are we now?" and "How soon shall we arrive?"

The saloon is the place in which ladies and gentlemen sit together. If a lady is so inconsiderate or selfish as to violate the rules of the boat, by inviting her husband or lover to take a seat in the ladies' cabin, there is no impropriety in sending the chambermaid to remind him that he must leave the room. This is often done, and always should be. We once saw a gentleman (or a pretended one) so pertinacious in remaining, (it is true his lady-love urged him "not to mind,") that the captain had to be brought to threaten him with forcible expulsion. This had the desired effect.

Such are the facilities of travelling, that a lady evidently respectable, plainly dressed, and behaving properly, may travel very well without a gentleman. Two ladies still better. On commencing the journey she should speak to the conductor, requesting him to attend to her and her baggage, and to introduce her to the captain of the boat, who will of course take charge of her during the voyage.

Before arriving at the wharf, she had best engage one of the servants of the boat, (promising him a shilling or two,) to obtain for her a porter or a hack, and to see that her baggage is safe. She must stipulate with the hackman that no stranger is to be put into the carriage with her. This is against the law, but notwithstanding, is often done, and the lady who has first engaged the coach, is liable to have for her riding-companions persons of improper character and vulgar appearance, and to be carried with them to their places in remote parts of the city, before she is conveyed to her own home. Previous to getting in, take the number of the coach, by writing it on a card with your pencil, and make your bargain with him as to the charge for conveying you and your baggage.

It would be well if the imposition and insolence of hack-drivers were *always* followed with the punishments provided by law. Ladies are naturally unwilling to appear at a magistrate's office. But it is the duty of every gentleman, as a good citizen, to see that the municipal regulations are never violated with impunity.

All trouble may be avoided on arriving, by sending for the captain of the boat, and requesting him to see you on shore, or to depute his clerk to that office.

In arriving at a rail-road depôt, be careful not to quit the cars till after they have positively stopped quite still. The time gained is but an instant, and the risk is very imminent of serious injury by falling, should your ankle twist in stepping out while there is the least motion.

On arriving at a hotel, ask immediately to see the proprietor; give him your name and address, tell how long you purpose staying, and request him to see that you are provided with a good room. Request him also to conduct you to the dining-room at dinner-time, and allot you a seat near his own. For this purpose, he will wait for you near the door, (do not *keep him waiting,*) or meet you in the ladies' drawing-room. While at table, if the proprietor or any other gentleman asks you to take wine with him, politely refuse.

If, on arriving at the wharf, you expect a gentleman to meet you, take a seat either on deck near the cabin-door, or just inside of the door, so that he may find you easily.

If you are to pursue your journey early in the morning, desire, over-night, the waiter who attends your room, to knock hard at your door an hour before the time of starting. Before you go down-stairs, ask for the chambermaid who has attended you, and give her a fee, (not less than a quarter-dollar,) putting it into her own hand yourself, and not commissioning another to convey it to her. Do not omit giving a quarter-dollar at least, to the waiter who attended your room, and one also to him who has served you at table.

Refrain from making acquaintance with any strangers, unless you are certain of their respectability. If a gentleman of whom you know nothing, endeavours to get into conversation with you, turn away, and make no reply. Avoid saying any thing to women in showy attire, with painted faces, and white kid gloves. Such persons have frequently the assurance to try to be very sociable with respectable ladies who are travelling alone. Keep aloof from them always.

If you have breakfasted early, it will be well to put some gingerbread-nuts or biscuits into your satchel, as you may become very hungry before dinner.

7

Carry but little money in your pocket—not more than will suffice for the expenses of the day. But for travelling, have another pocket, concealed *beneath* your upper petticoat, and *in that* keep the main portion of your cash. Be cautious of taking bank-notes in change—they may be such as you cannot pass. If they are offered to you, refuse them, and insist upon gold or silver.

Travelling in America, ladies frequently meet with little civilities from gentlemen, so delicately offered, that to refuse them would be rude. These incidental acts of politeness should always be acknowledged with thanks; but they should not be construed into a desire of commencing an acquaintance. If a lady obliged to travel alone, wishes to be treated with respect, her own deportment must in all things be quiet, modest and retiring.

If you have a servant with you, see that she gets her meals, and has a comfortable sleeping-place, or in all probability she will be neglected and overlooked. In a steamboat or a hotel, speak yourself to the head-waiter, and desire him to take her to the servants' table and attend to her; and tell the chambermaid to see her provided with a bed. If their lady forgets to look out for them, coloured women in particular have often no courage to look out for themselves.

CHAPTER X.

DEPORTMENT AT A HOTEL, OR AT A LARGE BOARDING-HOUSE.

Now that there is so much travelling in the summer, (and indeed at all seasons,) and so much living in public, to save the trouble and the expense of keeping house in private, it may be well to offer some hints on the propriety of manners that ought to be observed in places where you are always exposed to the inspection and to the remarks of strangers. These strangers, knowing you but slightly, or not at all, will naturally draw their inferences for or against you from what they see before their eyes; concluding that you are genteel or ungenteel, patrician or plebeian, according to the coarseness or the polish of your manners.

Yet strange to say, there are persons who indulge themselves in astounding acts of rudeness, from the supposition that a hotel is only a tavern, a sort of Liberty Hall, where every one has a right to "take their ease in their inn," if they pay for it. Have they no respect for themselves?

It is usual for members of the same party to meet in the ladies' drawing-room before they go in to breakfast, unless the party is large; and then it is not expected that half a dozen persons should be kept waiting for one or two late risers, or tardy dressers. When two or three of the party find themselves ready in the parlour, it will be best for them to proceed to the eating-room, and leave the others to follow at their convenience, by twos or by threes,—always seeing that a young lady, if a stranger, is not left to go in alone. Strangers at hotels can have no particular seats at breakfast and tea, as at these two repasts, they always come to table by instalments, and at no regular time. If a large party enters all at once, and they are *determined* to sit all together, they may occasion much inconvenience to persons already seated, or to the regular boarders, who have their allotted seats. Neither is there any necessity or advantage in six, eight, or ten people, who travel as one party, resolving to establish themselves at a hotel-table all side by side, in a row; particularly when it causes inconvenience to others. Certainly not more than three or four persons ranged in a line can join in the same conversation, or attend to the wants of their friends. Why then should they make any extraordinary point of occupying chairs next to each other. It would be better to divide their forces; and if they can, for half to sit on one side of the table, and the other half directly opposite. Or they will find that if the table is full, and they have to disperse still more widely, they had best do so with a good grace, rather than make any disturbance on the subject. When they quit the table to return to the drawing-room they may be very sure of all meeting again near the door.

Nine o'clock (or half-past) is the latest hour that

any guest at a hotel should come to breakfast; and few *Americans* have so little consideration as to detain the table and the servants till ten or eleven.* At a boarding-house, the guests are very soon made to understand that if they are late risers, they need expect nothing but the cold leavings of the breakfast. At a hotel they find more indulgence. You there choose from the bill of fare such dishes as you may prefer, and they will be brought to you, after you have been supplied with tea or coffee, and bread and butter to begin with. To each person is allowed a separate dish or plate of the articles selected; and it is understood to be for yourself alone, and that no other person has a right to partake of it, or to meddle with it in any way. Yet even from your own dish, never help yourself with the knife and fork or spoon you are eating with; but always use a spare one, with which the waiter will furnish you. Do not eat different sorts of relishes off the same plate. At a hotel there is no scarcity of plates, or of servants to change them. Always take butter with the butter-knife, and then do not forget to return that knife to the butter-plate. Carefully avoid cutting bread with your own knife, or taking salt with it from the salt-cellar. It looks as if you had not been accustomed to butter-knives and salt-spoons.

Ladies no longer eat salt-fish at a public-table.

---

* Nevertheless, it is not good manners to make any remark (even to a friend) on their coming to breakfast late or early. It is no concern of yours, and they have reasons of their own, undoubtedly.

The odour of it is now considered extremely ungenteel, and it is always very disagreeable to those who *do not* eat it. If you breakfast alone, you can then indulge in it.

Speak to the waiter in a distinct, but not in too loud a voice, and always civilly. Thank him for any little extra attention he may show you. If you do not like what he has brought you, or find that you cannot eat it, make your objection in a low voice, so as not to be heard by the neighbouring guests; and quietly desire him to bring you something else.

It is usual at a hotel-table for each waiter to have charge of three or four persons, and to attend to *their* wants exclusively. If you are a stranger, ask the waiter his name when he first comes to you; and unless he is not at hand, and you see another standing idle, do not call on any one else to attend you.

If the servants are coloured men, refrain from all conversation in their presence that may grate harshly on their feelings, by reminding them of their unfortunate African blood. Do not talk of them as "negroes,"* or "darkies." Avoid all discussions of abolition, (either for or against,) when coloured people are by. Also, quote none of their laughable sayings while they are present.

When the domestics are Irish, and you have occasion to reprove them for their negligence, forgetfulness, or blunders, do so without any reference to their

---

* Americans never really say *niggers*, though constantly accused of doing so by their British cousins. The word *negor* we have heard, but *nigger* never.

country. If you find one who is disrespectful or insolent, or who persists in asserting a falsehood, it is
safest to make no reply yourself, but to have the
matter represented to the proprietor of the house;
desiring that another waiter may be allotted to you.

It is ungenteel to go to the breakfast-table in any
costume approaching to full dress. There must be no
flowers or ribbons in the hair. A morning-cap should
be as simple as possible. The most genteel morning-
dress is a close gown of some plain material, with
long sleeves, which in summer may be white muslin.
A merino or cashmere wrapper, (grey, brown, purple,
or olive,) faced or trimmed with other merino of an
entirely different colour, such as crimson, scarlet,
green, or blue, is a becoming morning dress for winter.
In summer, a white cambric-muslin morning-robe is
the handsomest breakfast attire, but one of gingham
or printed muslin the most convenient. The coloured
dress may be made open in front, with short loose
sleeves and a pointed body. Beneath it a white
under-dress, having a chemisette front down to the
belt, and long white sleeves down to the wrist.
This forms a very graceful morning costume, the
white skirt appearing where the coloured skirt opens.

The fashion of wearing black silk mittens at breakfast is now obsolete. It was always inconvenient, and
neither useful nor ornamental.

After breakfast, it is customary for the ladies to
adjourn to the drawing-room, where they converse, or
read the papers, or receive early visiters, while the
chambermaids are putting the bed-chambers in order.

Some who are not accustomed to hotels, go immediately from the breakfast-table to their own apartment, sitting there among the flue and dust during the whole process of bed-making and room-sweeping; afraid to trust the chambermaid alone, lest she should steal something. This is absurd. They should know that the chambermaids (being all considered honest and responsible) are furnished with duplicate keys, by which they can at any time unlock the chamber-doors, and let themselves in, when the occupant is absent. Also, this palpable suspicion of their honesty is an insult to the girls, and is always felt as such. It is sufficient to lock the bureau, the wardrobe, and your trunks. When you go out, (that is, out of the house,) *then* lock the door of your room, lest some one passing by, should have curiosity to stroll in and look about, and meddle with what they see there.

Should you perceive that the dress of another lady is, by some accident, out of order—for instance, that a hook or a button has become unfastened; or that a string is visibly hanging out; a collar unpinned, and falling off; the corner of a shawl dragging along the floor; a skirt caught up; or a sleeve slipping down, immediately have the kindness to apprize her of it in a low voice, and assist her in repairing the mischance; and, if necessary, leave the room with her for that purpose.

We have seen a lady who, finding that a cluster of her false curls was coming down, had the courage to say so to a gentleman with whom she was conversing at a party. And going openly, and at once, to the nearest mirror, she calmly adjusted her borrowed locks, and returned to her seat with a good grace. Consequently, nobody laughed at the untoward accident; as might perhaps have been the case, had she seemed excessively confused and mortified, and awkwardly tried to hold on her curls till she got out of the room.

If you do not wish to be encumbered by carrying the key in your pocket, let it be left during your absence, with the clerk in the office, or with the barkeeper; and send to him for it on your return. Desire the servant who attends the door to show no person up to your room during your absence. If visiters wish to wait for your return, it is best they should do so in the parlour.

In going in and out, be careful to shut the parlour-doors after you, except in summer. Young ladies are often very inconsiderate in this respect, and cause much inconvenience, in cold weather, to those who do not like to sit with a draught of keen air blowing upon them. Even if you feel too warm yourself, it is rude to throw open a door, (much more to raise a window-sash,) without first enquiring if other ladies have no objection.

There is no impropriety in a lady commencing conversation with a stranger of genteel appearance. You can easily take occasion to mention your own name, and then, in return, she will communicate hers. But, unless you are previously certain of her respectability, have little to say to a woman who is travelling without a companion, and whose face is painted, who wears a profusion of long curls about her neck, who has a meretricious expression of eye, and who is over-dressed It is safest to avoid her. Also, you will derive no pleasure or advantage from making acquaintance with females who are evidently coarse and vulgar, even if you know that they are rich, live in a large house, and are of respectable character. Young girls who are loud, noisy, bold, and forward, (however fashionable they may be,) it is best also to avoid. They will not want your society, as they are generally all the time surrounded by "beaux," or else rattling over the keys of the piano.

In a public parlour, it is selfish and unmannerly to sit down to the instrument uninvited, and fall to playing or practising, without seeming to consider the probability of your interrupting or annoying the rest of the company, particularly when you see them all engaged in reading or in conversation. If you want amusement, you had better read, or occupy yourself with some light sewing or knitting-work.

If you have no book, you can ring the bell, and send to the reading-room to borrow a file of newspapers; but in most hotels, there are books belonging to the establishment, lying on a table in the ladies' parlour. Be sure not to carry any of these books upstairs, as they are intended solely for the drawing-room; and their removal from thence is interdicted. Also, never carry away the Directory, the Atlas, the City Guide, or any other book placed there for the convenience of strangers.

If you want pen and ink, or any sort of stationery,

you can obtain it immediately, by ringing for a servant to bring it you from the office. In ringing the bell, one pull is sufficient; and always pull the cord *downward*. If you jerk it out horizontally, and give successively several hard pulls in that direction, the cord is very likely to break, or the knob or tassel to come off in your hand. At the chief hotel in one of the New England cities, we saw a printed paper with directions in large type, pasted beside *every bell-pull in the house;* the directions specifying minutely the proper mode of bell-ringing. Could it be that this house was frequented by persons unaccustomed to bells?

To return to the too-prevalent evil of uninvited and ill-timed piano-playing, (much of which does not deserve the name of music,) we have always been at a loss to understand how a young stranger, (modest and unobtrusive in other things,) could walk up to the instrument, sometimes almost as soon as she arrives, and rattle "fast and furious" over the keys, drowning the voices of ladies and gentlemen who were talking, and therefore compelling them to cease their conversation; or if they pursued it, obliging them to raise their tone painfully; or to lose more than half, from the impossibility of hearing each other distinctly. To read when piano-playing is going on, is to most persons impossible. There are few readers who cannot so concentrate their attention on their book, as not to be disturbed by any *talking* that may occur in their vicinity; and if talking *does* withdraw their attention from the book, it is best that they should read only when alone in their apartment. But we have met with no one who could read in the neighbourhood of a played piano.

If the music is really very good, and accompanied by a fine voice, it is true that most readers will willingly close the book to listen. But if the playing is barely tolerable, or decidedly bad, and if the singing is weak and insipid, or harsh and screaming, or timeless and tasteless, who can possibly wish to hear it; except perhaps a doating father, or an injudicious mother, vain of her daughter because she is *hers*, and so anxious to show her off, that she encourages the girl to display even her deficiencies.

We believe that our beloved America is not yet the land of music; and that (with many exceptions) her children are generally not furnished with much capacity for it. If there was a true feeling for music, there would be more genius for that charming art, and there would be more composers of original airs, the number of which, in our country, is smaller than in any civilized nation in the world. It is true we have many excellent musicians, and many very good singers, but still, music is not the grand forte of Jonathan. Pity it were,—for he has "a nobler and a manlier one."

Now as "there is a time for all things," we persist in saying that the time and place for school-girls to hear their own music, or to prove that it is not worth hearing, is not in the drawing-room of a hotel, or in the presence of a company that can have no desire to hear them. What would be thought of a young lady, who in a public room, should suddenly come forward and "speak a speech;" or suddenly rise up, and commence, "loud and high," a reading of poetry, or recite a French fable, or repeat the multiplication table, or favour the company with a spontaneous *pas seul.* And yet we do not perceive that any of these feats would be a much greater evidence of deficiency in diffidence, (to call it by no bolder name,) than the practice of rattling, uninvited and unseasonably, over the keys of a piano. A really good musician is rarely obtrusive with her music, seldom playing unless she is asked; and then, of course, complying at once.*

We repeat that no lady should play or sing in company, unless she knows herself to be universally considered a good singer or player, and capable of something more than the mere series of lessons she has learnt from her music teacher. Also, some punishment should be devised for a young girl who cannot play, yet has the folly and assurance to seat herself at the piano of a public parlour, and annoy the company by an hour of tinking and tanking with one finger only. Yet this we have seen; and her mother present all the time.

The gratuitous exhibition of bad music is said by Europeans to be one of the peculiar characteristics of

---

* It is customary with professional or public musicians, when in private company, to volunteer a song or a piece; knowing that, out of delicacy, no one will *ask* them to give a gratuitous specimen of the art by which they live. This is polite and proper. It is always duly appreciated, and adds to the popularity of the per-former.

American young ladies. Let them then "reform it altogether."

Bring no large sewing into the ladies' drawing-room, and nothing that will produce clippings or litter. Whenever you have occasion to write more than a few lines, do it in your own apartment. It is well to have always there a small writing-case of your own, with paper, pens, ink, wafers, sealing-wax, envelopes, post-office stamps, &c. There are very neat little writing-cases, (to be purchased at the best stationers,) that are fitted with receptacles for all the above articles, excepting paper; the whole occupying no more space in your travelling-satchel than a needle-book. The ink is so secured, that there is no danger of its spilling. You may even carry these writing-cases in your pocket as conveniently as a card-case. As writing-paper should not be folded or rolled in packing, lay it flat in a small port-folio, and put it into your trunk. You will find great convenience, when from home, to have with you a little assortment of writing materials.

Except in cases of illness, it is well to decline invitations to visit ladies in their own apartments, unless you are very intimately acquainted with them, or have some particular business. Too much sociability may induce communications too confidential; and subsequent events may prove this confidence to be misplaced. Among the ladies staying at a hotel, there is always more harmony, when they all content themselves with meeting at table, or in the public drawing-room. Young ladies should not encourage daily morning visits from young men boarding at the same house, particularly if these visits are long. In our country, nearly every young man is obliged, in some way, to get his own living; and few can afford to idle away their mornings in loitering about parlours, and talking flirtation. A youth who passes his time in this manner, is a beau not worth having. A man that deserves to be called a *good match* has something else to do with his mornings. Ladies at hotels should be specially careful not to make acquaintance with gentlemen of whom they know nothing. If a man of notoriously dissipated or immoral character, presumes to request an introduction to a lady who is aware of his bad reputation, let her at once reply that not considering the acquaintance desirable, she must be excused for declining it. It is better thus to keep off an objectionable man, (even with the certainty of offending him,) than weakly to subject yourself to the annoyance and discredit (perhaps, still worse) of allowing him to boast of his intimacy with you.

In conversing with gentlemen at hotels, (and all other places,) try not to fall into the too common practice of talking to him nothing but nonsense. It is a problem difficult to solve, that so many ladies of good abilities and cultivated minds, and who always with their own sex talk like intelligent, sensible women, should, as soon as they get into conversation with a gentleman, seem immediately to take leave of rationality, and demean themselves like utter fools—giving way at once to something they call *excitement*, now the fashionable word for almost every feeling that is wrong.

We grieve to see a charming, modest, refined young lady, almost the moment a gentleman begins to talk to her, changing her whole demeanour, and quickly becoming bold, forward, noisy, and nonsensical; chattering at the top of her voice about nothing; and keeping up a continual laugh about nothing. Does she suppose he cannot understand her if she talks sense,—or does she think he will like her the better for regaling him with nothing but folly? She is, in all probability, egregiously mistaken, unless the gentleman is himself a simpleton.

Let it not be supposed that we have any objection to that sprightliness which is one of the most agreeable characteristics of youth. On the contrary, we are glad to see vivacity in women of all ages; and if they have a sprinkling of wit and humour, so much the better. But we wish them to do themselves justice; and not, when conversing with men, run wild, because it *is* with men; and give themselves up to all manner of folly, such as would be pointless, vapid, and insipid, if it was not seasoned with causeless laughter, and with eyes keeping time to the tongue, rolling about in perpetual motion at nothing. We do not wish ladies in conversing, even with men of sense, to confine themselves always to grave discussions on important subjects. On the contrary, gay and lively conversation is always pleasant, when well-timed. But those who have not a talent for wit and humour, had best not attempt it. Again, in listening to a woman of real wit, you will see that it is her hearers who laugh, and not herself.

Persons who have no turn for humour, and little perception of it, are apt to mistake mere coarseness for that amusing gift; and in trying to be diverting, often become vulgar—a word not too severe for things that are sometimes said and written by very good people who wish to be funny, and do not know how. For instance, there is no wit, but there is shocking ungentility, in a lady to speak of taking a "snooze" instead of a nap,—in calling pantaloons "pants," or gentlemen "gents,"—in saying of a man whose dress is getting old that he looks "seedy,"—and in alluding to an amusing anecdote, or a diverting incident, to say that it is "rich." All slang words are detestable from the lips of ladies.

We are always sorry to hear a young lady use such a word as "polking" when she tells of having been engaged in a certain dance too fashionable not long since; but happily, now it is fast going out, and almost banished from the best society. To her honour be it remembered, Queen Victoria has prohibited the polka being danced in her presence. How can a genteel girl bring herself to say, "Last night I was polking with Mr. Bell," or "Mr. Cope came and asked me to polk with him." Its coarse and ill-sounding name is worthy of the dance.

If you own a lap-dog or poodle, recollect that however charming it may be to yourself, others may regard it as an annoyance; therefore, try to do without it when you are in the parlour of a house that is not your own, and when the company present does not consist entirely of your own family. All but their

8

infatuated mistresses soon become very tired of the society of these animals. Poodles are generally peevish, whining, and snappish, prone to get under chairs and bite at feet, and to writhe about the skirts of dresses. Their faces often look old, withered, cross, and blear-eyed, seeming as if constantly troubled by the hair that dangles uncomfortably in their eyes; and they are seldom healthy. They have none of the honest, grateful, affectionate character common to dogs of larger growth. Though they often inspire their mistress with a love that becomes such a mania as to weaken her affection for all other things, they seldom make friends of any one else. We include what is called a King Charles's dog in the same category. For instance Jip—whose character is as true to nature, and as admirably drawn as that of Dora herself.

Should a visiter come in to see one of the boarders who may be sitting near you, change your place, and take a seat in a distant part of the room. It is ill-manners to remain, and listen to the conversation. It is best for the visited lady to meet her friend as soon as she sees her enter the room, and conduct her to a sofa or ottoman where they can enjoy their talk without danger of being overheard. After the visiter is gone, do not enquire her name of the friend she has just called on.

It is *not* well to call at the same time on two ladies both living at the same house, (so as to make one visit suffice for both,) unless they are intimate friends of each other, or unless your stay in the city will be very short. If one is taciturn, and the other conversable, she that is silent may imagine herself neglected, by the dialogue being chiefly between those who can talk fluently, as it certainly will be, if the third person only speaks when spoken to, and replies in monosyllables.

It is better to make a separate visit to each lady, on different days. There is another way, and a very good one. For instance, should Mrs. Canning wish to call on Mrs. Austin and Miss Lovel, both inmates of the same house, let her, when shown into the parlour, send up her name to Mrs. Austin first. When that lady comes down, and she and her friend have conversed about as long as the usual term of a morning call, Mrs. Canning will rise to depart, and when Mrs. Austin has seen her to the parlour door, Mrs. C. may say, "I will detain you no longer," or "I will encroach no longer on your time, but I am going now to send up for Miss Lovel."

Mrs. Austin then takes her leave, and goes up-stairs, (*her* part of the visit being over;) while Mrs. Canning returns to her seat in the parlour, having first rung the bell, and sent for Miss Lovel.

In this manner, two distinct visits may be politely made to two ladies living in the same hotel—and it is very customary.

Any lady that lives at a hotel can in some degree make a return for the civilities received from private families, by occasionally inviting a friend to dine or take tea with her. These dinners or teas are of course always charged in her bill. If she expects a friend, she will previously send to apprize the head-waiter that she wishes him to reserve a seat next to her own, for a lady. She should give her arm to her guest, in going to the table.

If a friend chances to call, whom she really wishes to stay and dine or drink tea with her, she should ask her guest to take off her bonnet as soon as she comes in; giving her the invitation at once, and not delaying it till the visiter is about taking her leave.

Even in a private house, such extemporaneous invitations (which if evidently sincere, are always gratifying, whether accepted or not) should be given *immediately*, as soon as the hostess meets her guest. There will then be time to order any improvement in the table arrangements that may be deemed necessary.

We often have occasion to repeat, that whatever is done at all, should be done well.

If, while in the parlour of the hotel, you wish to know if a person you are desirous of seeing is staying at the house, the easiest way to obtain the information, is not to enquire round of the ladies present, but to ring the bell, and desire the waiter to go and ask at the office. You can then send a message accordingly. It should be a card with a message pencilled on it.

By sending to the office you may learn where all the public places in the city and its environs are to be found. Also, where the churches are situated.

You may be sure that the most fashionable shops are in the main street.

At any stationer's, you can buy a small pocket-map of the city, folded in a little morocco case. This will be an almost indispensable aid in finding your way

In Philadelphia, the arrangement of the long streets that run east and west from the Delaware to the Schuylkill, has given occasion to the old rhyme of

> Market, Arch, Race and Vine,
> Chestnut, Walnut, Spruce and Pine.

If when about to ascend the stairs, you find that a gentleman is going up at the same time, draw back and make a sign for him to precede you. He will bow, and pass on before you. When coming down, do the same, that the gentleman may descend in advance of you.

A very polished man will not wait for a signal from the lady, but will bow and run up-stairs, passing her as a thing of course.

Do not idly detain a parlour newspaper on your lap, for half an hour or more, after you have done reading it. As soon as you have read all you want, replace it on the table, or transfer it to another lady, who may wish to read it, and who may have been waiting anxiously to see you lay it out of your hand. You have no right to monopolize any thing that is intended for the convenience of the whole company.

CHAPTER XI.

HOTEL DINNER.

IN dressing for a hotel dinner, it is not well to adopt a full evening costume, and to appear as if attired for a ball; for instance, with a coloured velvet gown; or one of a splendid brocade; or a transparent gauze material over a satin; or with short sleeves and bare neck in cold weather; or with flowers or jewels in the hair. Such costumes should be reserved for evening parties. If worn at the table d'hôte, it may be suspected you have no other place in which to display them. Your dress need not be more showy than you would wear when dining at a private house, particularly if you are a permanent boarder. There is no place where dress escapes with less scrutiny than at a great hotel. Still, it is bad taste to go to the dinner-table in ungenteel and unbecoming habiliments —such as a figured or party-coloured mousseline-de-laine, a thing which always has the effect of calico, and, like calico, gives an unlady-like look even to the most decided lady. In fact, what is it but woollen calico? And if it is accompanied by a very thin, flimsy collar, so small and narrow as to be scarcely visible, the neck and face will look dingy and ill-coloured for want of sufficient white to relieve it. No collar at all, but merely a coloured silk handkerchief. or a coloured dress, coming immediately against the neck, is disfiguring to all women, and men too.

Most American ladies beyond the age of thirty-five, look better in caps than without them, even if their hair shows no signs of middle age. Before that time, the females of our country begin to fade, evincing one effect of torrid summers and frozen winters. A tasteful and simply elegant cap (not one that is elaborate in its design, and loaded with ornament,) imparts a grace and softness to a faded face, and renders less conspicuous the inroads of time. A decidedly old lady, persisting in going with her head uncovered, is a pitiable object, and scarcely looks respectable. Worse still, when she takes to an auburn wig. Gray hair is seldom unbecoming to a man. To a woman it gives a masculine aspect, especially if worn without a cap; and if there is an attempt at long gray locks, or ringlets, the effect is strange, wild and ghastly. It is far more becoming for an elderly lady to give a dark shade to her temples, and the upper part of her forehead, by a plain, simple, and becoming dark-coloured braid, not intended to pass as her natural hair, (for it never does,) but merely that the face should be set off by a due proportion of shadow,—and not be all light or lightish. If a decidedly old lady prefers wearing her own gray hair, let her part it smoothly on her forehead, but make no attempt at curls, and be sure to add a cap to it. An elderly female should, as we have said, *always* wear a cap; and her cap should have tabs or broad strings to

tie under her chin. There is no use or beauty in a
lady looking older than is necessary, by wearing a
short-eared or round-eared cap, set back from her
head, and exposing all her cheeks even beyond her
ears, with the crease in her chin, and the deep
furrows or wrinkles on each side of her neck—all
which can be concealed by bringing forward the bow
of her cap tabs.

Let all ladies, old and young, avoid having their
caps trimmed with ribbons or flowers of what are called
high-colours; deep, heavy pinks and blues, and reddish
lilacs. These colours vulgarize every thing they are
intended to decorate. High-coloured ribbons, flowered
or figured, are decidedly vulgar.

A profusion of jewels at a public table is in very
bad taste, particularly if the jewellery is palpably
false—for instance, a large brooch with great mock
diamonds, or a string of wax beads meant for pearls.
Still worse, glass things imitating topazes or garnets
—or two or three gilt bracelets on one arm. A *large*
imitation gem always betrays its real quality by its size.

Endeavour to make your arrangements so as to be
dressed for dinner, and seated in the ladies' drawing-
room, about ten or fifteen minutes before the dining-
hour, that you may be ready to go in with the rest of
the company.

If you and your party are strangers, recently arrived, do not at once take the lead, and walk up to the
head of the table, regardless of dislodging and causing
inconvenience among the regular boarders, to whom
those seats have been allotted. But desire a servant

to show you a place. The head-waiter is usually at hand to arrange seats for the strangers, and he will attend to you. Persons not accustomed to hotels, frequently show a great craving for the seats near the head of the table. This is foolish. There are no places of honour; neither are the eatables better at one part of the table than another.

Nobody "sits below the salt." And every one has an equal chance of obtaining a share of the nicest articles on the table. What is most desirable is to have a seat in the vicinity of agreeable people, and you will more frequently find them about the middle, or lower end of the table, than at the top—that being the place usually most coveted by the least genteel of the guests. We have seen the Chief Magistrate of the Union, "the ruler of millions," simply take a seat near the door, at the lower end of a hotel-table, in Philadelphia, having arrived unexpectedly.

As we have said before, we perceive not the propriety or the convenience of a large party of strangers, on entering in a body, pertinaciously making their way to the upper end of the table, with a determination to obtain seats all in a row; as if the whole row together could join in the same conversation, or even *see* each other, when they sit on the same side.

In seating yourself, look down for a moment to see if you have placed the foot of your chair on the dress of the lady sitting next to you; and if you have done so, remove it immediately, that her dress may be in no danger of tearing when she attempts to rise.

Sit close to the table, but never lean your elbows upon it. To sit far from it, and reach out distantly, is very awkward. Having unfolded your napkin, secure it to your belt with a pin, to prevent its slipping down from your lap, and falling under the table. This may be done so that the pinning will not be perceptible. Bring with you a spare pin or two for this purpose,—or keep always a pincushion in your pocket. It is much better than to incur the risk of getting your dress greased or stained by the napkin deserting your lap. If such accidents *should* happen, pass them over slightly, and do not lose your temper. For the present, wipe the spot with your napkin, and dip the corner in water, and rub it lightly over the grease-mark. When dinner is over, you can finish repairing the injury in your own room. The coloured waiters are generally very clever at removing grease-spots from dresses. One of them will do it for you after dinner. The stain of wine or fruit may in most cases be taken out of a washable article by laying it immediately in cold water.

To eat in gloves or mittens was always foolish; fortunately it is no longer fashionable; but greatly the contrary.

Refrain from loud talking, or loud laughing. Young ladies truly genteel are never conspicuously noisy at a public table, or anywhere else. Still more carefully refrain from whispering, or exchanging significant glances. Whispers are always overheard, (even when the vulgar precaution is taken of screening your mouth with your hand,) and glances are always observed.* Joggings, nudgings, pinchings, sleeve-pull-ings, &c. are excessively unlady-like, and shamefully impudent when (as is often the case) the eye of the jogger is fixed upon the object of the jog. To put up an eye-glass at the face of a stranger, is very rude. So it is to make remarks in French.

When eating fish, first remove the bones carefully, and lay them on the edge of your plate. Then with your fork in your right hand, (the concave or hollow side held uppermost,) and a small piece of bread in your left, take up the flakes of fish. Servants, and all other persons, should be taught that the butter-sauce should not be *poured over* the fish, but put on one side of the plate, that the eater may use it pro-fusely or sparingly, according to taste, and be enabled to mix it conveniently with the sauce from the fish-castors. Pouring butter-sauce *over* any thing is now ungenteel.

Do not attempt removing a cover from a dish, that you may help yourself before the rest of the company. Leave all that to the waiters. Tell them what you want in a distinct, but not in a loud, conspicuous voice. In asking a servant to bring you a thing, add not the useless and senseless words "*will* you?" for instance, "Bring me the bread, will you?"—"Give me some water, will you?" Of course he will. Has he the

* A whisperer usually betrays herself by unconsciously fixing her eyes on the person she is secretly talking of. If you wish to inform your neighbour that a distinguished person is present, say softly, "Mr. C. is here, but do not look at him just now."

option of refusing? How you would be startled were he to answer, "*I will not.*" It is well always to say, even to servants, "I will thank you for the bread,—or the water." If you are a stranger in the house, ask, at the beginning, the servant who waits on you to tell you his name. This may save you some inconvenience. Where servants are numerous, they should always go by their surnames, and be called Wilson, Jackson, Thomson, or whatever it may be. This will prevent the confusion arising from half a dozen Johns, or as many Williams.

If the waiters are attentive, and in sufficient number, you will have, at a *good* hotel, little or no occasion to help yourself to any thing. Do not, under any circumstances, reach across the table, or rise on your feet to get at any particular dish you may want. Trouble no one of the company; but wait till you see a servant at hand. No man who is a gentleman ever puts the ladies in requisition to help him at table.

It is not customary at hotels for ladies to be assiduous in watching and supplying the plates of gentlemen. They can take care of themselves.

If in turning to speak to a waiter, you find him in the act of serving some one else, say, " *When you are at leisure*, I will thank you for some water,"—or whatever you may want.

It is selfish to be continually sending out of the room the man who waits near you, for the purpose of bringing extra things for yourself. Try to be satisfied with what you find on the table, and recollect that you are depriving others of his services, while you are dispatching him back and forward on errands to the kitchen.

Many persons hold silver forks awkwardly, as if not accustomed to them. It is fashionable to use your knife only while cutting up the food small enough to be eaten with the fork alone. While cutting, keep the fork in your left hand, the hollow or concave side downward, the fork in a very slanting position, and your fore-finger extended far down upon its handle. When you have done cutting up what you are going to eat, lay aside your knife, transfer the fork to your right hand, and take a small piece of bread in your left. If eating any thing soft, use your silver fork somewhat as a spoon, turning up the hollow side that the cavity may hold the food. If engaged in talking, do not, meanwhile, hold your fork bolt upright, but incline it downward, so as to be nearly on a level with your plate. Remember, always, to keep your own knife, fork, and spoon out of the dishes. It is an insult to the company, and a disgrace to yourself, to dip into a dish any thing that has been even for a moment in your mouth. To take butter or salt with your own knife is an abomination. There is always a butter-knife and a salt-spoon. It is nearly as bad to take a lump of sugar with your fingers.

In eating bread at dinner, break off little bits, instead of putting the whole piece to your mouth and biting at it.

No lady looks worse than when gnawing a bone, even of game or poultry. Few *ladies* do it. In fact. nothing should be sucked or gnawed in public; neither corn bitten off from the cob, nor melon nibbled from the rind.* It is very ungraceful to eat an orange at table, unless, having cut a bit off the top, you eat the inside with a tea-spoon—otherwise reserve it for the privacy of your own room. Always pare apples and peaches; and crack no nuts with your teeth. In eating cherries, put your half-closed hand before your mouth to receive the stones; then lay them on one side of your plate. To spit out the stones one at a time as you proceed with the cherries is very ungenteel. Get rid of plumb-stones in the same manner.

Do not eat incongruous and unsuitable things from the same plate, telling the waiter that "he need not change it, as it will do very well." The washing of a plate (more or less) is no object whatever in a large establishment, and it is expected that the guests will have clean ones very frequently.

It is an affectation of ultra-fashion to eat pie with a fork, and has a very awkward and inconvenient look. Cut it up first with your knife and fork both; then proceed to eat it with the fork in your right hand.

Much of this determined fork-exercise may be considered foolish. But it is fashionable.

If a lady wishes to eat lobster, let her request the waiter that attends her, to extract a portion of it from the shell, and bring it to her on a clean plate—also to place a castor near her.

---

* It is, however, customary in eating sweet potatoes of a large size, to break them in two, and taking a piece in your hand, to pierce down to the bottom with your fork, and then mix in some butter, continuing to hold it thus while eating it.

Novices in lobster sometimes eat it simply with salt, or with vinegar only, or with black pepper. This betrays great ignorance of the article. To prepare it according to the usual custom,—cut up, very small, the pieces of lobster, and on another plate make the dressing. First, mash together some hard-boiled yolk of egg, and some of the red coral of the lobster, with a little salt and cayenne. Mix in, with a fork, mustard to your taste; and then a liberal allowance of salad-oil, finishing with vinegar. Transfer the bits of lobster to the plate that has the dressing, and combine the whole with a fork. Lettuce salad is dressed in the same manner.

At a public table, a lady should never volunteer to dress salad for others of the company. Neither should she cut up a pie, and help it round. These things ought only to be done by a gentleman, or a servant.

If a gentleman with whom you are acquainted has dressed a salad, and offers the plate to you, take what you want, and immediately return to him the remainder; and do not pass it on to persons in your vicinity. It is *his* privilege, and not *yours* to offer it to others, as he has had the trouble of dressing it. And it is just that he should have a portion of it for himself, which will not be the case if you officiously hand it about to people around you. Leave it to him to dispose of as he pleases.

It was formerly considered ill-manners to refuse to take wine with a gentleman. Now that the fortunate increase of temperance has induced so many persons to abjure, entirely, the use of all liquors, it is no longer an offence to decline these invitations. If you have no conscientious scruples, and if you are acquainted with the gentleman, or have been introduced to him, (not else,) you may comply with his civility, and when both glasses are filled, look at him, bow your head, and taste the wine. If you are placed between a lady and gentleman who are taking wine together, lean back a little that they may see each other's faces. It is not customary, in America, for a lady to empty her glass,—or indeed, at a hotel, or boarding-house, to take wine with the same gentleman after the first day. Next time he asks, politely refuse, simply desiring him to excuse you. If he is a true gentleman, he will regard your refusal in its proper light, and not persist. We have often, at a public table, regretted to see ladies in the daily practice of taking wine with the same gentleman as often as invited. This "daily practice" is improper, indelicate, and we will say mean—for wine is expensive, and no lady should every day place herself under the same obligation to the same gentleman, even for a single glass. He will not respect her the more for doing so. On no consideration let any lady be persuaded to take *two* glasses of champagne. It is more than the head of an *American* female can bear. And she may rest assured that (though unconscious of it herself) all present will find her cheeks flushing, her eyes twinkling, her tongue unusually voluble, her talk loud and silly, and her laugh incessant. Champagne is very insidious; and two glasses may throw her into this pitiable condition.

If a stranger whom you do not know, and to whom

you have had no introduction, takes the liberty of asking you to drink wine with him, refuse at once, positively and coldly, to prove that you consider it an unwarrantable freedom. And so it is.

If you are helped to any thing whose appearance you do not like, or in which you are disappointed when you taste it, you, of course, at a hotel table, are not obliged to eat it. Merely leave it on your plate, without audibly giving the reason; and then, in a low voice, desire the waiter to bring you something else. It is well, while at table, to avoid any discussion of the demerits of the dishes. On the other hand, you may praise them as much as you please.

In refusing to be helped to any particular thing, never give as a reason that "you are afraid of it," or "that it will disagree with you." It is sufficient simply to *refuse;* and then no one has a right to ask why? While at table, all allusions to dyspepsia, indigestion, or any other disorders of the stomach, are vulgar and disgusting. The word "stomach" should never be uttered at any table, or indeed anywhere else, except to your physician, or in a private conversation with a female friend interested in your health. It is a disagreeable word, (and so are all its associations,) and should never be mentioned in public to "ears polite." Also, make no remarks on what is eaten by persons near you, (except they are children, and under your own care,) such as its being unwholesome, indigestible, feverish, or in any way improper. It is no business of yours; and besides, you are not to judge of others by yourself. No two constitutions are alike, and what

9

is very bad for *you*, may be perfectly innoxious to others. If persons are with you in whom you are much interested, and over whom you have influence, and they seem inclined to eat what is bad for them, refrain from checking them in presence of strangers. Above all, do not open your eyes, and hold up your hands, and exclaim against their folly, and want of self-control, and predict their certain sufferings from that cause. But if you *must* remonstrate, wait till you have quitted the table, and find yourself alone with the delinquent.

Never, while at table, (whether in public or private,) allow yourself to talk on painful or disgusting subjects. Avoid all discussions of sicknesses, sores, surgical operations, dreadful accidents, shocking cruelties, or horrible punishments. A love of such topics, evinces a coarse and unfeminine mind. It is rude in gentlemen at any time to introduce them before ladies; and a polished man never does so. The conversation at table should be as cheerful and pleasant as possible. Political and sectarian controversies ought to have no place there. Shakspeare truly says, "Unquiet meals make ill digestion."

Avoid the discussion at table of private affairs; either your own, or those of other people. Remember that "servants have ears," and frequently much more quickness of comprehension and retentiveness of memory than is generally supposed. So have children.

Abstain from picking your teeth at table. Notwithstanding that custom has allowed this practice in Europe, (even in fashionable society,) it is still a very disagreeable one, and to delicate spectators absolutely sickening to behold. Delay it till you are alone, and till you can indulge in it without witnesses. We know that it is quite possible to go on through a long life, and to have clean teeth, without ever once having been *seen* to pick them; and yet those teeth are really picked after every meal.

Should you chance to be extremely incommoded by some extraneous substance that has gotten between your teeth, you can remove it unperceived, by holding up your napkin or handkerchief before your mouth, so as effectually to conceal the process. When you take any thing out of your teeth, do not make the persons who are near you sick, by laying the disgusting particle on the side of your plate; but conceal it immediately. Still, nothing but "sheer necessity" can excuse any teeth-picking at table.

We have seen a young *lady*, at a very fashionable house in one of our great cities, pull a dish of stewed oysters close to her, and with a table-spoon fish out and eat the oysters one at a time; audibly sipping up their liquor from the said dish.

We have seen a young *gentleman* lift his plate of soup in both hands, hold it to his mouth and drink, or rather lap it up. This was at no less a place than Niagara.

We have heard of a well-dressed stranger at a great hotel in Boston, who having used his own knife for the butter, flew into a violent passion with the waiter for respectfully pointing out to him the silver butter-knife. Swearing that the knife he had been putting in his mouth was quite good enough, afterward, for any butter in the world, the *gentleman* flung the silver knife across the table, and broke it against the wall. For this exploit he had to pay five dollars.

A man that habitually rises on his feet to reach across the table for a dish, and pulls it to himself, instead of desiring the waiter to bring it to him, is unworthy the appellation of a gentleman. Ladies, of course, cannot be guilty of this abomination; but it is true that they sometimes extend their arms entirely too far, in trying to get at something which a servant would bring them if asked to do so.

Some persons behave coarsely at a public table because they are ignorant, and know no better. Some (far less excusable) are rude because they are too selfish to put any restraint on their inclinations, or to care for the convenience of others.

Some display, all the time, a vulgar determination to "get the full worth of their money." Some, who at a *private* dinner-table would be the most polite people imaginable, lay aside their good manners in a *public* dining-room; regarding a hotel as they would a tavern—a sort of Liberty Hall. And some are insolent by way of "showing their consequence,"—having, in reality, mixed so little with *true* people of consequence, as not to be aware that persons of high station are, with few exceptions, entirely free from the assumption of undue importance.

Servants are often very shrewd observers, and they always say that real gentlefolks "never take airs." Neither they do.

When the finger-glasses are sent round, dip a clean corner of your napkin into the water, and wet round your lips with it, but omit the disgusting foreign fashion of taking water into your mouth, rinsing and gurgling it round, and then spitting it back into the glass. Wait till you can give your mouth a regular and efficient washing up-stairs. Dip your fingers into the glass, rub them with the slice of lemon, or the orange-leaf that may be floating on the surface, and then wipe them on the napkin. We have heard of a man who saw finger-glasses for the first time in his life, when dining at one of the New York hotels. A slice of lemon floating on the top, he took up the bowl and drank the water, exclaiming as he set it down— "Well! if this isn't the poorest lemonade I ever tasted!"

On quitting the table, it is not necessary to fold up your napkin. Merely lay it on the table near your plate. The napkins will be immediately collected by the servants, carried to the laundry, and thrown at once into tubs of water, to take out the stains.

When dinner is over, and you see that nearly all the company, except two or three, have left the table, it is not well to be one of that two or three, and to remain to an indefinite period, loitering over the last pickings of a plate of nuts—nut-picking being always a tedious business. The waiters are, by this time, very tired of standing, and they (like all other people) are entitled to some consideration of their comfort. Even the attraction of a beau drinking his wine beside er, ought not to induce a young lady to outstay all

the company, with the pretext of being passionately
fond of nuts. She may indulge this passion at any
time by keeping a bag of them in her own room.

The English travellers who visit America are often
right in their remarks on many of our customs. And
instead of resenting these remarks, we might profit by
them, and reform.

For instance, it is true that the generality of Americans eat too fast, for their own health, and the comfort
of those about them; masticating their food very
slightly, and not allowing themselves time enough to
enjoy their meals. The French, however, eat faster
still, and can dispatch a surprising quantity of food in
less time than any people in the civilized world. If
we pattern after either nation in the customs of the
table, the *genteel* English are far better models than
most of their neighbours across the Channel. But the
best class of Americans are unsurpassed in the essen-
tials of all these observances. The English attach too
much importance to ceremonies merely conventional,
and for which there seems no motive but the ever-
changing decrees of fashion. Yet, on going to England, let every American lady take care to make
herself acquainted with these ceremonies; for her
ignorance of them will find no quarter there—and she
need not flatter herself that it will be passed over unnoticed.

In most hotels it is not customary to have hot cakes
or any warm dishes on the tea-table, except in cold
weather. We think, in a summer afternoon, they can
be easily dispensed with, and that ladies might be

satisfied with sweet cakes, fruit, preserves, and other things more delicate, and more suited to the hour, than the hot preparations they sometimes call for; and which, by not seeing them on the table, they may be assured do not come within scope of the tea-arrangements. It is expecting too much to suppose the cook will be willing to mix batter-cakes and bake them, or to scorch over the fire with broiling or stewing relishes, in a warm summer evening—or even to make toast, except for an invalid. Also, every one should know that a substantial meal (including tea and coffee) can generally be had at the nine o'clock supper-table. In houses where there is no nine o'clock supper, the tea-table is set out with greater profusion and variety.

At hotels, the interval between dinner and tea is usually short; the tea-hour being early, that the guests may have ample time to prepare for going to places of amusement. Yet there are ladies who, though spending all the evening at home, will remain sitting idly in the parlour till eight o'clock, (or later still,) keeping the table standing and servants waiting in attendance, that they may have a better appetite, and be able to make a heartier meal at their tea. This is selfish and inconsiderate, particularly as they might easily wait a little longer, and take their tea or coffee at the supper-table. Their appetites would then be still better. The servants certainly require rest, and should be exempt from all attendance in the ladies' eating-room, for an hour or two in the evening.

No lady can remain long in the drawing-room

talking to a gentleman after all the rest have retired for the night, without subjecting herself to remarks which it would greatly annoy her to hear—whether merited or not. Neither is it well for her to be seen continually sitting at the same window with the same gentleman.

Ladies and gentlemen who wish to hold private dialogues, should not for that purpose monopolize a centre-table; thereby preventing persons who wish to read from availing themselves of the light of the chandelier above it. Lovers who have proper consideration, (a rare occurrence,) always sit as far as possible from the rest of the company, and so they should—unless they can bring themselves to join in general conversation. That is, if the lovership is real. In many cases the semblance is only assumed to produce effect, and the talk has really nothing secret or mysterious about it, and might just as well be uttered audibly.

In making acquaintance with a stranger at a hotel, there is no impropriety (but quite the contrary) in enquiring of her from what place she comes. In introducing yourself give your name *audibly;* or what is still better, if you have a card about you, present that; and she should do the same in return. Before you enter into conversation on any subject connected with religion, it will be well to ask her to what church she belongs. This knowledge will guard you from indulging, inadvertently, in sectarian remarks which may be displeasing to her, besides producing a controversy which may be carried too far, and produce ill-feeling between the parties. We have known the mere question, "Have you been to church to-day?" when asked of a stranger at a Sunday dinner-table, bring on a dialogue of great asperity, and very annoying to the hearers. As it cannot possibly concern yourself whether the strangers at a hotel have been to church or not, or what church they have visited, omit catechising them at table on this or any other religious subject. We have never known a clergyman guilty of this solecism in good sense and good manners.

When you give a gratuity to a servant—for instance, to the man who waits on you at table, or he that attends your room, or to the chambermaid or the errand-boy—give it at no regular time, but whenever you think proper, or find it convenient. It is injudicious to allow them to suppose that they are to do you no particular service without being immediately paid for it. It renders them mercenary, rapacious, and neglectful of other boarders who are less profuse; not reflecting that the servants are hired to wait on the company, and are paid wages for doing so, by the proprietor of the establishment, and that it is therefore their duty to him, and to his guests, to exert themselves so to give satisfaction. Still, it is right and customary to pay them extra for conveying your baggage up and down stairs when you are departing from the house or returning to it. Carrying heavy baggage is very hard work even for strong men. If you are a permanent boarder, and from ill-health require extra attendance, it is well to give a certain

ium, monthl*f*, to each of the servants who wait upon
you; and then they will not expect any thing more,
except on extraordinary occasions. And to each of
them, separately, give the money with your own hand.
In short, whatever you give to any one, (servants or
others,) it is safest, when convenient, to bestow it in
person. There will then be no mistakes, no forget-
tings, and no temptation to embezzlement.

If you live in Philadelphia, you will find it very
convenient, in most cases, to send messages by a note
with a stamp on it, put into the city-post. There is
a mail-bag and a letter-box at all hotels, and at most
of the large boarding-houses. The errand-boy of the
hotel carries parcels, and takes such messages as
require an *immediate* answer. For a distance of any
consequence, he will expect from twelve to twenty-
five cents. For little errands in the immediate
neighbourhood, less will suffice. When a servant
brings you small change, do not tell him to keep it.
It is giving him the bad habit of expecting it always;
and at times when you may have occasion, yourself,
for that very change. It is the worst way of feeing
them. On leaving the house, and at Christmas, it is
customary to give a fee rather larger than usual, to
the servants who have been your attendants. But as
we have said before, give it with your own hands.

It is ungenerous and most unjustifiable to bribe
the servants to neglect other boarders, (whose place is
near yours,) for the purpose of their bestowing on you
a double share of attention. It is taking an undue
advantage, which in the end will come out badly.

All persons who go to hotels are not able to lavish large and frequent gratuities on the servants. But all, for the price they pay to the proprietor, are entitled to an ample share of attention from the domestics.

It is very mean and unladylike to gossip secretly with the servants, and question them about any of the other guests. Still worse, to repeat what they tell you, and give *them* as authority. Treat them always with kindness and civility, but have no confidential and familiar intercourse with them. To those you know, it is but common civility to bid good morning every day. Coloured people you may always gratify by saying a few words to them, now and then, in passing. They value this little kindness, and will not presume upon it like those from "the old country," who, if treated familiarly, will frequently take liberties, and lose all respect for you. Elderly coloured people, (particularly in the South,) like much to be called "aunt" or "uncle;" and it degrades no white lady to please them by doing so.

In all hotels, it is against the rule to take out of the ladies' drawing-room any books that may be placed there for the general convenience of the company, such as dictionaries, guide-books, directories, magazines, &c. If you borrow a file of newspapers from the reading-room, get done with them as soon as you can, lest they should be wanted there by the gentlemen; and as soon as you have finished, ring for a servant to carry them back.

Be careful, in cold weather, always to shut the

parlour-doors after you. If you think the room too warm, do not throw open either door or window, without first enquiring if it will cause inconvenience to any one present. It is a good practice to carry a pocket fan even in winter, in case you should chance to feel the heat more sensibly than any other lady in the room. If the heat of the grate causes you inconvenience, enquire if there is any objection to having the blower brought in and stood up before it. If not, ring the bell and order it.

If you have an anthracite fire in your chamber, and wish to extinguish it on retiring for the night, take the tongs, and lifting off some of the largest coals from the top, lay them beneath the grate. Then, with the shut-tongs or the poker, make a deep hollow in the centre of the fire; raking it into two hills, one on each side, leaving a valley down in the middle. It will begin to blacken immediately, and go out in a few minutes. If you cannot do this yourself, ring for a servant.

This is *the only way* to put out an anthracite fire, whether in a grate or a stove.—There is no other. Try it.

CHAPTER XII.

SHIP-BOARD.

THERE are few places where the looks and manners of the company are more minutely scanned than on ship-board; and few where the agreeability of a lady will be more highly appreciated. There is little or no variety of objects to attract attention. The passengers are brought so closely into contact with each other, and confined to so small a neighbourhood, or rather so many neighbours are crowded into so small a space, that all their sayings and doings are noticed with unusual attention, by those who are well enough to regard any thing but themselves. Sea-sickness is a very selfish malady,—and no wonder that it is so. Fortunately it is less prevalent than formerly, thanks to the improvements in cabin-room, ventilation, lodging, food, and many other things connected with ocean-travelling. A lady who is not of a bilious or dyspeptic habit, and who has taken precautionary medicine a few days before commencing the voyage, frequently escapes sea-sickness altogether; or at least gets well after the first day or two.

It is best not to be over-officious in offering your aid to the sick ladies, unless they are your intimate friends. The stewardess of a packet-ship is generally

all-sufficient; and much more capable of attending to
their wants than you can be. Sea-sickness renders
its victims very querulous; and few like to be continually reminded of their condition by enquiries too often
repeated of—"How do you find yourself now?" "Do
you feel any better?" or, "Do you think you could
not eat something?" To one very much prostrated
by the effects of the sea-motion, the mere replying to
these questions is an additional misery. Whatever
sympathy you may feel, at the time, for those afflicted
with the marine malady, remember that it is a disorder which never kills, but very frequently cures.

If you are sick yourself, say as little about it as
possible. And never allude to it at table, where you
will receive little sympathy, and perhaps render yourself disgusting to all who hear you. At no time talk
about it to gentlemen. Many foolish commonplace
sayings are uttered by ladies who attempt to describe
the horrors of sea-sickness. For instance this—"I
felt all the time as if I wished somebody to take me
up, and throw me overboard." This is untrue—no
human being ever really *did* prefer drowning to sea-
sickness.

When the ship is actually in danger, this malady is
always frightened away; the feelings of the mind
entirely overpowering those of the body.

Try to avoid supposing that every fresh gale is a
violent storm; but confide in the excellence of the
ship, and the skill of its navigators. Yet, though not
afraid yourself, remember that others may be so, and
do not try to show your courage by indulging in undue

gayety. Mirth is out of place when the sky is over-cast with gloom, the wind blowing hard, and the waves "running mountains high," and foaming and roaring all round the vessel.

If there is truly a violent tempest, and if the danger is real and imminent, trust to that Almighty Power who is with you always,—on the sea, and on the land; and silently and fervently implore his protection.

No captain likes to be teazed with importunities concerning the probable length of the passage. You may be sure he will do all he can to make it as short as possible. In rough weather, refrain from asking, whenever you see him, "If there is any danger?" If there really is, he will certainly let you know it in time.

Endeavour to live harmoniously with your fellow-passengers. Avoid such national allusions as may give offence to the foreigners. If you find that any of them are in the frequent practice of sneering at your own country, or speaking of it disrespectfully, repress your resentment, resort to no recrimination, but refrain from further conversation with that individual, and leave him to the gentlemen. If a female foreigner is in the habit of gratuitously abusing America, endeavour calmly to convince her that her ideas of your country are erroneous. If she will not be convinced, (as is most likely, if she is an *ungenteel* Englishwoman,) give up the attempt, and leave her to herself. If you have a taste for the ridiculous, you will regard her prejudices and the expression of them only as objects of amusement.

Avoid all arguments with a woman of irritable disposition, lest you are drawn in yourself to defend your opinion too warmly. You will soon find whether or not you can convince her, or whether she is likely to convince you. And it is worse than useless for both to continue protracting the argument, when they know that the opinion of neither will be shaken. Also, it is foolish to keep on repeating the same ideas, with no change but in a few of the words.

Long and turbulent discussions are peculiarly annoying on ship-board, particularly in rainy weather, when for the weary and pent-up audience, "there's no door to creep out."

It is certainly advisable for every lady on ship-board to endeavour to make herself as agreeable as she can, and not to suppose that all her "whims and oddities" will be excused because she is suffering "the pains and penalties" of the sea, and is therefore not "a responsible being." If free from sickness, a lady may propose or promote many pleasant little amusements and occupations; such as playing children's games on deck, or taking a part in chess, chequers, and backgammon in the cabin. Ladies sometimes form a regular little coterie, for assembling at certain hours, and employing themselves in knitting, bead-work, light-sewing, &c. while a gentleman reads aloud to them in some entertaining book. In the evening, vocal concerts will be an agreeable variety, as there are always some persons on board who can sing. And when the weather is fine, and the ship steadily laying her course, a moonlight dance on deck is delightful.

A young lady should improve the opportunity of learning the names of the principal parts of the ship. It is a silly boast at the end of the voyage, (and yet we have heard such boasts,) to say that you do not know the fore-mast from the main-mast; and that you have no idea where the mizen-mast is, much less the bow-sprit. And even if a fair damsel should be able to distinguish the fore-topsail from the jib, and to know even the flying-jib, and have learnt the difference between the compass and the quadrant, and the log-line and the lead-line, we opine that "the gentlemen" will think none the worse of her; to say nothing of the satisfaction it will afford herself to listen with some comprehension to talk concerning the ship, and to read understandingly a few of the numerous excellent novels that treat of "life on the ocean wave."

If you have, unfortunately, the rude and unamiable habit of laughing whenever you see any one get a fall, leave it off when on ship-board,—where falls are of continual occurrence from the rolling of the vessel, and the steepness of the stairs. We never could tell why a fall, even on the ice, should be regarded as a subject of mirth, when the chance is that it may produce a serious hurt, and is always attended with some pain or some annoyance at least. Low-bred women always say they cannot help laughing at such sights. We think *ladies* ought always to help it, and hasten at once to the relief of the sufferer, to ascertain if they are hurt

Be washed and dressed *neatly* every day. This

10

can generally be managed with the assistance of the female servants—even if you *are* sick.

A piano never sounds well on ship-board—the cabins are too small, and the ceilings too low. To the sick and nervous, (and all who are sea-sick become *very* nervous,) this instrument is peculiarly annoying. Therefore be kind enough to spare them the annoyance. You can practise when the weather is fine, and the invalids are on deck. Pianos have been abolished in many of the finest ships. Such instruments as can be carried on deck, and played in the open air, are, on the contrary, very delightful at sea, when in the hands of good performers—particularly on a moonlight evening.

In going to England, take with you no American reprints of English books, unless you intend leaving them on board the ship. If you attempt to land them, they will be seized at the custom-house. American books by American authors are *not* prohibited.

Make no attempt to smuggle any thing. You may be detected and disgraced. The risk is too great, and the advantage too little.

When you leave your state-room to sit in the ladies' cabin, do not fall to relating the particulars of your sickness, or complaining of the smallness of your apartment, the rolling of the ship, or the roughness of the waves. These inconveniences are unavoidable, and must always be expected in a sea-voyage; and talking about them too much seems to magnify their evils.

If there is any deficiency in accommodations or

attentions, either try as well as you can to do without them, or in a kind and considerate manner endeavour to obtain them of the servants, if not too inconvenient, or against the ship's regulations.

It is very inconsiderate to have things cooked at luncheon time purposely for yourself. Ladies who are quite well will sometimes order baked apples, stewed prunes, buttered toast, arrow-root, cups of tea or coffee, &c.,—notwithstanding that the lunch-table is always profusely spread with a variety of cold articles; and that when dinner is cooking at the same time, the small size of the kitchen renders any extra preparations very inconvenient to the preparers.

CHAPTER XIII.

LETTERS.

THE practice of inclosing letters in envelopes is now universal; particularly as when the letter is single no additional postage is charged for the cover. The postage now is in almost every instance pre-paid, it being but three cents when paid by the writer, and five if left to the receiver. Therefore, none but very poor or very mean people send unpaid letters. Letter-stamps for the United States post should be kept in a little box on your writing-table. You can get them always by sending to the post-office—from a dollar's worth or more, down to fifty or twenty-five cents' worth, at a time. In a second box, keep stamps for the city or penny post, which transmits notes from one part of the town to another. And in a third, stamps to go on the covers of newspapers.

Sealing with wax is found to be very insecure for letters that are carried by steamers into warm climates—the wax melting with the heat, and sticking the letters to each other, so that they cannot be separated without tearing. Wafers are better.

It would be very convenient to use the post-office stamp as a seal, but the clerks in that establishment charge extra postage for the trouble of turning the letter to mark the stamp. This subjects the receiver to the payment of two additional cents.

In writing upon business exclusively your own, for instance to make a request, to ask for information, to petition for a favour, or to solicit an autograph, it is but right not only to pay the postage of your own letter, but to enclose a stamp for the answer. This is always done by really polite and considerate people. You have no right, when the benefit is entirely your own, to cause any extra expense to the receiver of the letter—not even the cost of three cents to pay the postage back again. It is enough to tax their time by requiring them to write to you and send off the reply. Also, in corresponding with a relative, or very intimate friend, to whom even a small expense is of more importance than to yourself, you may enclose a stamp for the answer. Do so always in writing to poor people. Be careful not to allow yourself to get entirely out of post-office stamps. Replenish your stock in time. If the gum on the back seems too weak, go over it afresh with that excellent cement, "Perpetual Paste." Embossed or bordered envelopes are not often used except in notes of ceremony—or when the acquaintance is slight. The same with ornamented note-paper. Intimate friends and relatives use paper that is handsome, but plain. Letters of business are generally enclosed in yellow or buff-coloured envelopes. Some of these yellow envelopes are large enough to contain a folio sheet when folded.

Notes *not* to be sent by post, are usually sealed with wax—the seal very small. But a *small* wafer is admissible—a white one looks best for a note. In folding your note or letter, see that it is not too large to go into the envelope. It is customary to write the direction on the envelope only. Nevertheless, if the letter is to go a long distance by post, the envelope may be worn off, or torn off accidentally, or get so damaged in the letter-bag as to be rendered illegible. The surest and safest way is to put the address on the letter also; or if the sheet is full, to find a corner for the direction, either at the beginning or end.

We have seen no *good* letter-paper at less price than twenty-five cents per quire; and for that it ought to be *very* good. If of lower cost, you may find it soft and fuzzy, so that the pen will not move freely, (the nib wearing out directly,) or so thin that you cannot write on both sides of the sheet. In paper, as in most other things, the best is the cheapest. If the tint is bluish, the writing will not be so legible as on a pure white. The surface should be smooth and glossy. For letter writing *ruled* paper is rarely used, except by children. In writing for the press, no other is so convenient. A page of ruled lines to slip beneath, is indispensable to those who cannot otherwise write straight. They are to be had for a few cents at every stationer's. It is well to get three different sizes. If you write a small hand, the lines should be closer together than if your writing is large. If you are addressing a friend and have much to say, and expect to fill the sheet, begin very near the top of the first page. But if your letter is to be a short one, commence lower down, several inches from the top. If a *very* short letter of only a few lines, begin but a little above the middle of the page. Crossing a letter all over with transverse lines is obsolete. It is intolerable to read, and there is no excuse for it now, when postage is so low, and every body pays their own.

Write the date near the right-hand side of the first page, and place it about two lines higher than the two or three words of greeting or accosting with which letters usually commence. Begin the first sentence a little below those words, and farther toward the right than the lines that are to follow. It is well in dating *every* letter to give always your exact residence—that is, not only the town you live in, but the number and street. If your correspondent has had *but one* notification of your present place of abode, she may have forgotten the number, and even the street. Your letter containing it may not be at hand as a reference, and the answer may, in consequence, be misdirected—or directed in so vague a manner that it will never reach you. We have known much inconvenience (and indeed loss) ensue from not specifying with the date of *each* letter the exact dwelling-place of the writer. But if it is *always* indicated at the top of *every one*, a reference to *any* one of your letters will furnish your proper address. If you are in the country, where there are no streets or numbered houses, give the name of the estate and that of the nearest post-town;

also the county and state. All this will occupy a long line, but you will find the advantage. If your letter fills more than one sheet, number each page. Should you have no envelope, leave, on the inside of the third page, two blank spaces where the seal is to come. These spaces should be left rather too large than too small. Lest you should tear the letter in *breaking* it open, it is best to *cut* round the seal. We have seen letters that were actually illegible from the paleness of the ink. If you write from your own house this is inexcusable, as you ought always to be *well* supplied with that indispensable article; and in a city you can easily send to a stationer's and buy it. It is still better to make it yourself; than which nothing is more easy. The following receipt *we know, by experience, to be superlative.* Try it.

Buy at a druggist's four ounces of the best blue Aleppo nut-galls; half an ounce of green copperas; and half an ounce of clean, white gum-arabic. These three articles must be pulverized in a mortar. Put them into a large, clean, white-ware pitcher, and pour on a quart of.boiling water. Stir the whole with a stick that will reach to the bottom, and set the pitcher in a warm place; covering it lightly with a folded newspaper. In about an hour, stir it again very hard; and repeat the stirring several times during the day. Let it remain in the pitcher several days, or a week, till it becomes an excellent black; the blackening will be accelerated by keeping the pitcher in the sun; for instance, in a sunny balcony. Stir it, down to the bottom, two or three times a day—always with a stick. Use nothing of metal in making this ink. When it is very black, and writes well, pour it off carefully from the bottom, (which must have rested undisturbed for two or three hours previous,) passing it through a funnel into pint-bottles. Before you cork them, put into each a large tea-spoonful of brandy, to prevent moulding, or a few drops of lavender. A small tea-spoonful of cloves, (slightly broken,) placed in the bottom of each bottle, before the ink is poured in, will answer the same purpose. Scouring the pitcher with soap and sand, after throwing away the dregs of the ink, will completely clear off the stains.

Ink-stands should be washed out, before they are filled anew.

There is no ink superior to this in blackness or smoothness. You can make it at less than half the cost of that which you buy in the shops. It looks blacker the next day after using, and never fades. If it becomes rather too thick, dilute it slightly with water, and stir it down to the bottom.

Never use *blue* ink. If the letter chances to get wet, the writing will be effaced. Serious losses have resulted from business letters being written in blue ink.

If you make a mistake in a word, draw your pen through it, or score it so as to be quite illegible, and then interline the correction, placing a caret beneath. This will be better than scratching out the error with your penknife, and afterward trying to write a new word in the identical place; an attempt which rarely succeeds, even with the aid of pounce-powder, which is pulverized gum-sandarac.

At the end of the letter, somewhat lower than your signature, (which should be very near the right-hand edge of the page,) add the name and address of the person for whom the letter is designed, and to whom it will thus find its way, even if the envelope should be defaced, or torn off and lost. Write your own name rather larger than your usual hand, and put a dot or dash after it.

Some of the ensuing paragraphs are taken (with permission of the publisher) from a former work of the author's.

In folding a letter, let the breadth (from left to right) far exceed the height. A letter folded tall is ridiculous, and one verging towards squareness looks very awkward. It is well to use a folder (or paper-knife) to press along the edges of the folds, that they may be smooth and straight. If one is looser than another, or if there is the slightest narrowing in, or widening out, toward the edge of the turn-over, the letter will have an irregular, unsightly appearance. Pieces of ruled lines may be so cut that you can slip them under the back of a letter after it is folded, and then you will be in no danger of writing the direction crooked, or uneven.

Write the name of your correspondent about the middle of the back, and very clearly and distinctly. Then give the number and street on the next line, a little nearer to the right. Then the town in *large* letters, extending still nearer to the right. If a country-town, give next (in letters a little smaller) the name of the *county* in which it is situated. This is very necessary, as in some of our states there is more than one town of the same name, and "Washingtons" all over the Union. Lastly, at the very bottom, and close to the right, indicate the state or district by its usual abbreviation,—for instance, *Me.* for Maine*—*N. H.* New Hampshire—*Vt.* Vermont—*Mass.* Massachusetts—*R. I.* Rhode Island— *Ct.* or *Conn.* Connecticut—*N. Y.* New York—*N. J.* New Jersey—*Pa.* or *Penna.* Pennsylvania—*Del.* Delaware—*Md.* Maryland—*Va.* Virginia—*N. C.* North Carolina—*S. C.* South Carolina—*Ga.* or *Geo.* Georgia —*Ala.* Alabama—*Miss.* Mississippi—*Mo.* Missouri— *La.* Louisiana—*Tenn.* Tennessee—*Ky.* Kentucky— *O.* Ohio—*Ind.* Indiana—*Ill.* Illinois—*Mich.* Michigan—*Ark.* Arkansas—*Wis.* Wisconsin—*Io.* Iowa— *Tex.* Texas—*Flo.* Florida—*Cal.* California—*Or.* Oregon—*Minn.* Minnesota—*Utah*—*D. C.* District of Columbia.

To these may be added the abbreviations of the British possessions in North America: *U. C.* Upper Canada—*L. C.* Lower Canada—*N. S.* Nova Scotia— *N. B.* New Brunswick—*N. P.* New Providence.

In directing a letter to a foreign country, give the whole name, as France, Spain, Belgium, England, Ireland, Scotland, &c. We have towns in America called after all manner of European towns. For in-

---

* When the name of the state is short, you may give all the letters that compose it, as Maine—Ohio—Iowa—Texas—Utah.

stance, a letter directed to our Havre-de-Grace, might, if Maryland was not designated, find its way to Havre-de-Grace in France; Rome in the state of New York might be taken to Rome in Italy,—York in Pennsylvania to York in England, &c.   We know an instance of a gentleman directing an important letter to Boston, and, forgetting to add *Mass.* (for Massachusetts) at the bottom, the letter actually went from Philadelphia to the small town of Boston in Lincolnshire, England. In writing *from* Europe, finish the direction with the words *United States of North America.*

When you send a letter by a private opportunity, (a thing which is already almost obsolete since the days of cheap postage,) it will be sufficient to introduce very near the lower edge of the left-hand corner of the back, simply the name of the gentleman who carries it, written small.   It is now considered old-fashioned to insert on the back of such a letter—"Politeness of Mr. Smith"—"Favoured by Mr. Jones"—"Honoured by Mr. Brown."   If the letter is to cross the sea, by mail or otherwise, write the name of the vessel on the left-hand corner of the outside.

When a letter is to go to New York city, always put the words New York *in full,* (and not N. Y.,) written large.   Much confusion is caused by the name of this state and its metropolis being the same.   It has been well-suggested that the name of the state of New York should be changed to Ontario—a beautiful change.   In directing to any of the towns in the state of New York, then put N. Y. after the name of the town, as Hudson, N. Y.,—Syracuse, N. Y., &c.

In sending a letter to the metropolis of the Union, direct for Washington, D. C.

In directing to a clergyman, put *Rev.* (Reverend) before his name. If a bishop, *Right Reverend.* To an officer, immediately after his name put U. S. A. for United States Army, or U. S. N. for United States Navy—having preceded his name with *Gen.*, *Col.*, *Capt.*, *Lieut.*, according to his rank.

The title Hon. (Honourable) is always used in directing to a member of congress, a member of the cabinet, a judge of the supreme court, an ambassador, or the governor of a state. For the Chief Magistrate of the Union, you may direct simply to the President of the United States. The term "Excellency" is now but little used.

For a gentleman holding a professorship in a university, preface his name with *Prof.* or *Professor.* The title of "Professor" does not really belong to all men who teach any thing, or to every man that exhibits a show—or to mesmerists, and spiritual knockers. Do not give it to them.

For sealing letters no light is so convenient as a wax taper in a low stand. A lamp, or candle, may smoke or blacken the wax. To seal well, your wax should be of the finest quality. Red wax of a bright scarlet colour is the best. Low-priced wax consumes very fast; and when melted, looks purplish or brownish. When going to melt sealing-wax, rest your elbow on the table to keep your hand steady. Take the stick of wax between your thumb and finger, and hold it a little above the light, so that it barely touches the point of the flame. Turn the stick round till it is equally softened on all sides. Then insert a little of the melted wax *under* the turn-over part of the letter, just where the seal is to come. This will render it more secure than if the sole dependence was on the outside seal. Or instead of this little touch of wax, you may slip beneath the turn-over a small wafer, either white or of the same colour as the wax. Then begin at the outer edge of the place you intend for the seal; and move the wax in a circle, which must gradually diminish till it terminates in the centre. Put the seal exactly to the middle of the soft wax, and press it down hard, but do not screw it round. Then withdraw it suddenly. Do not use motto seals unless writing to a member of your own family, or to an intimate friend. For common service, (and particularly for letters of business,) a plain seal, with simply your initials, is best.

For a note always use a very small seal. In addressing one of your own family, it is not necessary to follow scrupulously all these observances. In writing to persons decidedly your inferiors in station, avoid the probability of mortifying them by sending mean, ill-looking notes.

Remember also (what, strange to say, some people calling themselves ladies seem not to know) that a note commenced in the first person must continue in the first person all through. The same when it begins in the third person. We have heard of invitations to a party being worded thus:—

Mrs. Welford's compliments to Mrs. Marley, and requests the pleasure of her company on Thursday evening.

Yours sincerely,

E. WELFORD.

Notes of invitation should always designate both the day of the week and that of the month. If that of *the month only* is specified, one figure may perhaps be mistaken for another; for instance, the 13th may look like the 18th, or the 25th like the 26th. We know instances where, from this cause, some of the guests did not come till the night *after* the party.

There are some very sensible people who, in their invitations, tell frankly what is to be expected, and if they really ask but *a few* friends, they at once give the names of those friends, so that you may know whom you are to see. If you are to meet no more than can sit round the tea-table, they signify the same. If they expect twenty, thirty, or forty persons, they say so—and do not leave you in doubt whether to dress for something very like a party, or for a mere family tea-drinking.

If it is a decided music-party, by all means specify the same, that those who have no enjoyment of what is considered fashionable music, may stay away.

Always reply to a note of invitation the day after you have received it. To a note on business send an answer the same day. After accepting an invitation, should any thing occur to prevent your going, send a second note in due time.

Do not take offence at a friend because she does not invite you every time she has company. Her regard for you may be as warm as ever, but it is probably inconvenient for her to have more than a certain number at a time. Believe that the omission is no evidence of neglect, or of a desire to offend you; but rest assured that you are to be invited on other occasions. If you are *not*, then indeed you may take it as a hint that she is no longer desirous of continuing the acquaintance. Be dignified enough not to call her to account; but cease visiting her, without taking her to task and bringing on a quarrel. But if you *must* quarrel, let it not be in writing. A paper war is always carried too far, and produces bitterness of feeling which is seldom entirely eradicated, even after apologies have been made and accepted. Still, when an offence has been given in writing, the atonement should be made in writing also.

Much time is wasted (particularly by young ladies) in writing and answering such epistles as are termed "letters of friendship,"—meaning long documents (frequently with crossed lines) filled with regrets at absence, asseverations of eternal affection, modest deprecations of your humble self, and enthusiastic glorifyings of your exalted correspondent; or else wonderments at both of you being so much alike, and so very congenial; and anticipations of rapture at meeting again, and lamentations at the slow progress of time, till the extatic hour of re-union shall arrive— the *postscript* usually containing some confidential allusion to a lover, (either real or supposed,) and perhaps a kind enquiry about a real or supposed lover of your friend's.

Now such letters as these are of no manner of use but to foster a sickly, morbid feeling, (very often a fictitious one,) and to encourage nonsense, and destroy all relish for such true friendship as is good and wholesome.

A still worse species of voluminous female correspondence is that which turns *entirely* upon love, or rather on what are called "beaux;" or entirely on hate—for instance, hatred of step-mothers. This topic is considered the more *piquant* from its impropriety, and from its being carried on in secret.

Then there are young ladies born with the organ of letter-writing amazingly developed, and increased by perpetual practice, who can scarcely become acquainted with a gentleman possessing brains, without volunteering a correspondence with him. And then ensues a long epistolary dialogue about nothing, or at least nothing worth reading or remembering; trenching closely on gallantry, but still not quite *that;* affected flippancy on the part of the lady; and unaffected impertinence on that of the gentleman, "which serves her right"—alternating with pretended poutings on her side, and half or whole-laughing apologies on his. Sometimes there are attempts at moralizing, or criticising, or sentimentalizing—but nothing is ever elicited that, to a third person, can afford the least amusement or improvement, or excite the least interest. Yet, strange to say, gentlemen have been inveigled into this sort of correspondence, even by ladies who

11

have made a business of afterward selling the letters for publication, and making money out of them. And such epistles have actually been printed. We do not suppose they have been read. The public is very stubborn in refusing to read what neither amuses, interests, or improves—even when a publisher is actually so weak as to print such things.

No young lady ever engages in a correspondence with a gentleman that is neither her relative or her betrothed, without eventually lessening herself in his eyes. Of this she may rest assured. With some men, it is even dangerous for a lady to write a note on the commonest subject. He may show the superscription, or the signature, or both, to his idle companions, and make insinuations much to her disadvantage, which his comrades will be sure to circulate and exaggerate.

Above all, let no lady correspond with a married man, unless she is obliged to consult him on business; and from that plain, straight path let her not diverge. Even if the wife sees and reads every letter, she will, in all probability, feel a touch of jealousy, (or more than a touch,) if she finds that they excite interest in her husband, or give him pleasure. This will inevitably be the case if the married lady is inferior in intellect to the single one, and has a lurking consciousness that she is so.

Having hinted what the correspondence of young ladies ought *not* to be, we will try to convey some idea of what it ought. Let us premise that there is no danger of *any* errors in grammar or spelling, and but few faults of punctuation, and that the fair writers are aware that a sentence should always conclude with a period or full stop, to be followed by a capital letter beginning the next sentence; and that a new paragraph should be allotted to every change of subject, provided that there is room on the sheet of paper. And still, it is well to have always at hand a dictionary and a grammar, in case of unaccountable lapses of memory. However, persons who have read much, and read to advantage, generally find themselves at no loss in orthography, grammar, and punctuation. To spell badly is disgraceful in a lady or gentleman, and it looks as if they had quitted reading as soon as they quitted school.

To write a legible and handsome hand is an accomplishment not sufficiently valued. And yet of what importance it is! We are always vexed when we hear people of talent making a sort of boast of the illegibility of their writing, and relating anecdotes of the difficulty with which it has been read, and the mistakes made by its decipherers. There are persons who affect bad writing, and boast of it, because the worst signatures extant are those of Shakspeare, Bonaparte, and Byron. These men were great in spite of their autographs, not because of them. The caliph Haroun Alraschid, who was well imbued with Arabic learning, sent an elegantly written letter to Charlemagne, with a splendid cover and seals; not being aware that the European emperor's signature was made by dipping his thumb into the ink and giving a smear—sealing with the hilt of his dagger.

The "wording" of your letter should be as much like conversation as possible, containing (in a condensed form) just what you would be most likely to talk about if you saw your friend. A letter is of no use unless it conveys some information, excites some interest, or affords some improvement. It may be handsomely written, correct in spelling, punctuation, and grammar, and yet stiff and formal in style—affectedly didactic, and therefore tiresome—or mawkishly sentimental, and therefore foolish. It may be refined, or high-flown in words, but flat and barren in ideas, containing nothing that a correspondent cares to know.

Read over each page of your letter, as you finish it, to see that there are no errors. If you find any, correct them carefully. In writing a familiar letter, a very common fault is tautology, or a too frequent repetition of the same word—for instance, "Yesterday I received a letter from sister Mary, which was the first letter I have received from sister since she left." The sentence should be, "Yesterday I received a letter from my sister Mary, the first since she left us."

Unless you are writing to one of your own family, put always the pronoun "*my*" before the word "sister." Say also—"my father," "my mother," and not "father," "mother," as if they were also the parents of your correspondent.

To end the sentence with the word "left," (for departed,) is awkward and unsatisfactory—for instance, "It is two days since he left." Left what? It is one of the absurd innovations that have crept in among us of late years, and are supposed to be fashionable. Another is the ridiculous way of omitting the possessive S in words ending with that letter; for instance, "Sims' Hotel" instead of "Sims's Hotel" —"Jenkins' Bakery" for "Jenkins's Bakery." Would any one, in talking, say they had stayed at Sims' Hotel, or that they bought their bread at Jenkins' Bakery. This is ungrammatical, as it obliterates the possessive case, and is therefore indefinite; and moreover, it looks and sounds awkwardly.

Many persons who think themselves good grammarians put on their cards "The Misses Brown,"— "The Misses Smith." Those who *really* are so, write "The Miss Browns"—"The Miss Smiths"—the plural being always on the substantive, and never on the adjective. Would we say "the whites glove" instead of "the white gloves"—or the "blues ribbon" for the "blue ribbons." Does any lady in talking say, "The two Misses Brown called to see me?"

It is also wrong to say "two *spoons*ful," instead of two *spoon*fuls. Thus, "two spoonsful of milk" seems to imply two separate spoons with milk in each; while "two spoonfuls of milk" gives the true idea—one spoon twice filled.

Avoid in writing, as in talking, all words that do not express the true meaning. We are sorry to say that sometimes even among educated people, when attempting smartness or wit, we find a sort of conventional slang that has, in truth, a strong tinge of vulgarity, being the wilful substitution of bad words or bad phrases for good ones. When we find them

issuing from the lips or the pen of a *lady*, we fear she
is unfortunate in a reprobate husband, or brother,
from whom she must have learnt them. Yet even
reprobates dislike to hear their wives and sisters talking coarsely.

Unless you know that your correspondent is well
versed in French, refrain from interlarding your letters
with Gallic words or phrases.

Do not introduce long quotations from poetry.
Three or four lines of verse are sufficient. One line,
or two, are better still. Write them rather smaller
than your usual hand, and leave a space at the beginning and end; marking their commencement and
termination with inverted commas, thus " "

One of our young relatives when seven or eight
years old, tried her hand at story-writing. In finishing the history of a naughty girl, much addicted to
falsehood, the terminating sentence ran thus:—

"Arabella did not cure herself of this fault; but
when she grew up, and became an authoress, she never
marked her quotations."

If your letter is longer than can be comprised in
one sheet, number the pages, placing the number near
the upper corner. If engaged in a regular correspondence on business or other things, or in writing from a
foreign country to your family at home, number not
only the pages, but the letter itself, putting that figure
in the centre at the top of the first page. Thus, if
your friend, having received No. 10, finds the next
letter that comes to hand is No. 12, she will know
that No. 11 is missing, and will tell you so in her

reply. Keep a memorandum of the letters you have sent, that you may know how to number the next. Before commencing a long letter, it is well to put down on a slip of paper, a list of the subjects you intend to write on.

Unless to persons living in the same house, do not inclose one letter in another. And even then, it is not always safe to do so. Let each letter be transmitted on its own account, by mail, with its own full direction, and its own post-office stamp. We know an instance where the peace of a family was entirely ruined by one of its members suppressing enclosed letters. Confide to no one the delivery of an important letter intended for another person. It is better to trust to the mail, and send a duplicate by the next post.

To break the seal of a letter directed to another person is punishable by law. To read *secretly* the letter of another is morally as felonious. A woman who would act thus meanly is worse than those who apply their eyes or ears to key-holes, or door-cracks, or who listen under windows, or look down from attics upon their neighbours; or who, in a dusky parlour, before the lamps are lighted, ensconce themselves in a corner, and give no note of their presence while listening to a conversation not intended for them to hear.

We do not conceive that, unless he authorizes her to do so, (which he had best not,) a wife is justifiable in opening her husband's letters, or he in reading hers. Neither wife nor husband has any right to entrust to the other the secrets of their friends; and letters may contain such secrets.   Unless under extraordinary circumstances, parents should not consider themselves privileged to inspect the correspondence of grown-up children.   Brothers and sisters always take care that their epistles shall not be unceremoniously opened by each other.   In short, a letter is the property of the person to whom it is addressed, and nobody has a right to read it without permission.

If you are shown an autograph signature at the bottom of a letter, be satisfied to look at *that only;* and do not open out, and read the whole—unless desired.

Some years ago, in one of our most popular magazines, were several pages containing fac-simile signatures of a number of distinguished literary women— chiefly English.   We saw an original letter, from a lady, who complained that some mischievous person had taken *her* magazine out of the post-office before it reached her, and shamefully *scribbled women's names* in it, disfiguring it so as to render it unfit for binding; therefore she desired the publisher to send her a clean copy in place of it.

In putting up packets to send away, either tie them round and across, with red tape, (sealing them also where the tape crosses,) or seal them without any tape.   If the paper is strong, the wax good, and the contents of the parcel not too heavy, sealing will in most cases be sufficient.   Twine or cord may cut the paper, and therefore is best omitted.   Never put up a parcel in newspaper.   It looks mean and disrespectful, and will soil the articles inside.

Keep yourself provided with different sorts and sizes of wrapping-paper.

A large packet requires more than one seal; the seals rather larger than for a letter.

Put up newspapers, for transmission, in thin whitish or brownish paper, pasting the cover, and leaving one end open. Newspaper-stamps cost but one cent, and are indispensable to the transmission of the paper.

Avoid giving letters of introduction to people whose acquaintance cannot possibly afford any pleasure or advantage to those whose civilities are desired for them, or who have not leisure to attend to strangers. Artists, authors, and all other persons to whom "time is money," and whose income stops whenever their hands and eyes are unemployed, are peculiarly annoyed by the frequency of introductory letters, brought by people with whom they can feel no congeniality, and whom they never would have sought for. Among the children of genius, but few are in a situation to entertain strangers *handsomely*, as it is called, which means, *expensively*. Many are kept always in straitened circumstances, from the incessant demands on their time and attention. And in numerous instances, letters are asked and given with no better motive than the gratification of idle curiosity.

We advise all persons obtaining an introductory letter to a painter, to ascertain, before presenting it, what branch of the art he professes. We have been asked whether a certain artist (one of the most distinguished in London) painted "figures, flowers, or landscapes." Also, no one should presume to request an introduction to an authoress, if they are ignorant whether she writes prose or verse. Not that they are expected to talk to her, immediately, on literary subjects. Far from it; but if they know nothing of her works, they deserve no letter. In America, books, or at least newspapers, are accessible to all who can read.

Bores are peculiarly addicted to asking letters of introduction, in accordance with their system of "bestowing their tediousness" upon as many people as possible. We pity the kind friends from whom these missives are required, and who have not courage to refuse, or address enough to excuse themselves plausibly from complying.

We have known instances of stupid, vulgar persons, on preparing to visit another city, obtaining letters to families of the really highest class, and receiving from them the usual civilities, which they knew not how to appreciate.

On the other hand, how pleasant it is, by means of an introductory letter, to bring together two kindred spirits, whose personal intercourse must inevitably produce mutual satisfaction, who are glad to know each other, glad to meet frequently, and grateful to the friend who has made them acquainted.

Letters of introduction should not be sealed. To do so is rude, and mean. If you wish to write on the same day to the same person, take another sheet, write as long an epistle as you please, seal it, and send it *by mail*.

It is best to deliver an introductory letter in person, as the lady or gentleman whose civilities have been requested in your behalf, may thus be spared the trouble of calling at your lodgings, with the risk of not finding you at home. This is very likely to happen, if you *send* instead of taking it yourself. If you *do* send it, enclose a card with your residence. Also, it is more respectful to go yourself, than to expect them to come to you.

As soon as you are shown into the parlour, send up the letter, and wait till the receiver comes to you.

When a letter is brought to you by a private hand, the usual ceremony is to defer reading it till the bringer has departed, unless he desires you to read it at once, which he will, if it is evidently a short letter. If a long one, request him to excuse you a moment while you look at the beginning, to see if your correspondent is well.

On farewell cards, it is usual to write with a pencil the letters " t. t. l.," " to take leave"—or " p. p. c.," " pour prendre congé." A lady complained to us that an acquaintance of hers, about to leave town, had left a card for her with " p. d. a." upon it. Not understanding the meaning of these letters, she had applied to a friend for explanation, who told her they meant " poor dear adieu." " Now," continued she—" I cannot understand why a mere acquaintance should be so familiar as to call me ' poor dear ;' why am I a poor dear to her ?" We relieved her by explaining that " pour dire adieu" was French for " to bid adieu."

To conclude—let nothing induce you to give a letter of introduction to any person whose moral character is disreputable.

CHAPTER XIV.

PRESENTS.

HAVING accepted a present, it is your duty, and ought to be your pleasure, to let the giver see that you make use of it as intended, and that it is not thrown away upon you. If it is an article of dress, or of personal decoration, take occasion, on the first *suitable* opportunity, to wear it in presence of the giver. If an ornament for the centre-table, or the mantel-piece, place it there. If a book, do not delay reading it. Afterward, speak of it to her as favourably as you can. If of fruit or flowers, refer to them the next time you see her.

In all cases, when a gift is sent to you, return a note of thanks; or at least a verbal message to that effect.

Never enquire of the giver what was the price of her gift, or where she bought it. To do so is considered exceedingly rude.

When an article is presented to you for a specified purpose, it is your duty to use it for *that* purpose, and for no other, according to the wish of the donor. It is mean and dishonourable to give away a present; at least without first obtaining permission from the original giver. You have no right to be liberal or generous at the expense of another, or to accept a gift with

a secret determination to bestow it *yourself* on somebody else. If it is an article that you do not want,
that you possess already, or that you cannot use for
yourself, it is best to say so candidly, at once; ex-
pressing your thanks for the offer, and requesting
your friend to keep it for some other person to whom
it will be advantageous. It is fit that the purchaser
of the gift should have the pleasure of doing a kindness with her own hand, and eliciting the gratitude of
one whom she knows herself. It is paltry in you to
deprive her of this pleasure, by first accepting a present,
and then secretly giving it away as from yourself.

There are instances of women whose circumstances
did not allow them to indulge often in delicacies, that
on a present of early fruit, or some other nice thing
being sent to them by a kind friend, have ostenta-
tiously transferred the gift to a wealthy neighbour,
with a view of having it supposed that they had
bought it themselves, and that to *them* such things
were no rarities. This is contemptible—but it is sometimes done.

Making a valuable present to a rich person is in
most cases, a work of supererogation; unless the gift
is of something rare or *unique*, which cannot be purchased, and which may be seen and used to more
advantage at the house of your friend than while in
your own possession. But to give an expensive article
of dress, jewellery, or furniture to one whose means
of buying such things are quite equal (if not superior)
to your own, is an absurdity; though not ·a very
uncommon one, as society is now constituted. Such

gifts elicit no real gratitude, for in all probability, they may not suit the pampered taste of those to whom fine things are no novelties. Or they may be regarded (however unjustly) as baits or nets to catch, in return, something of still greater cost.

There are persons, who, believing that presents are generally made with some mercenary view, and being unwilling themselves to receive favours, or incur obligations, make a point of repaying them as soon as possible, by a gift of something equivalent. This at once implies that they suspect the motive. If sincere in her friendship, the donor of the first present will feel hurt at being directly paid for it, and consider that she has been treated rudely, and unjustly. On the other hand, if compensation *was* secretly desired, and really expected, she will be disappointed at receiving nothing in return. Therefore, we repeat, that among persons who can conveniently provide themselves with whatever they may desire, the bestowal of presents is generally a most unthankful business. If you are in opulent circumstances, it is best to limit your generosity to such friends only as do not abound in the gifts of fortune, and whose situation denies them the means of indulging their tastes. By them such acts of kindness will be duly appreciated, and gratefully remembered; and the article presented will have a double value, if it is to them a novelty.

Gratitude is a very pleasant sensation, both for those who feel and to those who excite it. No one who confers a favour can say *with truth*, that "they want no thanks." They always do.

We know not why, when a young lady of fortune is
going to be married, her friends should all be expected
to present her with bridal gifts. It is a custom that
sometimes bears heavily on those whose condition
allows them but little to spare. And from that little
it may be very hard for them to squeeze out enough
to purchase some superfluous ornament, or some bauble
for a centre-table, when it is already glittering with
the gifts of the opulent;—gifts lavished on one who is
really in no need of such things; and whose marriage
confers no benefit on any one but herself. Why should
she be rewarded for gratifying her own inclination in
marrying the man of her choice? Now that it is
fashionable to display all the wedding-gifts arranged
in due form on tables, and labelled with the names of
the donors, the seeming necessity of giving something
expensive, or at least elegant, has become more onerous
than ever. For instance, poor Miss Cassin can barely
afford a simple brooch that costs about five dollars;
but she strains the utmost capacity of her slender purse
to buy one at ten dollars, that it may not disgrace the
brilliant assemblage of jewellery that glitters on the
bridal table of her wealthy friend Miss Denham. And
after all, she finds that her modest little trinket looks
really contemptible beside the diamond pin given by
Mrs. Farley the millionaire. After all, she sees
no one notice it, and hears no one say that it is even
neat and pretty. To be sure, the bride, when it was
sent with a note on the preceding day, did vouchsafe
a polite answer. But then, if poor Miss C. does not
make a wedding present to rich Miss D., it might be

supposed that Miss C. cannot afford it. Neither she can. And her making the effort elicits perhaps some satirical remarks, that would be very mortifying to Miss Cassin if she heard them.

We repeat, that we cannot exactly perceive why, when the union of a couple of lovers, in many cases, adds to the happiness, honour, and glory of the married pair alone, their friends should think it a duty to levy on themselves these contributions; so often inconvenient to the givers, and not much cared for by the receivers.

When the young couple are not abounding in what are called "the goods of this world," the case is altered; and it may then be an act of real kindness for the opulent friends of the bride to present her with any handsome article of dress, or of furniture, that they think will be acceptable. What we contend is, that on a marriage in a wealthy family, the making of presents should be confined to the immediate relatives of the lady, and only to such of *them* as can well afford it.

Much of the money wasted in making ostentatious gifts to brides whose fathers have already given them a splendid outfit, might be far better employed, in assisting to purchase the *trousseaus* and the furniture of deserving young women in humble life, on their marriage with respectable tradesmen or mechanics. How many ladies of fortune have it in their power to do this—yet how seldom it is done!

At christenings, it is fortunately the sponsors only that are expected to make gifts to the infant. Therefore, invite no persons as sponsors, who cannot well afford this expense; unless you are sufficiently intimate to request them, privately, not to comply with the custom; being unwilling that they should cause themselves inconvenience by doing so.

The presentation of Christmas and New-Year's gifts is often a severe tax on persons with whom money is not plenty. It would be well if it were the universal custom to expect and receive no presents from any but the rich.

In making gifts to children, choose for them only such things as will afford them somewhat of lasting amusement. For boys, kites, tops, balls, marbles, wheelbarrows, carts, gardening utensils, and carpenter's tools, &c. Showy toys, that are merely to look at, and from which they can derive no enjoyment but in breaking them to pieces, are not worth buying. Little girls delight in little tea-sets, and dinner-sets, in which they can "make feasts," miniature kitchen-utensils, to play at cooking, washing, &c.; and dolls so dressed that all the clothes can be taken off and put on at pleasure. They soon grow tired of a doll whose glittering habiliments are sewed fast upon her. A wax doll in elegant attire is too precarious and expensive a plaything to make them happy; as they are always afraid of injuring her. We knew a little girl for whom a magnificent wax doll, splendidly dressed, was brought from France; and for an hour she was highly delighted. But next morning she was found still more happy in carrying about her favourite baby, a sofa-pillow, with an old shawl pinned round it for a

12

frock; feeling perfect freedom to toss it about as she pleased. Children like their doll-babies to be very substantial, and rather heavy than light. A large, well-made *rag*-doll is for a small child far better than any other—occasionally putting a clean new face upon it.

We have seen country children perfectly satisfied with a doll that was nothing but a hard ear of Indian corn, arrayed in a coarse towel pinned round it. A little farm-house boy, of three years old, made a pet of a large squash, which he dressed in a pocket-handkerchief, and called Phebe Ann. We heard him say, as he passed his hand over its lumpy neck, "Poor Phebe Ann! what hives she has!"

To an intelligent child, no gifts are so valuable as entertaining books—provided they really *are* entertaining. Children are generally wise enough to prefer an amusing book in a plain cover, to a dull one shining with gold. When children are able to read fluently, they lose much of their desire for mere picture-books. If the cuts are badly executed, and give ugly, disagreeable ideas of the characters in the stories, they only trouble and annoy the little readers, instead of pleasing them. Some of the most popular juvenile books have no pictures inside, and no gilding outside. Bad engravings, (beside uselessly enhancing the price,) spoil the taste of the children. We highly recommend to the publishers of juvenile books to omit the cuts entirely, if they cannot afford very good ones. Many children have better judgment in these things than their parents suppose; and some of them more than the parents themselves.

Children have less enjoyment than is supposed in being taken to shops to choose gifts for themselves, or even in laying out their own money. It is always a long time before they can decide on what to buy, and as soon as they have fixed upon one thing, they immediately see something they like better. And often, after getting home, they are dissatisfied with their choice, and sorry they bought it. Also, they frequently wear out the patience of the shopkeepers; being desirous of seeing every thing, and pondering so long before they can determine on buying any thing.

It is every way better to go to the shops without them, buy what you think proper, and then give them an agreeable surprise by the presentation.

Young ladies should be careful how they accept presents from gentlemen. No truly modest and dignified woman will incur such obligations. And no gentleman who really respects her will offer her any thing more than a bouquet, a book, one or two autographs of distinguished persons, or a few relics or mementos of memorable places—things that derive their chief value from associations. But to present a young lady with articles of jewellery, or of dress, or with a costly ornament for the centre-table, (unless she is his affianced wife,) ought to be regarded as an offence, rather than a compliment, excusable only in a man sadly ignorant of the refinements of society. And if he is so, she should set him right, and civilly, but firmly, refuse to be his debtor.

Yet, we are sorry to say, that there are ladies so

rapacious, and so mean, that they are not ashamed to give broad hints to gentlemen, (particularly those gentlemen who are either very young or very old,) regarding certain beautiful card-cases, bracelets, essence-bottles, &c. which they have seen and admired,— even going so far as to fall in love with elegant shawls, scarfs, splendid fans, and embroidered handkerchiefs. And their admiration is so violent, and so reiterated, that the gentleman knows not how to resist; he therefore puts them in possession of a gift far too costly for any woman of delicacy to accept.   In such cases, the father or mother of the young lady should oblige her to return the present.   This has been done.

There are ladies who keep themselves supplied with certain articles of finery, (for instance, white kid gloves,) by laying ridiculous wagers with gentlemen, knowing that, whether winning or losing, the gentleman, out of gallantry, always pays.   No lady should ever lay wagers, even with one of her own sex.   It is foolish and unfeminine—and no man likes her any the better for indulging in the practice.

Some young ladies, who profess a sort of daughterly regard for certain wealthy old gentlemen, are so kind as to knit purses or work slippers for them, or some other nick-nacks, (provided always that the "dear old man" has a character for generosity,) for they know that he will reward them by a handsome present of some bijou of real value.   And yet they may be assured that the kind old gentleman (whom "they mind no more than if he was their pa") sees through the whole plan, knows why the purse was knit, or the slippers worked, and esteems the kind young lady accordingly.

Another, and highly reprehensible way of extorting a gift, is to have what is called a philopena with a gentleman. This very silly joke is when a young lady, in cracking almonds, chances to find two kernels in one shell; she shares them with a beau; which ever first calls out "*philopena*," on their next meeting, is entitled to receive a present from the other; and she is to remind him of it till he remembers to comply. So much nonsense is often talked on the occasion, that it seems to expand into something of importance; and the gentleman thinks he can do no less, than purchase for the lady something very elegant, or valuable; particularly if he has heard her tell of the munificence of other beaux in their philopenas.

There is great want of delicacy and self-respect in philopenaism, and no lady who has a proper sense of her dignity *as a lady* will engage in any thing of the sort.

In presenting a dress to a friend whose circumstances are not so affluent as your own, and who you know will gladly receive it, select one of excellent quality, and of a colour that you think she will like. She will feel mortified, if you give her one that is low-priced, flimsy, and of an unbecoming tint. Get an ample quantity, so as to allow a piece to be cut off and laid by for a new body and sleeves, when necessary. And to make the gift complete, buy linen for the body-lining; stiff, glazed muslin for the facings; buttons, sewing-silk, and whatever else may be wanted. This will save her the cost of these things.

When you give a dress to a poor woman, it is far better to buy for her a substantial new one, than to bestow on her an old thin gown of your own. The poor have little leisure to sew for themselves; and second-hand fine clothes last them but a very short time before they are fit only for the rag-bag.

If you are going to have a party, and among your very *intimate* friends is one whose circumstances will not permit her to incur the expense of buying a handsome new dress for the occasion, and if she has no choice but to stay away, or to appear in a costume very inferior to that of the other ladies, you may (if you can well afford it) obviate this difficulty by presenting her with a proper dress-pattern, and other accessories. This may be managed anonymously, but it will be better to do it with her knowledge. It will be a very gratifying mark of your friendship; and she ought to consider it as such, and not refuse it from a feeling of false pride. Of course, it will be kept a secret from all but yourselves. In the overflow of gratitude *she* may speak of it to others, but for *you* to mention it would be ungenerous and indelicate in the extreme. We are glad to say that ladies of fortune often make gifts of party-dresses to their less-favoured friends.

In sending a present, always pay in advance the expense of transmitting it, so that it may cost nothing at all to the receiver. You may send by the Mail a package of any size, weighing not more than four pounds, paying the postage yourself at the office from whence it goes. It will then be delivered at the door of your friend, without further charge.

CHAPTER XV.

CONVERSATION.

CONVERSATION is the verbal interchange of thoughts and feelings. To form a *perfect* conversationist, many qualifications are requisite. There must be knowledge of the world, knowledge of books, and a facility of imparting that knowledge; together with originality, memory, an intuitive perception of what is best to say, and best to omit, good taste, good temper, and good manners. An agreeable and instructive talker has the faculty of going "from gay to grave, from lively to serene," without any apparent effort; neither skimming so slightly over a variety of topics as to leave no impression of any, or dwelling so long upon one subject as to weary the attention of the hearers. Persons labouring under a monomania, such as absorbs their whole mind into one prevailing idea, are never pleasant or impressive talkers. They defeat their own purpose by recurring to it perpetually, and rendering it a perpetual fatigue. A good talker should cultivate a temperance in talking; so as not to talk too much, to the exclusion of other good talkers. Conversation is dialogue, not monologue. It was said of Madame de Stael that she did not converse, but delivered orations.

To be a perfect conversationist, a good voice is indispensable—a voice that is clear, distinct, and silver-toned. If you find that you have a habit of speaking too low, "reform it altogether." It is a bad one; and will render your talk unintelligible.

Few things are more delightful than for one intelligent and well-stored mind to find itself in company with a kindred spirit—each understanding the other, catching every idea, and comprehending every allusion. Such persons will become as intimate in half an hour, as if they had been personally acquainted for years.

On the other hand, the pleasure of society is much lessened by the habit in which many persons indulge, of placing themselves always in the opposition, controverting every opinion, and doubting every fact. They talk to you as a lawyer examines a witness at the bar; trying to catch you in some discrepancy that will invalidate your testimony; fixing their scrutinizing eyes upon your face "as if they would look you through," and scarcely permitting you to say, "It is a fine day," without making you prove your words. Such people are never popular. Nobody likes perpetual contradiction, especially when the subject of argument is of little or no consequence. In young people this dogmatic practice is generally based upon vanity and impertinence. In the old it is prompted by pride and selfishness. We doubt if in the present day the talk and manners of Johnson would have been tolerated in really good society.

Unless he first refers to it himself, never talk to a

gentleman concerning his profession; at least do not question him about it. For instance, you must not expect a physician to tell you how his patients are affected, or to confide to you any particulars of their maladies. These are subjects that he will discuss only with their relatives, or their nurses. It is also very improper to ask a lawyer about his clients, or the cases in which he is employed. A clergyman does not like always to be talking about the church. A merchant, when away from his counting-house, has no wish to engage in business-talk with ladies; and a mechanic is ever willing "to leave the shop behind him." Every American is to be supposed capable of conversing on miscellaneous subjects; and he considers it no compliment to be treated as if he knew nothing but what the Scotch call his "bread-winner." Still, there are some few individuals who like to talk of their bread-winner. If you perceive this disposition, indulge them, and listen attentively. You will learn something useful, and worth remembering.

Women who have begun the world in humble life, and have been necessitated to give most of their attention to household affairs, are generally very shy in talking of housewifery, after their husbands have become rich, and are living in style, as it is called. Therefore, do not annoy them by questions on domestic economy. But converse as if they had been ladies always.

Lord Erskine, having lived a bachelor to an advanced age, finally married his cook, by way of securing her services, as she had frequently threatened to leave him. After she became Lady Erskine she lost all knowledge of cookery, and it was a mortal affront to hint the possibility of her knowing how any sort of eatable should be prepared for the table.

Never remind any one of the time when their situation was less genteel, or less affluent than at present, or tell them that you remember their living in a small house, or in a remote street. If they have not moral courage to talk of such things themselves, it is rude in you to make any allusion to them.

On the other hand, if invited to a fashionable house, and to meet fashionable company, it is not the time or place for you to set forth the comparative obscurity of your own origin, by way of showing that you are not proud. If *you* are not proud, it is most likely that your entertainers may be, and they will not be pleased at your ultra-magnanimity in thus lowering yourself before their aristocratic guests. These communications should be reserved for *tête-à-têtes* with old or familiar friends, who have no more pride than yourself.

When listening to a circumstance that is stated to have actually occurred to the relater, even if it strikes you as being very extraordinary, and not in conformity to your own experience, it is rude to reply, "Such a thing never happened to *me*." It is rude because it seems to imply a doubt of the narrator's veracity; and it is foolish, because its not having happened to *you* is no proof that it could not have happened to any body else. Slowness in belief is sometimes an evidence of ignorance, rather than of knowledge. People who have read but little, travelled but little, and seen but little of the world out of their own immediate circle, and whose intellect is too obtuse to desire any new accession to their own small stock of ideas, are apt to think that nothing can be true unless it has fallen under their own limited experience. Also, they may be so circumstanced that nothing in the least out of the common way is likely to disturb the still water of their pond-like existence.

A certain English nobleman always listens incredulously when he hears any person descanting on the inconveniences of travelling on the continent, and relating instances of bad accommodations and bad fare; uncomfortable vehicles, and uncomfortable inns; the short beds and narrow sheets of Germany; the slow and lumbering diligence-riding of France; the garlicky stews of Spain with a feline foundation; the little vine-twig fires in the chilly winters of Northern Italy; and various other ills which the flesh of travellers is heir to;—the duke always saying, "Now really *I* never experienced any of these discomforts, much as I have traversed the continent. None of these inconveniences ever come in my way." And how should they, when, being a man of enormous wealth, he always travels with a cavalcade of carriages; a retinue of servants; a wagon-load of bedding and other furniture; a cook, with cooking-utensils, and lots of luxurious eatables to be cooked at stopping-places— his body-coach (as it is called) being a horse-drawn palace. What inconveniences can possibly happen to *him?*

When you hear a gentleman speak in praise of a lady whom you do not think deserving of his commendations, you will gain nothing by attempting to undeceive him; particularly if she is handsome. Your dissenting from his opinion he will, in all probability, impute to envy, or ill-nature; and therefore the only impression you can make will be against yourself.

Even if you have reason to dislike the lady, recollect that few are without some good points both of person and character. And it will be much better for you to pass over her faults in silence, and agree with him in commending what is really commendable about her. What he would, perhaps, believe implicitly if told to him by a man, he would attribute entirely to jealousy, or to a love of detraction if related by a woman. Above all, if a gentleman descants on the beauty of a lady, and in your own mind you do not coincide with his opinion, refrain, on your part, from criticizing invidiously her face and figure, and do not say that "though her complexion may be fine, her features are not regular;" that "her nose is too small," or "her eyes too large," or "her mouth too wide." Still less disclose to him the secret of her wearing false hair, artificial teeth, or tinging her cheeks with rouge. If she is a bold, forward woman, he will find that out as soon as yourself, and sooner too,—and you may be sure that though he may amuse himself by talking and flirting with her, he in reality regards her as she deserves.

If a foreigner chances, in your presence, to make an unfavourable remark upon some custom or habit peculiar to your country, do not immediately take fire and resent it; for, perhaps, upon reflection, you may find that he is right, or nearly so. All countries have their national character, and no character is perfect, whether that of a nation or an individual. If you know that the stranger has imbibed an erroneous impression, you may calmly, and in a few words, endeavour to convince him of it. But if he shows an unwillingness to be convinced, and tells you that what he has said he heard from good authority; or that, before he came to America, "his mind was made up," it will be worse than useless for you to continue the argument. Therefore change the subject, or turn and address your conversation to some one else.

Lady Morgan's Duchess of Belmont very properly checks O'Donnell for his ultra-nationality, and advises him not to be always running a tilt with every Englishman he talks to, continually seeming as if ready with the war-cry of "St. Patrick for Ireland, against St. George for England."

Dr. Johnson was speaking of Scotland with his usual severity, when a Caledonian who was present, started up, and called out, "Sir, *I* was born in Scotland." "Very well, sir," said the cynic calmly, "I do not see why so small a circumstance should make any change in the national character."

English strangers complain (and with reason) of the American practice of imposing on their credulity, by giving them false and exaggerated accounts of certain things peculiar to this country, and telling them, as truths, stories that are absolute impossibilities;

the amusement being to see how the John Bulls swallow these absurdities. Even General Washington diverted himself by mystifying Weld the English traveller, who complained to him at Mount Vernon of musquitoes so large and fierce that they bit through his cloth coat. "Those are nothing," said Washington, "to musquitoes I have met with, that bite through a thick leather boot." Weld expressed his astonishment, (as well he might;) and, when he "put out a book," inserted the story of the boot-piercing insects, which he said *must* be true, as he had it from no less a person than General Washington.

It is a work of supererogation to furnish falsehoods for British travellers. They can manufacture them fast enough. Also, it is ungenerous thus to sport with their ignorance, and betray them into ridiculous caricatures, which they present to the English world in good faith. We hope these tricks are not played upon any of the best class of European travel-writers.

When in Europe, (in England particularly,) be not over sensitive as to remarks that may be made on your own country; and do not expect every one around you to keep perpetually in mind that you are an American; nor require that they should guard every word, and keep a constant check on their conversation, lest they should chance to offend your republican feelings. The English, as they become better acquainted with America, regard us with more favour, and are fast getting rid of their old prejudices, and opening their eyes as to the advantages to be derived from cultivating our friendship instead of

13

provoking our enmity. They have, at last, all learn that our language is theirs, and they no longer compliment newly-arrived Americans on speaking English "quite well." It is not many years since two young ladies from one of our Western States, being at a party at a very fashionable mansion in London, were requested by the lady of the house to talk a little American; several of her guests being desirous of hearing a specimen of that language. One of the young ladies mischievously giving a hint to the other, they commenced a conversation in what school-girls call *gibberish;* and the listeners, when they had finished, gave various opinions on the American tongue, some pronouncing it very soft, and rather musical; others could not help saying candidly that they found it rather harsh. But all agreed that it resembled no language they had heard before.

There is no doubt that by the masses, better English is spoken in America than in England.

However an Englishman or an Englishwoman may boast of their intimacy with "the nobility and gentry," there is one infalliable rule by which the falsehood of these pretensions may be detected. And that is in the misuse of the letter H, putting it where it should not be, and omitting it where it should. This unaccountable practice prevails, more or less, in all parts of England, but is unknown in Scotland and Ireland. It is never found but among the middle and lower classes, and by polished and well-educated people is as much laughed at in England as it is with us. A relative of ours being in a stationer's shop in St. Paul's

Church Yard, (the street surrounding the cathedral,) heard the stationer call his boy, and tell him to "go and take the babby out, and give him a *hairing*—the babby having had no *hair* for a week." We have heard an Englishman talk of "taking an *ouse* that should have an *ot* water pipe, and a *hoven*." The same man asked a young lady "if she had *eels* on her boots." We heard an Englishwoman tell a servant to "bring the *arth* brush, and sweep up the *hashes*." Another assured us that "the American ladies were quite *hignorant* of *hetiquette*."

We have actually seen a ridiculous bill sent seriously by a Yorkshireman who kept a livery-stable in Philadelphia. The items were, *verbatim*—

	D. C.
anosafada	2 50
takinonimome	0 37

No reader can possibly guess this—so we will explain that the first line, in which all the words run into one, signifies "An orse af a day,"—or "A horse half a day." The second line means "takin on im ome,"—or "Taking of him home."

English travellers are justly severe on the tobacco-chewing and spitting, that though exploded in the best society, is still too prevalent among the million. All American ladies can speak feelingly on this subject, for they suffer from it in various ways. First, the sickening disgust without which they cannot witness the act of expectoration performed before their faces. Next, the danger of tobacco-saliva falling on their dresses in the street, or while travelling in steamers and rail-cars. Then the necessity of walking through the abomination when leaving those conveyances; treading in it with their shoes; and wiping it up with the hems of their gowns. We know an instance of the crown of a lady's white-silk bonnet being bespattered with tobacco-juice, by a man spitting out of a window in one of the New York hotels. A lady on the second seat of a box at the Chestnut-street theatre, found, when she went home, the back of her pelisse entirely spoilt, by some man behind not having succeeded in trying to spit past her—or perhaps he did not try. Why should ladies endure all this, that men may indulge in a vulgar and deleterious practice, pernicious to their own health, and which they cannot acquire without going through a seasoning of disgust and nausea?

. It is very unmannerly when a person begins to relate a circumstance or an anecdote, to stop them short by saying, "I have heard it before." Still worse, to say you do not wish to hear it at all. There are people who set themselves against listening to any thing that can possibly excite melancholy or painful feelings; and profess to hear nothing that may give them a sad or unpleasant sensation. Those who have so much tenderness for themselves, have usually but little tenderness for others. It is impossible to go through the world with perpetual sunshine over head, and unfading flowers under foot. Clouds will gather in the brightest sky, and weeds choke up the fairest primroses and violets. And we should all endeavour to prepare ourselves for these changes, by listening with sympathy to the manner in which they have affected others.

No person of good feelings, good manners, or true refinement, will entertain their friends with minute descriptions of sickening horrors, such as barbarous executions, revolting punishments, or inhuman cruelties perpetrated on animals. We have never heard an officer dilate on the dreadful spectacle of a battle-field; a scene of which no description can ever present an adequate idea; and which no painter has ever exhibited in all its shocking and disgusting details. Physicians do not talk of the dissecting-room.

Unless you are speaking to a physician, and are interested in a patient he is attending, refrain in conversation from entering into the particulars of revolting diseases, such as scrofula, ulcers, cutaneous afflictions, &c. and discuss no terrible operations— especially at table. There are women who seem to delight in dwelling on such disagreeable topics.

If you are attending the sick-bed of a friend, and are called down to a visiter, speak of her illness with delicacy, and do not disclose all the unpleasant circumstances connected with it; things which it would grieve her to know, may, if once told, be circulated among married women, and by them repeated to their husbands. In truth, upon most occasions, a married woman is not a safe confidant. She will assuredly tell every thing to her husband; and in all probability to his mother and sisters also—that is, every thing concerning her friends—always, perhaps, under a strict injunction of secrecy. But a secret entrusted to more than two or three persons, is soon diffused throughout the whole community.

A man of some humour was to read aloud a deed. He commenced with the words, "Know one woman by these presents." He was interrupted, and asked why he changed the words, which were in the usual form, "Know all men by these presents." "Oh!" said he, "'tis very certain that all men will soon know it, if one woman does."

Generally speaking, it is injudicious for ladies to attempt arguing with gentlemen on political or financial topics. All the information that a woman can possibly acquire or remember on these subjects is so small, in comparison with the knowledge of men, that the discussion will not elevate them in the opinion of masculine minds. Still, it is well for a woman to desire enlightenment, that she may comprehend something of these discussions, when she hears them from the other sex; therefore let her listen as understandingly as she can, but refrain from controversy and argument on such topics as the grasp of a female mind is seldom capable of seizing or retaining. Men are very intolerant toward women who are prone to contradiction and contention, when the talk is of things considered out of their sphere; but very indulgent toward a modest and attentive listener, who only asks questions for the sake of information. Men like to dispense knowledge; but few of them believe that in departments exclusively their own, they can profit

much by the suggestions of women. It is true there
are and have been women who have distinguished
themselves greatly in the higher branches of science
and literature, and on whom the light of genius has
clearly descended. But can the annals of woman
produce a female Shakspeare, a female Milton, a
Goldsmith, a Campbell, or a Scott? What woman
has painted like Raphael or Titian, or like the best
artists of our own times? Mrs. Damer and Mrs.
Siddons had a talent for sculpture; so had Marie of
Orleans, the accomplished daughter of Louis Philippe.
Yet what are the productions of these talented ladies
compared to those of Thorwaldsen, Canova, Chantrey,
and the master chisels of the great American statu-
aries. Women have been excellent musicians, and
have made fortunes by their voices. But is there
among them a Mozart, a Bellini, a Michael Kelly, an
Auber, a Boieldieu? Has a woman made an improvement on steam-engines, or on any thing connected
with the mechanic arts? And yet these things have
been done by men of no early education—by self-
taught men. A good tailor fits, cuts out, and sews
better than the most celebrated female dress-maker.
A good man-cook far excels a good woman-cook.
Whatever may be their merits as assistants, women
are rarely found who are very successful at the head
of any establishment that requires energy and originality of mind. Men make fortunes, women make
livings. And none make poorer livings than those
who waste their time, and bore their friends, by
writing and lecturing upon the equality of the sexes,

and what they call "Women's Rights." How is it that most of these ladies live separately from their husbands; either despising them, or being despised by them?

Truth is, the female sex is really as inferior to the male in vigour of mind as in strength of body ; and all arguments to the contrary are founded on a few anomalies, or based on theories that can never be reduced to practice. Because there was a Joan of Arc, and an Augustina of Saragossa, should females expose themselves to all the dangers and terrors of "the battle-field's dreadful array." The women of the American Revolution effected much good to their country's cause, without encroaching upon the province of its brave defenders. They were faithful and patriotic ; but they left the conduct of that tremendous struggle to abler heads, stronger arms, and sterner hearts.

We envy not the female who can look unmoved upon physical horrors—even the sickening horrors of the dissecting-room.

Yet women are endowed with power to meet misfortune with fortitude ; to endure pain with patience ; to resign themselves calmly, piously, and hopefully to the last awful change that awaits every created being ; to hazard their own lives for those that they love ; to toil cheerfully and industriously for the support of their orphan children, or their aged parents ; to watch with untiring tenderness the sick-bed of a friend, or even of a stranger ; to limit their own expenses and their own pleasures, that they may have something to bestow on deserving objects of charity ; to smooth the ruggedness of man; to soften his asperities of temper; to refine his manners; to make his home a happy one; and to improve the minds and hearts of their children. All this women can—and do. And this .s their true mission.

In talking with a stranger, if the conversation should turn toward sectarian religion, enquire to what church he belongs; and then mention your own church. This, among people of good sense and good manners, and we may add of true piety, will preclude all danger of remarks being made on either side which may be painful to either party. Happily we live in a land of universal toleration, where all religions are equal in the sight of the law and the government; and where no text is more powerful and more universally received than the wise and incontrovertible words—"By their fruits ye shall know them." He that acts well is a good man, and a religious man, at whatever altar he may worship. He that acts ill is a bad man, and has no true sense of religion; no matter how punctual his attendance at church, if of that church he is an unworthy member. Ostentatious sanctimony may deceive man, but it cannot deceive God.

On this earth there are many roads to heaven; and each traveller supposes his own to be the best. But they must all unite in one road at the last. It is only Omniscience that can decide. And it will then be found that no sect is excluded because of its faith; or if its members have acted honestly and conscientiously according to the lights they had, and molesting no one for believing in the tenets of a different church. The religion of Jesus, as our Saviour left it to us, was one of peace and good-will to men, and of unlimited faith in the wisdom and goodness, and power and majesty of God. It is not for a frail human being to place limits to his mercy, and say what church is the only true one—and the only one that leads to salvation. Let all men keep in mind this self-evident truth—"He can't be wrong whose life is in the right;" and try to act up to the Divine command of "doing unto all men as you would they should do unto you."

In America, no religious person of good sense or good manners ever attempts, in company, to controvert, uncalled for, the sectarian opinions of another. No clergyman that is a gentleman, (and they all are so, or ought to be,) ever will make the drawing-room an arena for religious disputation, or will offer a single deprecatory remark, on finding the person with whom he is conversing to be a member of a church essentially differing from his own. And if clergymen have that forbearance, it is doubly presumptuous for a woman, (perhaps a silly young girl,) to take such a liberty. "Fools rush in, where angels fear to tread."

Nothing is more apt to defeat even a good purpose than the mistaken and ill-judged zeal of those that are not competent to understand it in all its bearings.

Truly does the Scripture tell us—"There is a time for all things." We know an instance of a young lady at a ball attempting violently to make a proselyte of a gentleman of twice her age, a man of strong sense and high moral character, whose church (of which he was a sincere member) differed materially from her own. After listening awhile, he told her that a ball-room was no place for such discussions, and made his bow and left her. At another party we saw a young girl going round among the matrons, and trying to bring them all to a confession of faith.

Religion is too sacred a subject for discussion at balls and parties.

If you find that an intimate friend has a leaning toward the church in which you worship, first ascertain truly if her parents have no objection, and then, but not else, you may be justified in inducing her to adopt your opinions. Still, in most cases, it is best not to interfere.

In giving your opinion of a new book, a picture, or a piece of music, when conversing with a distinguished author, an artist or a musician, say modestly, that "so it appears to *you*,"—that "it has given *you* pleasure," or the contrary. But do not positively and dogmatically assert that it *is* good, or that it *is* bad. The person with whom you are talking is, in all probability, a far more competent judge than yourself; therefore, listen attentively, and he may correct your opinion, and set you right. If he fail to convince you, remain silent, or change the subject. Vulgar ladies have often a way of saying, when disputing on the merits of a thing they are incapable of understanding, "Any how, *I* like it," or, "It is quite good enough for *me*."—Which is no proof of its being good enough for any body else.

In being asked your candid opinion of a person, be very cautious to whom you confide that opinion; for

ıf repeated as yours, it may lead to unpleasant consequences. It is only to an intimate and long-tried
friend that you may safely entrust certain things,
which if known, might produce mischief. Even very
intimate friends are not always to be trusted, and
when they have actually told something that they
heard under the injunction of secrecy, they will consider it a sufficient atonement to say, "Indeed I did
not mean to tell it, but somehow it slipped out;" or,
" I really intended to guard the secret faithfully, but
I was so questioned and cross-examined, and bewil-
dered, that I knew not how to answer without dis-
closing enough to make them guess the whole. I am
very sorry, and will try to be more cautious in future.
But these slips of the tongue will happen."

The lady whose confidence has been thus betrayed, should be "more cautious in future," and
put no farther trust in she of the slippery tongue—
giving her up, entirely, as unworthy of farther friendship.

No circumstances will induce an honourable and
right-minded woman to reveal a secret after promising
secrecy. But she should refuse being made the
depository of any extraordinary fact which it may be
wrong to conceal, and wrong to disclose.

We can scarcely find words sufficiently strong to
contemn the heinous practice, so prevalent with low-
minded people, of repeating to their friends whatever
they hear to their disadvantage. By low-minded
people, we do not exclusively mean persons of low
station. The low-minded are not always "born in a

garret, in a kitchen bred." Unhappily, there are (so-called) ladies—ladies of fortune and fashion—who will descend to meannesses of which the higher ranks ought to be considered incapable, and who, without compunction, will wantonly lacerate the feelings and mortify the self-love of those whom they call their friends, telling them what has been said about them by other friends.

It is sometimes said of a notorious tatler and mis-chief-maker, that "she has, notwithstanding, a good heart." How is this possible, when it is her pastime to scatter dissension, ill-feeling, and unhappiness among all whom she calls her friends? She may, perhaps, give alms to beggars, or belong to sewing circles, or to Bible societies, or be officious in visiting the sick. All this is meritorious, and it is well if there is some good in her. But if she violates the charities of social life, and takes a malignant pleasure in giving pain, and causing trouble—depend on it, her show of benevo-lence is mere ostentation, and her acts of kindness spring not from the heart. She will convert the sew-ing circle into a scandal circle. If she is assiduous in visiting her sick friends, she will turn to the worst account, particulars she may thus acquire of the sanctities of private life and the humiliating mysteries of the sick-chamber.

If indeed it can be possible that tatling and mis-chief-making may be only (as is sometimes alleged) a bad habit, proceeding from an inability to govern the tongue—shame on those who have allowed themselves to acquire such a habit, and who make no effort to subdue it, or who have encouraged it in their children, and perhaps set them the example.

If you are so unfortunate as to know one of these pests of society, get rid of her acquaintance as soon as you can. If allowed to go on, she will infallibly bring you into some difficulty, if not into disgrace. If she begins by telling you—"I had a hard battle to fight in your behalf last evening at Mrs. Morley's. Miss Jewson, whom you believe to be one of your best friends, said some very severe things about you, which, to my surprise, were echoed by Miss Warden, who said she knew them to be true. But I contradicted them warmly. Still they would not be convinced, and said I must be blind and deaf not to know better. How very hard it is to distinguish those who love from those who hate us!"

Instead of encouraging the mischief-maker to relate the particulars, and explain exactly what these severe things really were, the true and dignified course should be to say as calmly as you can—"I consider no person my friend, who comes to tell such things as must give me pain and mortification, and lessen my regard for those I have hitherto esteemed, and in whose society I have found pleasure. I have always liked Miss Jewson and Miss Warden, and am sorry to hear that they do not like *me*. Still, as I am not certain of the exact truth, (being in no place where I could myself overhear the discussion,) it will make no difference in my behaviour to those young ladies. And now then we will change the subject, never to resume it. My true friends do not bring me such tales."

By-the-bye, tatlers are always listeners, and are frequently the atrocious writers of anonymous letters, for which they should be expelled from society.

Let it be remembered that all who are capable of detailing unpleasant truths, (such as can answer no purpose but to produce bad feeling, and undying enmity,) are likewise capable of exaggerating and misrepresenting facts, that do not seem quite strong enough to excite much indignation. Tale-bearing always leads to lying. She who begins with the first of these vices, soon arrives at the second.

Some prelude these atrocious communications with—"I think it my duty to tell how Miss Jackson and Mrs. Wilson talk about you, for it is right that you should know your friends from your enemies." You listen, believe, and from that time become the enemy of Miss Jackson and Mrs. Wilson—having too much pride to investigate the truth, and learn what they really said.

Others will commence with—"I'm a plain-spoken woman, and consider it right, for your own sake, to inform you that since your return from Europe, you talk quite too much of your travels."

You endeavour to defend yourself from this accusation, by replying that "having seen much when abroad, it is perfectly natural that you should allude to what you have seen."

"Oh! but there should be moderation in all things. To be candid—your friend Mrs. Willet says she is tired of hearing of France and Italy."

"Why then does she always try to get a seat next

to me, and ask me to tell her something more of those countries ?"

"Well, I don't know. People are so deceitful! There is Mr. Liddard, who says you bore him to death with talking about England."

"And yet whenever I do talk about England, I always find him at the back of my chair. And when I pause, he draws me on to say more."

"Men are such flatterers! Well, I always tell the plain truth. So it is best you should know Colonel Greenfield declares that since your return from Europe you are absolutely intolerable. Excuse my telling you these things. It is only to show that every body else thinks just as I do. Mrs. Gray says it is a pity you ever crossed the Atlantic."

Do not excuse her—but drop her acquaintance as soon as you can, without coming to a quarrel, in which case you will most probably get the worst. A plain-spoken woman is always to be dreaded. Her cold-blooded affectation of frankness is only a pretext to introduce something that will wound your feelings; and then she will tell you "that Mrs. A. B. C. and D., and Mr. E. and Mr. F. also, have said a hundred times that you are a woman of violent temper, and cannot listen to advice without flying into a passion."

And she will quietly take her leave, informing you that she is your best friend, and that all she has said was entirely for your own good, and that she shall continue to admonish you whenever she sees occasion.

A plain-spoken woman will tell you that you were

thought to look very ill at Mrs. Thomson's party, your dress being rather in bad taste; that you ought to give up singing in company, your best friends saying that your style is now a little old-fashioned; that you should not attempt talking French to French ladies, as Mr. Leroux and Mr. Dufond say that your French is not quite Parisian, &c. &c. She will say these things upon no authority but her own.

When any one prefaces an enquiry by the vulgarism, "If it is a fair question?" you may be very certain that the question is a most *un*fair one—that is, a question which it is impertinent to ask, and of no consequence whatever to the asker.

If a person begins by telling you, "Do not be offended at what I am going to say," prepare yourself for something that she knows will certainly offend you. But as she has given you notice, try to listen, and answer with calmness.

It is a delicate and thankless business to tell a friend of her faults, unless you are certain that, in return, you can bear without anger to hear her point out your own. She will undoubtedly recriminate.

It is not true that an irritable temper cannot be controlled. It can, and is, whenever the worldly interest of the *enragée* depends on its suppression.

Frederick the Great severely reprimanded a Prussian officer for striking a soldier at a review. "I could not refrain," said the officer. "I have a high temper, your majesty, and I cannot avoid showing it, when I see a man looking sternly at me." "Yes, you can," replied the king. "I am looking sternly at you, and I am giving you ten times as much cause of offence as that poor soldier—yet you do not strike *me*."

A naturally irritable disposition can always be tamed down, by a strong and persevering effort to subdue it, and by determining always to check it on its first approaches to passion. The indulgence of temper renders a man (and still more a woman) the dread and shame of the whole house. It wears out the affection of husbands, wives, and children—of brothers and sisters; destroys friendship; disturbs the enjoyment of social intercourse; causes incessant changing of servants; and is a constant source of misery to that most unhappy of all classes, poor relations.

That a violent temper is generally accompanied by a good heart, is a popular fallacy. On the contrary, the indulgence of it hardens the heart. And even if its ebullitions are always succeeded by " compunctious visitings," and followed by apologies and expressions of regret, still it leaves wounds that time cannot always efface, and which we may forgive, but cannot forget..

Ill-tempered women are very apt to call themselves nervous, and to attribute their violent fits of passion to a weakness of the nerves. -This is not true. A real nervous affection shows itself " more in sorrow than in anger," producing tears, tremor, and.head-ache, fears without adequate cause, and general depression of spirits—the feelings becoming tender to a fault.

When a woman abandons herself to terrible fits of anger with little or no cause, and makes herself **a** frightful spectacle, by turning white with rage, rolling up her eyes, drawing in her lips, gritting her teeth, clenching her hands, and stamping her feet, depend on it, she is not of a nervous, but of a furious temperament. A looking-glass held before her, to let her see what a shocking object she has made herself, would, we think, have an excellent effect. We have seen but a few females in this revolting state, and only three of them were ladies—but we have heard of many.

When the paroxysm is over, all the atonement she can make is to apologize humbly, and to pray contritely. If she has really any goodness of heart, and any true sense of religion, she will do this promptly, and prove her sincerity by being very kind to those whom she has outraged and insulted—and whose best course during these fits of fury is to make no answer, or to leave the room.

As out of nothing, nothing can come, to be a good conversationist, you must have a well-stored mind, originality of ideas, and a retentive memory. Without making a lumber-room of your head, and stuffing it with all manner of useless and unnecessary things not worth retaining, you should select only such as are useful or ornamental, interesting or amusing. Your talk must flow as if spontaneously; one subject suggesting another, none being dwelt upon too long. Anecdotes may be introduced with much effect. They should be short, and related in such words as will give them the most point. We have heard the same anec dote told by two persons. With one it became prosy and tiresome, and the point was not perceptible from its being smothered in ill-chosen words. With the other narrator, the anecdote was "all light and spirit; soon told, and not soon forgotten." Brevity is the soul of wit, and wit is the soul of anecdote. And where wit is wanting, humour is an excellent substitute. Every body likes to laugh, or ought to. Yet there is a time for all things; and after listening to a serious or interesting incident well related, it is exceedingly annoying to hear some silly and heartless girl follow it with a ridiculous remark, intended to be funny—such as "Quite solemncolly!"—or, "We are all getting into the doldrums."

You may chance to find yourself in a company where no one is capable of appreciating the best sort of conversation, and where to be understood, or indeed to keep them awake, you must talk down to the capacities of your hearers. You must manage this adroitly, or they may find you out, and be offended. So, after all, it is, perhaps, safest to go on and scatter pearls where wax beads would be equally valued. Only in such society, do not introduce quotations from the poets, especially from Shakspeare, or your hearers may wonder what queer words you are saying. Another time, and with congenial companions, you can indulge in "the feast of reason, and the flow of soul."

If placed beside a lady so taciturn that no effort on your part can draw her out, or elicit more than a monosyllable, and that only at long intervals, you may safely conclude that there is nothing in her, and leave her to her own dullness, or to be enlivened by the approach of one of the other sex. That will make her talk.

14

Few persons are good talkers who are not extensive and miscellaneous readers. You cannot attentively read the best authors without obtaining a great command of words, so that you can always, with ease and fluency, clothe your ideas in appropriate language.

Knowledge is of course the basis of conversation— the root whose deepened strength and vigour gives life to the tree, multiplicity to its branches, and beauty to its foliage.

Much that is bad and foolish in women would have no existence if their minds were less barren. In a waste field, worthless and bitter weeds will spring up which it is hard to eradicate; while a soil that is judi- ciously cultivated produces abundant grain, luxuriant grass, and beautiful flowers.

There are ladies so exceedingly satisfied with them- selves, and so desirous of being thought the special favourites of Providence, that they are always desiring to hold out an idea "that pain and sorrow can come not near them," and that they enjoy a happy exemp- tion from "all the ills that flesh is heir to." They complain of nothing, for they profess to have nothing to complain of. They feel not the cold of winter, nor the heat of summer. The temperature is always exactly what *they* like. To them the street is never muddy with rain, nor slippery with ice. Unwhole- some food agrees perfectly with *them*. They sleep soundly in bad beds, or rather no beds are bad. Travelling never fatigues them. Nobody imposes on them, nobody offends them. Other people may be ill —they are always in good health and spirits. To

them all books are delightful—all pictures beautiful—
all music charming. Other people may have trouble
with their children—*they* have none. Other people
may have bad servants—*theirs* are always excellent.

Now if all this were true, the lot of such persons
would indeed be enviable, and we should endeavour to
learn by what process such complete felicity has been
attained—and why they see every thing through such
a roseate medium. But it is not true. This is all
overweening vanity, and a desire "to set themselves
up above the rest of the world." We have always
noticed that these over-fortunate, over-happy women
have, in reality, a discontented, care-worn look, re-
sulting from the incessant painful effort to seem what
they are not. And if any body will take the trouble,
it is very easy to catch them in discrepancies and
contradictions. But it is not polite to do so. Therefore let them pass.

As mothers are always on the *qui vive*, (and very
naturally,) be careful what you say of their children.
Unless he is a decidedly handsome man, you may give
offence by remarking, "The boy is the very image of
his father." If the mother is a vain woman, she would
much rather hear that all the children are the very
image of herself. Refrain from praising too much
the children of another family, particularly if the two
sets of children are cousins. It is often dangerous to
tell a mother that "little Willy is growing quite handsome." She will probably answer, "I had hoped my
child was handsome always." With some mothers it
is especially imprudent to remark that "little Mary

looks like her aunt, or her grandmother." Again, if you prudently say nothing about the looks of the little dears, you may be suspected and perhaps accused of taking no interest in children. Young ladies, when in presence of gentlemen, are too apt to go on the other extreme, and over-act their parts, in the excessive fondling and kissing and hugging of children not in the least engaging, or even good-looking. We cannot believe that any female, not the mother, can really fall into raptures with a cross, ugly child. But how pleasant it is to play with and amuse, an intelligent, affectionate, and good-tempered little thing, to hear its innocent sayings, and to see the first buddings of its infant mind.

When you are visiting another city, and receiving civilities from some of its inhabitants, it is an ill re-quital for their attentions to disparage their place, and glorify your own. In every town there is some-thing to praise; and in large cities there is a great deal to amuse, to interest, and to give pleasure. Yet there are travellers who (like Smelfungus) are never satisfied with the place they are in—who exclaim all the time against the east winds of Boston, the sea-air of New York, the summer heats of Philadelphia, the hilly streets of Baltimore, and the dusty avenues of Washington. We have heard people from New Or-leans call Philadelphia the hottest city in the Union, and people from Quebec call it the coldest. If there are two successive days of rain, then poor Philadelphia is the rainiest of all places. If it snows twice in two weeks, then it is the snowiest. If a fire breaks out, it is the city of fires. If there is an Irish fight in Moyamensing, it is the city of perpetual riots. By-the-bye, after that summer when we really had several successive riots up-town, and down-town, we saw an English caricature of the City of Brotherly Love, where the spirit of William Penn, in hat and wig, was looking down sadly from the clouds at the rioters, who were all represented as Quakers, in strait, plain clothes, and broad brims, knocking each other about with sticks and stones, firing pistols, and slashing with bowie-knives. Alas, poor Quakers! how guiltless ye were of all this! It is a common belief in England, that of this sect are *all* the people of Pennsylvania.

In talking to an elderly lady, it is justly considered very rude to make any allusion to her age; even if she is unmistakeably an old woman, and acknowledges it herself. For instance, do not say—"This silk of yours is very suitable for an elderly person"—or—"Will you take this chair?—an old lady like you will find it very comfortable"—or—"Look, baby—is not that grandma?"—or—"I told the servant to attend first to you, on account of your age"—or—"Children, don't make such a noise—have you no respect for old people?"

All this we have heard.

CHAPTER XVI.

INCORRECT WORDS.

EVERY one who sees much of the world must observe with pain and surprise various unaccountable instances of improper and incorrect words that sometimes disfigure the phraseology of females who have gone through a course of fashionable education, and mixed in what is really genteel society. These instances, it is true, are becoming every day more rare; but we regret that they should exist at all. Early impressions are hard to eradicate. Bad habits of speaking are formed in childhood: sometimes from the society of illiterate parents, but more frequently from that of nurses and servants; and if not corrected or shaken off in due time, will cling like burrs to the diction of women who are really ladies in every thing else. Such women will say "that there," and "this here"— "them girls"—"them boys"—"I don't want no more"—"I didn't hear nothing about it"—"I didn't see nobody there"—"I won't do so no more." And other similar violations of grammar; and grammar is never more palpably outraged than when two negatives are used for an affirmative. It is surely shorter and easier to say, "I want no more"—"I heard nothing about it"—"I saw nobody there"—"I will do so no more."

Another grammatical error, less glaring, but equally incorrect, is the too common practice of converting a certainty into an uncertainty by saying, "I have no doubt but he was there." As if his being there was your only doubt. You should say, "I have no doubt of his being there." "I have no doubt but that he wrote it," seems to signify that you do doubt his writing it, and that you are nearly sure he did not. The proper phrase is, "I have no doubt of his writing it." "I do not doubt but that she knew it long ago," implies that you do doubt her having known it. It should be, "I do not doubt her knowing it long ago." Leave out *but*, when you talk of doubting.

No word is proper that does not express the true meaning. For instance, it is not right to call a township a town. A township is a section of land that may consist entirely of forests and farms, and may not comprise even a small village or hamlet. A town resembles a city in being closely built up with streets of adjoining houses. Men cannot go fishing or hunting in a *town*, though they may in a township. We are surprised to find this misapplication of the word among some of the most distinguished of the New-England *literati*. Perhaps it explains Jonathan's perplexity in one of the old Yankee Doodle songs:

> "He said he couldn't see the town,
> There were so many houses."

We hope it is not necessary to caution our readers

against the most provincial of Yankee provincialisms, such as, ' _ hadn't ought," or "I shouldn't ought"—or "It warn't," instead of "It was not"—or the exclamations, "Do tell!" or "I want to know," ejaculated as a token of surprise the moment after you have told, and made known. The common English habit, or rather a habit of the common English, of using continually the words "you know," and "you know," is very tiresome, particularly when they are talking of something that you cannot possibly be acquainted with. Check them by saying, "No, I do not know." They also make great use of the word "monstrous"—ugly as that word is. Do not imitate them in saying that you are "monstrous glad," or "monstrous sorry," or "monstrous tired," or that a young lady is "monstrous pretty." We have heard even "monstrous little."

We advise our New-England friends to eschew, both in speaking and writing, all Yankee phrases that do not convey the exact meaning of the words. For instance, to "*turn out* the tea," instead of to "*pour* it out." There can be no turn given, in this process, to the spout or handle of the tea-pot. On the contrary, it cannot pour well unless it is held straight. To "cut the eggs," instead of to beat them. The motion of beating eggs does not cut them. "Braiding eggs," is still worse. But we believe that this braiding is not the same as cutting. What is it?

Two young officers were travelling in the far West, when they stopped to take supper at a small road-side tavern, kept by a very rough Yankee woman. The landlady, in a calico sun-bonnet, and bare feet, stood at the head of the table to pour out. She enquired of her guests, "if they chose long sweetening, or short sweetening in their coffee." The first officer, supposing that "long sweetening" meant a large portion of that article, chose it accordingly. What was his dismay when he saw their hostess dip her finger deep down into an earthen jar of honey that stood near her, and then stir it (the finger) round in the coffee. His companion, seeing this, preferred "short sweetening." Upon which the woman picked up a large lump of maple sugar that lay in a brown paper on the floor beside her, and biting off a piece, put it into his cup. Both the gentlemen dispensed with coffee that evening. This anecdote we heard from the sister of one of those officers.

"Emptyings" is not a good name for yeast. "Up chamber, up garret, down cellar," are all wrong. Why not say, "up in the chamber, up in the garret, down in the kitchen, down in the cellar?" &c. Why should a mirthful fit of laughter be called "a gale!" "Last evening we were all in such a gale!"

Snow and ice are not the same. Therefore a snowball should not be called an ice-ball, which latter might be a very dangerous missile.

Pincushions are pincushions, and not pin-balls, unless they are of a globular shape. If in the form of hearts, diamonds, &c., they are not balls.

When you are greatly fatigued, say so—and not that you are "almost beat out." When the Yankees are "beat out," the English are quite "knocked up."

The English are "starved with cold"—Americans only starve with hunger. They may perish with cold; but unless hunger is added, they will not starve.

It is wrong to say that certain articles of food are healthy or unhealthy. Wholesome and unwholesome are the right words. A pig may be healthy or unhealthy while alive; but after he is killed and becomes pork, he can enjoy no health, and suffer no sickness.

If you have been accustomed to pronounce the word "does" as "doos," get rid of the custom as soon as you can. Also, give up saying "pint" for "point," "jint" for "joint," "anint" for "anoint," &c. Above all, cease saying "featur, creatur, natur, and raptur."

In New England it is not uncommon to hear the word "ugly" applied to a bad temper. We have heard, "He will never do for president, because he is so ugly." On our observing that we had always considered the gentleman in question, as rather a handsome man, it was explained that he was considered ugly in disposition.

A British traveller, walking one day in a suburb of Boston, saw a woman out on a door-step whipping a screaming child. "Good woman," said the stranger, "why do you whip that boy so severely." She answered, "I *will* whip him, because he is so ugly." The Englishman walked on; but put down in his journal that "American mothers are so cruel as to beat their children, merely because they are not handsome."

No genteel Bostonian should call Faneuil Hall, "Old

Funnel," or talk of the " Quinsey market," instead of
Quincy, or speak of "Bacon street," or "Bacon Hill."
That place was so called from a beacon, or signal-pole
with a light at the top, and never was particularly
celebrated for the pickling and smoking of pork.

The word " slump," or " slumped," has too coarse
a sound to be used by a lady.

When you have exchanged one article for another,
say so, and not that you have " traded it."

Do not say, " I should admire to read that book,"
" I should admire to hear that song," " I should
admire to see the president."   Substitute, " I should
like to read that book," " I should like to hear that
song," " I should like to see the president."

Using the word " love" instead of "like" is not peculiar to the ladies of any section of the Union.   But
they may assure themselves it is wrong to talk of
loving any thing that is eatable.   They may *like* terrapins, oysters, chicken-salad, or ice-cream ; but they
need not *love* terrapins or oysters, or *love* chicken-
salad.

We remember, in the farce of Modern Antiques,
laughing at an awkward servant-girl bringing in a
dish of salad to a supper-table, before the company
had assembled, and, after taking a large bite, turning
her foolish face toward the audience, and saying, " I
loves beet-root."

Even if you are a provincial New-Yorker, give up
calling the door-step or porch by the ancient Dutch
name of "stoop," (stoep,) and do not talk of going out
on the stoop, or sitting in the stoop.   When a load of

wood or coal is put down at your door, say not that it is "dumped." Never speak of visiting friends that "live to Brooklyn," or "live to Newark." They live *at* those places, not *to* them. The word "muss" sounds badly, when a young lady says, "her scarf is mussed," or her collar is "mussed"—or that her bureau drawers are all in a muss. The English synonyme, "mess," has *rather* a better sound. Be it also remembered that a stool is not a bench. A bench holds several people, a stool but one.

When you mean that an article of dress (a bonnet or a cap) is neat and pretty, do not say that it is cunning. An inanimate object cannot be cunning. To be cunning requires some mind. We are sorry to say that we have heard females who, when they intend to be witty, talk of taking a snooze, (which means a nap,) and speak of a comic anecdote as being "rich," and of a man in faded clothes as looking "seedy." We have heard Philadelphia ladies speak of a "great big" house, or a "great big" ship; and there are still some who *expect* what has already come to pass—as, "I expect it rained somewhere last night" —"I expect she arrived yesterday"—"I expect he went to Baltimore." In all these cases the proper term is "I suppose," and not "I expect."

The word "mayhap" (instead of perhaps) is a positive vulgarism. It is of English origin, but is only used in England by very low people—and by English writers, never.

We have little tolerance for young ladies, who, having in reality neither wit nor humour, set up for

both, and having nothing of the right stock to go upon,
substitute coarseness and impertinence, (not to say
impudence,) and try to excite laughter, and attract
the attention of gentlemen, by talking slang. Where
do they get it? How do they pick it up? From low
newspapers, or from vulgar books? Surely not from
low companions?

We have heard one of these ladies, when her collar
chanced to be pinned awry, say that it was put on
drunk—also that her bonnet was drunk, meaning
crooked on her head. When disconcerted, she was
"floored." When submitting to do a thing unwillingly, "she was brought to the scratch." Sometimes
"she did things on the sly." She talked of a certain
great vocalist "singing like a beast." She believed
it very smart and piquant to use these vile expressions.
It is true, when at parties, she always had half a dozen
gentlemen about her; their curiosity being excited as
to what she would say next. And yet she was a
woman of many good qualities; and one who boasted
of having always "lived in society."

We think that gentlemen lose a particle of their
respect for young ladies who allow their names to be
abbreviated into such cognomens as Kate, Madge,
Bess, Nell, &c. Surely it is more lady-like to be
called Catharine, Margaret, Eliza, or Ellen. We
have heard the beautiful name Virginia degraded into
Jinny; and Harriet called Hatty, or even Hadge.

A very silly practice has been introduced of writing
Sally, Sallie—Fanny, Fannie—Mary, Marie—Abby,
Abbie, &c. What would our grand-parents have

thought of Pollie, Mollie, Peggie, Kittie, Nancie?
Suppose young men were to adopt it, and sign themselves, Sammie, Billie, Dickie, Tommie, &c.!

By-the-bye, unless he is a relation, let no young
lady address a gentleman by his christian name. It
is a familiarity which he will not like.

CHAPTER XVII.

BORROWING.

ANY article you are likely to want on more than one occasion, it is better to buy than to borrow. If your own, you can have it always at hand: you will lay yourself under no obligation to a lender, and incur no responsibility as to its safety while in your possession. But when you *do* borrow, see that the article is speedily returned. And, under no consideration, take the liberty of lending it to any person whatever, before restoring it to the owner. Apologies and expressions of regret are no compensation, should it be out of your power to replace it if injured or lost.

When you ask to borrow a thing, do not say, "Will you *loan* it to me?" The word "loan" is, by good talkers, and good writers, never used but as a substantive: notwithstanding that Johnson gives it as a verb also, but only on one obscure authority—and Johnson is not now regarded as infallible. To *lend*, not to *loan*, is the usual and proper expression. As a substantive it is generally employed in a commercial and political sense, or to denote a large sum borrowed for a public and important purpose. It is true you can say, "May I request the loan of your fan?" "Will you permit me to ask the loan of this book?" But it is much easier and smoother to say simply, "Will you lend me your fan for a few minutes?" "Will you be kind enough to lend me this book?"

No articles, perhaps, are more frequently borrowed than umbrellas, and none are returned with so little punctuality. Frequently, a borrowed umbrella is never thought of by the borrower, till after the weather clears up; the lender, most probably, suffering inconvenience for want of it. Often it is detained till the next rain, when the lender has to take the trouble of sending for it. And then it is very possible it may not be found at all; some person in the mean time having nefariously carried it off. In such a case, it is a matter of common honesty for the careless borrower to replace that umbrella with a new one; as she is not to suppose that empty expressions of regret or unmeaning apologies will be sufficient compensation for a substantial loss.

To avoid any difficulties concerning umbrellas, it is safest, in cloudy weather, not to leave home without one. Many persons venture out beneath a threatening sky, unwilling to encumber themselves with an umbrella, which (possibly) they may not chance to require before they got home. Their dependance is on stopping in at the house of a friend, and borrowing one there. But is it not better to incommode yourself a little by carrying a closed umbrella, even if you should *not* find occasion to use it, than to hasten rapidly through the street to reach a shelter when you find the rain beginning to drop; and afterwards to deprive your friend, even temporarily, of an article which the wet weather may render it inconvenient to spare. Also, you may be caught by a sudden shower, at a considerable distance from the dwelling of the person with whom you are acquainted, and you may find the omnibuses all full, (as they generally are when it rains,) and no other vehicle in sight. Therefore, when the wind is in a rainy quarter, and the sky louring, be always on the safe side, and take an umbrella with you on leaving home.

Every lady should own a small light umbrella, or else a very large parasol, of extra size, covered with strong India silk that will not easily tear or fade, and that may be used, on occasion, for either sun or rain; and that will not be cumbrous to carry, though quite large enough to shelter *one* person. In truth, we have found but few umbrellas, however large, that could effectually cover *two* persons (unless they were people of very small size) so that the rain did not drop upon the off-shoulder of one or the other. You cannot be well screened by an umbrella, unless you carry it all the time steadily in your *own* hands, and over yourself alone. And politeness requires that you should give your companion the best of the shelter. So when two ladies go out together, the clouds portending rain, let each take an umbrella for herself, and then much injury to bonnets and shawls may be avoided.

These small light umbrellas are excellent to travel with, and especially useful in the transit from car to steamboat, or even from the house to the carriage. When not in "actual service," keep this umbrella beside you with your shawl and your travelling satchel.

15

It will be useful during the journey, if packed away in a trunk.*

When you purchase an umbrella, desire that, before sending it home, your name be engraved on the little plate at the termination of the handle, or else on the slide. "To make assurance doubly sure," you may get the name painted in full in small white or yellow letters on the *inside* of one of the gores of silk. These letters will not be conspicuous on the outside, but they will always serve to identify the umbrella. Your residence (if permanent) may be added. When about to travel, sew a small card with your address near the bottom of one of the gores inside. This card may be changed when staying at a new place. With these precautions, and a little care, (unless you are habitually thoughtless and forgetful,) you may carry an umbrella from Maine to Florida without losing it.

All the members of a family should be provided with at least one rain-umbrella of their own, and these should be kept up-stairs when not likely to be wanted. There is always great danger of their being purloined, or *borrowed*, if left in the hall. Persons who would not, for the world, be known to pilfer a single cent, are by no means particular with regard to detaining an umbrella or a book.

Umbrellas for the kitchen can now be had as low as

---

* In buying a *handsome* parasol or umbrella, see that it has a folding-joint in the middle of the stick, and that this joint works easily, so that there may be no difficulty in packing it in a trunk or box. To prevent the silk being rubbed, tie up the parasol in a smooth linen case, previous to packing.

seventy-five cents, or one dollar. If of coloured cotton (brown or blue) and highly glazed, they will turn off a moderate rain very well, but a drenching shower may cause the dye or colouring to run in streams. For very common use, though higher in price, the best are of oil-cloth, or of brown unbleached linen. The handsomest umbrellas are of blue or brown India silk, with steel frames, and a small silver name-plate on the handle. A green silk umbrella will soon be spoiled by the rain, and none look so badly in a short time. We have known a lady's bonnet entirely ruined by the drippings from a green parasol, hastily put up as a small screen from a sudden shower. No colour stands the sun and damp so badly as green.

After borrowing an umbrella, fail not to send it back immediately, unless you have previously ascertained from the owner that it will not be wanted for two or three hours. In that case, you will have time to dry it before it goes home; and this should de done as soon as possible, that it may be returned in good order. If left in the entry or hall, it may be carried off; or, in plain words, stolen. Let it be dried under your own inspection, spreading it wide open, and standing it on the floor. If dried fast, and in an expanded position, the wetting will not perceptibly injure it. But if left shut and standing up closed, with the wet soaking into the umbrella, it will dry in discoloured streaks, and be spoiled. If the spring or any other part of a borrowed umbrella gets broken or injured while in your possession, be sure to have it repaired before sending home. There is a meanness verging on dishonesty in leaving this to be done by the owner.

If the cheap or common umbrellas are given up to the care of the domestics, and kept in the kitchen, in all probability they will soon disappear altogether, and be no longer forthcoming when wanted. They will lend them to their friends, and lose them in various ways. The umbrellas should be kept in some small room or closet up-stairs; and when required, the servants should come and ask for them; bringing them back when done with, and dried.

When you go out to tea, even in a summer evening, carry a shawl on your arm to throw over your shoulders before coming out into the night-air. This will preclude the necessity of borrowing one of your friend, should the weather have changed and grown cooler. Also, to prevent any risk from damp pavements, take with you a pair of over-shoes, (India-rubber, of course,) or else a pair of inside-soles, such as you can conveniently slip into your pocket. We have found no inside-soles equal to those of lamb-skin with the wool left on the upper-side; the under-side of the skin being coated with India-rubber varnish to render them water-proof. These soles are both warm and dry, and are far pleasanter than cork soles covered with flannel, and more lasting. But if you are obliged to borrow things to wear home, see that they are sent back next morning, if not the same evening, and in good order—the shawl well-dried from the damp, and folded smoothly, and the over-shoes cleaned nicely.

Always take a fan with you on going to a place of

public amusement. You will be sure to require it, and it is better than to depend on fanning yourself with the bill or programme, or borrowing the fan of a more provident friend, and perhaps forgetting to return it.

With regard to the practice of borrowing articles of household use, it is generally a custom "more honoured in the breach than the observance," particularly when living in a place where all such things can be easily obtained by sending to the shops. There are persons who, with ample means of providing themselves with all that is necessary for domestic service, are continually troubling their neighbours for the loan of a hammer, a screw-driver, a gimlet, a carpet-stretcher, a bed-stead screw, a fluting-iron, a preserving kettle, jelly-moulds, ice-cream freezers, &c. &c. If these or any other articles *must* be borrowed, let them be returned promptly, and in good order.

If, in consequence of the unexpected arrival of company, any thing for the table is borrowed of a neighbour, such as tea, coffee, butter, &c., see that it is punctually returned; equal in quantity, and in quality; or rather superior. Habitual borrowers are very apt to forget this piece of honesty, either neglecting to return the things at all, or meanly substituting inferior articles—or perhaps laying themselves under such an imputation without actually deserving it, should the lender be ill-natured or untruthful. There is a homely proverb, "To go a-borrowing is to go a-sorrowing."

We have been told of a very aristocratic but very economical lady, in one of our large cities, who was in the almost daily practice of borrowing things of a neighbour to whom she never condescended to speak. On one occasion she borrowed the use of that neighbour's fire to roast a pair of fowls.

Avoid borrowing change, or small sums. It is possible that you may really forget to repay them; but then it is also possible that you may be suspected of forgetting wilfully. So do not trust much to your memory. It is a true remark, that there are few instances of a borrower being so oblivious as to offer twice over the return of a small loan, forgetting that it had been paid already.

In borrowing a dress as a pattern, it is safest not to try it upon yourself, lest some part of the body should be stretched or frayed. Also, in trying on a bonnet or cap that is not your own, refrain from tying the strings; as every tying will give them additional wrinkles or rumples, and perhaps somewhat soil them. Never put on another person's gloves.

Should you be staying at a boarding-house, do not depend on "the lady in the next room," or any other lady, to lend you things which you can procure quite as easily as she can. Keep yourself always provided with pen, ink, and paper, envelopes, wafers, sealing-wax, pencils, post-office stamps, &c. Also with sewing implements.

When a friend lends you a handkerchief, a collar, or any other washable article, see that it is nicely washed, and done up, before returning it to her,—and do so promptly. If an article of jewellery, carry it back to her yourself, and put it into her own hand, to

preclude all risk of loss. She will not be so ungenerous as to tell any person that she has lent it to you;
and will for a while afterward, refrain from wearing
it herself, in any company where it may be recognized.

Should a visiter accidentally leave her handkerchief
at your house, have it washed and ironed before restoring it to her.

On borrowing a book, immediately put a cover upon
it—and let the cover be of clean, smooth, white or
light-coloured paper. What is called nankeen paper
is best and strongest for this purpose. Newspaper, or
any paper that is printed, makes a vile book-cover.
Beside its mean and dirty appearance, the printing-
ink will not only soil your own hands while reading,
but will do more injury to the binding than if it was
left uncovered.

To cover a book neatly—take a sheet of nice paper
of more than sufficient size, and lay the book open
upon it. Cut a notch or indentation at the top and
bottom of this paper, so as to admit the back of the
book, making the notch exactly the width of the back,
and two or three inches deep. Fold down the edges
of the paper straightly, smoothly, and evenly, over
the edges of the binding or cover. Fold the corners
of the paper nicely underneath, (trimming off the
superfluous paper that turns under,) making them lie
as flat as possible. You may secure all the folds at
the corners with small wafers, pins, or paste-cement.
If you use pins, take care to stick them so as not to
scratch the inside of the binding, or to prick and tear
the fly-leaves. The paper-cover should not only be

strong, but smooth also; if coarse and rough, it will injure the binding. When you send the book home, put it up neatly, so as to make a well-looking package; secured with either a string or a seal, and direct it to the owner.

If the book is a pamphlet, and the sewing-thread gives way, sew it again, with a large needle and a strong brown thread—not white cotton. If not sewed immediately, it will fall apart, and some leaves may drop out, and be lost. If, by any unlucky accident, a leaf is torn, lay the two pieces nicely together, and sew them, lightly, with a rather fine thread. But if one side of the torn page is blank, it will be best to mend it by pasting a small narrow slip of white paper underneath, so as to unite the torn edges neatly.

You may have excellent paste or cement, continu ally at hand, by buying at a druggist's an ounce of the *best and cleanest* gum tragacanth, with a little bit of corrosive sublimate not larger than a grain of corn, and dissolving them in a large half-pint of clear water, either warm or cold. Pick the gum tragacanth very clean, freeing it carefully from all dust and impurities. Put it with the corrosive sublimate into a white or queensware vessel having a close cover, and holding a pint, to allow for swelling. Pour on the water; cover it closely; and stir it *with a stick*, several times during the day. When sufficiently dissolved, the paste will be smooth throughout. The corrosive sublimate will cause it to keep good for a year or more; and it is an excellent and most convenient cement for all purposes, from wall-paper to artificial

flowers. It must on no account be kept in a metal
vessel or be stirred with a metal spoon, as it will then
turn black. No house should be without this paste—
and it should find a place in every library and office.
When it is nearly used up, and becomes dry at the
bottom, pour on a little water, and it will dissolve
again.

Make no remarks with pen or pencil on the margin
of any book that does not belong to yourself. Whatever may be your own opinion of certain passages,
you have no right to disturb other readers by obtrud-
ing upon them these opinions, unasked for. The
pleasure of reading a book from a public library, is
frequently marred by finding, as you proceed, that
some impertinent fools have been before you, and
scribbled their silly comments all through; or indulged in sneers and vituperations directed at the
author. You may lessen this annoyance by turning
over all the leaves before you begin reading, and
erasing all the marginal remarks with India rubber;
and this will also be an act of kindness to the next
reader after yourself. When written with ink, (as is
often the case,) there is no remedy; and you must
endure the infliction of being annoyed throughout the
book by these gratuitous criticisms. In a book, even
belonging to yourself, it is well to use the pencil
sparingly; and only to correct an error of the press,
or a chronological mistake of the author. All readers
like to form their own opinions as they go along,
without any prompting from those who have preceded
tnem.

Never, on any consideration, allow yourself to lend a borrowed book. If requested to do so, it should be a sufficient excuse to say that "it is not your own." But if still urged, persist in declining steadily; for it is a liberty you have no right to take with any article belonging to another. Even if the owner is your sister, you should lend nothing of hers without first obtaining her permission. Whatever you borrow yourself, should pass safely from your hands to those of the owner. If a friend of yours is very desirous of reading a borrowed book, and has no other means of obtaining it, and you think you can depend on her carefulness and punctuality, (not else,) you may promise "to request for her the favour." And when the owner has consented, (and not till then,) you may transfer the book to the new borrower with strict injunctions to take great care of it, and to return it as soon as possible.

I have known a borrowed book travel round a whole circle of relations and acquaintances, till, when sent home at last, it was literally worn out by dint of use. And this when nearly the whole set were persons who could well afford to buy all they were desirous of reading. Many ladies like very well to read when they can do so at the cost of their friends; but they seem to regard the purchase of any thing to improve the mind, or amuse the fancy, as throwing away money which they would expend more to their satisfaction in articles of personal decoration. And is it not melancholy to see an intelligent child craving in vain for books, while bedizened with finery to gratify the vanity of an ostentatious mother?

If, with the permission of the owner, you have lent a borrowed book to a person who, having lost or injured it, still has the presumption to ask you to intercede for the loan of another, you are bound to refuse the request; and do so with civility but steadiness, assigning the true reason. It may be a salutary lesson to that borrower.

Remember never to send home any article in a wrapper of newspaper. Keep always in the house a supply of good wrapping-paper, bought for the purpose, and also of balls of twine. For putting up small things, what is called shoe-paper is very useful. It is both nice and cheap, selling from fifty to sixty cents per ream, according to the size, and there are twenty quires in a ream. There are varieties of stronger and larger wrapping-paper for articles that require such, and for parcels that are to be sent to far-off places, or to go by public conveyances. Such packages are best secured by red tape and sealing-wax. At every stationer's may be purchased all varieties of paper.

Be particularly careful of borrowed magazines, as the loss of one number spoils a whole set, and you may find great difficulty in replacing a lost number. Even a newspaper should be punctually returned. The owner may wish to file it, or to send it away to a friend. If lost or defaced while in your possession, send to the publishing-office and buy another. It is unsafe to leave the book you are reading in the parlour of a hotel. Always carry it away with you, whenever you quit the room—otherwise you will be likely to see it no more.

In America, books are so cheap (not to mention the numerous public libraries) that in most instances all who can afford it had better buy than borrow, particularly such works as are worth a second reading. If you find your books accumulating inconveniently, give away a portion of them to some lover of reading, who, less fortunate than yourself, is unable to expend much money with the booksellers.

I have often wondered to see a fair young stranger sitting day after day, idle and listless in the drawing-room of a hotel, when she might have known that there were bookstores in the immediate neighbourhood.

If, while in your possession, a borrowed book is irreparably injured, it is your duty to replace it by purchasing for the owner another copy. And, if that cannot be procured, all you can do is to buy a work of equal value, and to present *that*, as the only compensation in your power. Observe the same rule with all borrowed articles, lost or injured. The lender is surely not the person to suffer from the carelessness of the borrower. Leave no borrowed books in the way of children, and never give a young child a book to play with. Eat no cake or fruit over an open book, lest it be greased or stained. And take care not to blister or spoil the binding by putting it down in a wet place, for instance, on a slopped table.

Some young ladies have a bad habit of biting their fingers, especially if they rejoice in handsome hands; and the same ladies, by way of variety, are prone to

biṭe the corners of books, and the edges of closed fans.
So it is dangerous to trust these articles in their
vicinity. We have seen the corners of an elegant
Annual nearly bitten off at a centre-table in the
course of one evening. And we have seen ice-cream
eaten and wine drank over an open port-folio of
beautiful engravings.

By-the-bye, in taking up a print to look at it, always
extend it carefully with both hands, that the paper may
be in no danger of cracking or rumpling, which it
cannot escape if held but in one hand, particularly if
there is a breeze blowing near it. To show a large
engraving without risk of injury, spread it out smoothly
on a table; keeping it flat by means of books or other
weights, laid carefully down on the corners, and, if the
plate is *very* large, at the sides also. And let no one
lean their elbows upon it.

It is an irksome task to show any sort of picture to
people who have neither taste, knowledge, nor enjoyment of the art. There are persons (ungenteel ones,
it is true) who seem to have no other pleasure, when
looking at a fine print or picture, than in trying to
discover in the figures or faces, fancied resemblances
to those of some individuals of their own circle:
loudly declaring for instance, that, "Queen Victoria is
the very image of Sarah Smith;" "Prince Albert an
exact likeness of Dick Brown;" "the Duke of Wellington the very ditto of old Captain Jones," &c. &c. To
those "who have no painting in their souls," there is
little use in showing or explaining any fine specimen
of that noblest of the fine arts. We have heard a

gentleman doubting whether a capital portrait of Franklin was not General Washington in his every-day dress. We could fill pages with the absurd remarks we have heard on pictures, even from persons who have had a costly education put at them. There are ladies who can with difficulty be made to understand the difference between a painting and an engraving—others who think that "the same man always makes both." Some call a coloured print a painting—others talk* of themselves *painting pictures* in albums—not understanding that, properly speaking, they are water-colour drawings when done on paper and with transparent tintings—while *pictures* are painted with oil or opaque colours on canvas or board. Frescoes are painted on new walls before the plastering is quite dry, so that the colours incorporate at once with the plaster, and dry along with it; acquiring in that manner a surprising permanency.

There is another very common error, that of calling

---

* We were a few years since, told by one of our principal book-sellers that a young lady came into his store when he chanced to be at the counter himself, and, showing him a small English prayer-book elegantly bound, and with fine engravings, she enquired if he had any exactly like that. On his replying in the negative, she desired that he would get precisely such a prayer-book *made for her*, in time for church on Sunday morning—(it was then Friday) —as she had set her mind on it. It must have just such pictures, and just such a beautiful gilt cover. He endeavoured in vain to convince her of the utter impossibility of performing this feat of having one single book printed, and bound, with plates engraved purposely for it, and all in the space of a day and a half. She seemed much displeased, and went away, in search, as she said, of a bookseller that was more obliging.

a diorama a panorama.   A panorama, correctly speaking, is a large circular representation of one place only,
(such as Rome, Athens, Thebes, Paris,) comprising as
much as the eye can take in at a view.   The spectators, looking from an elevated platform in the centre,
see the painting all around them in every direction,
and appearing the size of reality, but always stationary.
The panoramas exhibited successively in London by
Barker, Burford, Catherwood and others, are admirable and truthful views of the places they represent;
and after viewing them a few minutes, you can
scarcely believe that you are not actually there, and
looking at real objects.   A few of these triumphs of
perspective and colouring, have been brought to America.   It were much to be wished that an arrangement could be made for conveying every one of these
fine panoramas successively across the Atlantic, and
exhibiting them in all our principal cities.   It would
be a good speculation.

It is difficult to imagine whence originated the
mistake of calling a diorama a panorama, which it
is *not*.   A diorama is one of those numerous flat-
surface paintings of which we have had so many, (and
some few of them very good,) and which, moving on
unseen rollers, glide or slide along, displaying every
few minutes a new portion of the scenery.

The error has grown so common that persons fall
habitually into it, though knowing all the time that it
is an error.   To correct it, let the exhibiters of dio-
ramas cease to call them *panoramas*, and give them
their proper name, both in their advertisements and

in their verbal descriptions. Sebron's magnificent
representation of the departure of the Israelites, that
looked so amazingly real, was not a diorama, for it
did not move, and not a panorama, for it was not circular. But it was a colossal picture, so excellent
that at the first glance it seemed to be no picture at
all, but the real scene, with the real people.

CHAPTER XVIII.

OFFENCES.

IF the visits of an acquaintance become less frequent than formerly, the falling off is nòt always to be imputed to want of regard for you, or to having lost all pleasure in your society. The cause may be want of time, removal to a distance, precarious health, care of children, absence from town, family troubles, depressed fortunes, and various other circumstances. Also, with none of these causes, visiting may gradually and almost insensibly decline, and neither of the parties have the slightest dislike to each other. If no offence has been intended, none should be taken; and when you chance to meet, instead of consuming the time in complaints of estrangement, meet as if your intercourse had never been interrupted, and you will find it very easy to renew it; and perhaps on a better footing than before. The renewal should be marked by a prompt interchange of special invitations— followed by visits.

Unless your rooms are spacious, you cannot have what is called a large general party. Some of your acquaintances must be omitted, and all that are left out. are generally offended. Therefore it is not well ever to have such parties, unless your accommodations are ample. *Squeezes* are out of fashion in the best American society. We have heard of parties at great houses in London, where, after the rooms were crowded to suffocation, a large portion of the company had to pass the evening on the stairs; and where coaches, unable to draw up from the immense number of these vehicles that were in advance, had to remain all night at the foot of the line, with ladies sitting in them. When morning came, they had to turn back, and drive home, the carriages being all they saw of the party.

It is better to give two or three moderate entertainments in the course of the season, than to crowd your rooms uncomfortably; and even then to risk giving offence to those who could not be added to the number.

If such offence has been given, try to atone for it by inviting the offended to dine with you, or to pass an evening, and asking at the same time a few pleasant people whom you know she likes.

You may have a very intimate and sincere friend who does not find it convenient to send for you every time she has company. If, in all things else, she treats you with uniform kindness, and gives reason to believe that she has a true affection for you, pass over these occasional omissions of invitation, and do not call her to account, or treat her coolly when you see her. True friendship ought not depend upon *parties*. It should be based on a better foundation.

If no answer is returned to a note of invitation, be not hasty in supposing that the omission has sprung from rudeness or neglect. Trust that your friend is neither rude nor neglectful; and believe that the answer was duly sent, but that it miscarried from some accidental circumstance.

A friend may inadvertently say something that you do not like to hear, or may make a remark that is not pleasant to you. Unless it is prefaced with a *previous* apology; or unless she desires you "not to be offended at what she is going to say;" or unless she informs you that "she considers it her duty always to speak her mind,"—you have no right to suppose the offence premeditated, and therefore you should restrain your temper, and calmly endeavour to convince her that she is wrong; or else acknowledge that she is right. She ought then to apologize for what she said, and you should immediately change the subject, and never again refer to it. In this way quarrels may be prevented, and ill-feeling crushed in the bud. When what is called "a coolness" takes place between friends, the longer it goes on the more difficult it is to get over. But "better late than never." If, on consideration, you find that *you* were in the wrong, let no false pride, no stubborn perverseness prevent you from making that acknowledgement. If your friend, on her part, first shows a desire for reconciliation, meet her half-way. A vindictive disposition is a bad one, and revenge is a most unchristian feeling. People of sense (unless the injury is very great, and of lasting consequences) are easy to appease, because they generally have good feelings, and know how **to** listen to reason.   Dr. Watts most truly says—

> "The wise will let their anger cool,
>   At least before 'tis night;
> But in the bosom of a fool,
>   It burns till morning light."

Should you chance to be thrown into the presence of persons who have proved themselves your enemies, and with whom you can have no intercourse, say nothing either *to* them or *at* them; and do not place yourself in their vicinity.   To talk *at* a person, is mean and vulgar.   Those who do it are fully capable of writing anonymous and insulting letters; and they often do so.   High-minded people will always be scrupulously careful in observing toward those with whom they are at variance, all the ceremonies usual in polite society—particularly the conventional civilities of the table.

If you have, unfortunately, had a quarrel with a friend, talk of it to others as little as possible; lest in the heat of anger, you may give an exaggerated account, and represent your adversary in darker colours than she deserves.   You may be very sure these mis-representations will reach her ear, and be greatly magnified by every successive relater.   In this way a trifle may be swelled into importance; a mole-hill may become a mountain; and a slight affront may embitter the feelings of future years.   "Blessed are the peace-makers,"—and a mutual friend, if well-disposed toward both opponents, generally has it in her power to effect

a reconciliation, by repeating, kindly, any favourable
remark she may chance to have heard one of the
offended parties make on the other. In truth, we
wish it were the universal custom for all people to tell
other people whatever good they may hear of them—
instead of the wicked and hateful practice of telling
only the bad. Make it a rule to repeat to your friends
all the pleasant remarks that (as far as you know) are
made on them, and you will increase their happiness,
and your own popularity. We do not mean that you
should flatter them, by reciting compliments that are
not true; but truth is not flattery, and there is no
reason why agreeable truths should not always be
told. There would then be far more kind feeling in
the world. Few persons are so bad as not to have
some good in them. Let them hear of the good.
Few are so ugly as not to have about them something
commendable even externally, if it is only a becoming
dress. Let them hear of that dress. Flattery is
praise without foundation. To tell a person with
heavy, dull gray eyes, that her eyes are of a bright
and beautiful blue; to talk of her golden locks to a
woman with positive red hair of the tint called
carroty; to tell a long, thin, stoop-shouldered girl,
that she possesses the light and airy form of a sylph;
or a short-necked, fat one that her figure has the
dignity of an empress; to assure a faded matron
that she looks like a young girl; to fall into raptures on listening to bad music, or when viewing a
drawing that depicts nothing intelligible; or praising
album poetry that has neither "rhyme nor reason,"—

all this is gross flattery, which the object (if she has any sense) will easily detect, and suspect that you are trying experiments on her vanity and credulity.

Still where agreeable qualities *really* exist, it is not amiss to allude to them delicately. It will give pleasure without compromising veracity.

When any thing complimentary is said to you, acknowledge it by a bow and smile, but do not attempt an answer unless you can say something in return that will be equally sincere and pleasant. Most probably you cannot; therefore look gratified, and bow your thanks, but remain silent. Few ladies are distinguished, like the Harriet Byron of Grandison, "for a very pretty manner of returning a compliment." Do not reject the compliment by pretending to prove that you do not deserve it. But if it is a piece of bare-faced flattery, the best answer is to look gravely, and say or do nothing.

Should you chance accidentally to overhear a remark to your disadvantage, consider first if there may not be some truth in it. If you feel that there is, turn it to profitable account, and try to improve, or to get rid of the fault, whatever it may be. But never show resentment at any thing not intended for your ear. unless it is something of such vital importance as to render it necessary that you should come forward in self-defence. These instances, however, are of rare occurrence.

If you are so placed that you can hear the conversation of persons who are talking about you, it is very mean to sit there and listen. Imme diately remove to a distance far enough to be out of hearing.

It is a proverb that listeners seldom hear any good of themselves. It were a pity if they should. Eaves-dropping or listening beneath an open window, the crack of a door, or through a key-hole, are as dishonourable as to pick pockets.

CHAPTER XIX.

OBLIGATIONS TO GENTLEMEN.

IN her intercourse with gentlemen, a lady should take care to avoid all pecuniary obligations. The civility that a gentleman conventionally owes to a lady is a sufficient tax—more she has no right to expect, or to accept. A man of good sense, and of true politeness, will not be offended at her unwillingness to become his debtor. On the contrary, he will respect her delicacy, and approve her dignity; and consent at once to her becoming her own banker on all occasions where expense is to be incurred. This is the custom in Europe; and is, in most cases, a very good one.

When invited to join a party to a place of amusement, let her consent, if she wishes; but let her state expressly that it is only on condition of being permitted to pay for her own ticket. If she steadily adheres to this custom, it will soon be understood that such is always her commendable practice; and she can then, with perfect propriety, at any time, ask for a seat among friends who intend going. To this accommodation she could not invite herself, if in the continual habit of visiting public places at the expense of others. The best time for a lady to pay for herself is to put her money into the hand of the gentleman *previous* to their departure for the place of performance. He will not be so rude as to refuse to take it. If he does refuse, she should evince her resentment by going with him no more.

Young men of limited means are frequently drawn into expenses they can ill afford, by being acquainted with young ladies who profess a passion for equestrian exercises—a most inconvenient passion for one who has not a horse of her own, or who lives in a family where no horses are kept. If her gentleman is obliged to hire, not only a horse for himself, but also one for the lady, let her have sufficient consideration *not* to propose to him that they should take rides together—and let her not draw him into an invitation, by her dwelling excessively on the delight of horseback excursions. In cities, these rides are expensive luxuries to those who keep no horses. Few city ladies ride well, (even if they have been at riding-school,) for want of daily practice out of doors. They are not exactly at ease on the horse, and always seem somewhat afraid of him; at least till they are "off the stones," and out in the open country. While in the streets, the rare sight of a lady on horseback attracts much attention, and a crowd of boys gathers round to see her mount her steed, or alight from it. This to a young lady of delicacy is very embarrassing, or ought to be.

In the country, the case is totally different. There, "practice makes perfect." The ladies, being accustomed to riding their own horses from childhood, acquire the art without any trouble, have no fear, feel perfectly at home in the saddle, and therefore sit gracefully, and manage their steeds easily. And as every country gentleman has a riding-horse of his own, he can accompany a lady without the expense of hiring.

Lay no wagers with gentlemen, and have no philopenas with them. In betting with a lady, it is customary for the gentleman to pay whether he wins or loses. What then does the wager imply, but a rapacious and mean desire on the part of the lady to " get a present out of him"—as such ladies would express it. No delicate and refined female ever bets at all. It is a very coarse and masculine way of asserting an opinion or a belief; and always reminds gentlemen of the race-course, or the gaming-table.

We disapprove of ladies going to charity-fairs in the evening, when they require a male escort—and when that escort is likely to be drawn into paying exorbitant prices for gifts to his fair companion—particularly, if induced to do so from the fear of appearing mean, or of being thought wanting in benevolence. In the evening, the young ladies who "have tables," are apt to become especially importunate in urging the sale of their goods—and appear to great disadvantage as imitation-shop-keepers, exhibiting a boldness in teazing that no real saleswoman would presume to display. Then the crowd is generally great; the squeezing and pushing very uncomfortable; and most of the company far from genteel. Ladies who *are* ladies, should only visit fancy-fairs in the day-time, when they can go without gentlemen; none of whom

take much pleasure in this mode of raising money; or
rather of levying contributions for special purposes.
There are other ways that are more ·lady-like, more
effective, less fatiguing, and more satisfactory to all
concerned—and far less detrimental to the interests
of the numerous poor women who get their living by
their needles, or by their ingenuity in making ornamental nick-nacks for sale, and who ask but a fair
price for them.   Dress-makers are frequently induced
to keep back portions of silk, the rightful property of
their customers, who may afterwards be put to great
inconvenience for want of them, when the dress is to
be altered or repaired.   And these pieces are given to
the ladies who go about begging for materials to make
pincushions, &c. for fancy-fairs.   This is dishonest.
Let them go to a store and buy small pieces of silk,
velvet, ribbon, and whatever they want for these
purposes.

If you have occasion to send by a gentleman a
package to a transportation-office, give him along
with it the money to pay for its carriage. If you
borrow change, (even one cent,) return it to him
punctually.   He ought to take it as a thing of course,
without any comment.   When you commission him to
buy any thing for you, if you know the price, give the
money beforehand; otherwise, pay it as soon as he
brings the article.   Do all such things promptly, lest
they should escape your memory if delayed.

When visiting a fancy-store with a gentleman, refrain from excessively admiring any handsome or
expensive article you may chance to see there.   Above

all, express no wish that you were able to buy it, and no regret that you cannot, lest he should construe those extreme tokens of admiration into hints that you wish him to buy it for you. To allow him to do so, would on your part be very mean and indelicate, and on his very foolish.

It ought to be a very painful office (and is a very improper one) for young ladies to. go round soliciting from gentlemen subscriptions for charitable purposes. Still it is done. Subscription-papers should only be offered by persons somewhat advanced in life, and of undoubted respectability—and then the application should be made, exclusively, to those whose circumstances are known to be affluent. People who have not much to give, generally prefer giving that little to objects of charity within their own knowledge. Who is there that does not know a poor family? And without actually giving money, (which in too many instances, is immediately appropriated by a drunken husband to supply himself with more drink,) much may be done to procure a few comforts for a miserable wife and children.

When you ask money for a charitable purpose, do so only when quite alone with the person to whom you apply. It is taking an undue advantage to make the request in presence of others—particularly if, as before observed, there is not wealth as well as benevolence. There is a time for all things—and young ladies are deservedly unpopular when, even in the cause of charity, they seize every opportunity to levy contributions on the purses of gentlemen.

It is wrong to trouble gentlemen with commissions that may cause them inconvenience or expense. In the awful days of bandboxes, unfortunate young men riding in stages were sometimes required to convey one of these cumbrous receptacles of bonnets and caps a day's journey upon their knees, to save it from rain outside. Sometimes an immense package containing an immense shawl. We knew an officer who, by particular desire, actually carried *three* great shawls several hundred miles; each bundle to be delivered at a different house in "the City of Magnificent Distances." But as to officers, "sufferance is the badge of all their tribe." Now these shawls should all have been sent by the public line, even if the transportation *did* cost something.

We repeat, that a lady cannot be too particular in placing herself under obligations to a gentleman. She should scrupulously avoid it in every little thing that may involve him in expense on her account. And he will respect her the more.

CHAPTER XX.

CONDUCT TO LITERARY WOMEN.

On being introduced to a female writer, it is rude to say that "you have long had a great *curiosity* to see her." Curiosity is not the right word. It is polite to imply that, "knowing her well by reputation, you are glad to have an opportunity of making her personal acquaintance." Say nothing concerning her writings, unless you chance to be alone with her. Take care not to speak of her first work as being her best; for if it is really so, she must have been retrograding from that time; a falling off that she will not like to hear of. Perhaps the truth may be, that you yourself have read only her *first* work; and if you tell her this, she will not be much flattered in supposing that you, in reality, cared so little for her first book, as to feel no desire to try a second. But she will be really gratified to learn that you are acquainted with most of her writings; and, in the course of conversation, it will be very pleasant for her to hear you quote something from them.

If she is a writer of fiction, and you presume to take the liberty of criticising her works, (as you may at her own request, or if you are her intimate friend,) refrain from urging that certain incidents are *improba-*

ble, and certain characters *unnatural*. Of this it is impossible for you to judge, unless you could have lived the very same life that she has; known exactly the same people; and inhabited with her the same places. Remember always that "Truth is stranger than fiction." The French say—"Le vrai n'est pas toujours le plus vraisemblable,"—which, literally translated, means that "Truth is not always the most truth-like." Also, be it understood that a woman of quick perception and good memory can see and recollect a thousand things which would never be noticed or remembered by an obtuse or shallow, common-place capacity. And the intellect of a good writer of fiction is always brightened by the practice of taking in and laying up ideas with a view toward turning them to professional use. Trust in her, and believe that she *has* painted from life. A sensible fictionist always does. At the same time, be not too curious in questioning her as to the identity of her personages and the reality of her incidents. You have no right to expect that she will expose to you, or to any one else, her process of arranging the story, bringing out the characters, or concocting the dialogue. The machinery of her work, and the hidden springs which set it in motion, she naturally wishes to keep to herself; and she cannot be expected to lay them bare for the gratification of impertinent curiosity, letting them become subjects of idle gossip. Be satisfied to take her works as you find them. If you like them, read and commend them; but do not ask her to conduct you behind the scenes, and show you the mysteries of

her art—for writing is really an art, and one that
cannot be acquired, to any advantage, without a certain amount of talent, taste, and cultivation, to say
nothing of genius.   What right have you to expect
that your literary friend will trust you with "the
secrets of her prison-house," and put it into your
power to betray her confidence by acquainting the
world that a certain popular novelist has informed
you with her own lips ("but it must on no account be
mentioned, as the disclosure would give mortal offence,
and create for her hosts of enemies,") that by her
character of Fanny Gadfly she really means Lucy
Giddings; that Mr. Hardcastle signifies Mr. Stone;
that Old Wigmore was modelled on no less a person
than Isaac Baldwin; that Mrs. Baskings was taken
from Mrs. Sunning; and Mrs. Babes from Mrs. Chil-
ders—&c. &c.   Also, do not expect her to tell you on
what facts her incidents were founded, and whether
there was any truth in them, or if they were mere
invention.

Be not inquisitive as to the length of time con-
sumed in writing this book or that—or how soon the
work now on hand will be finished.   It can scarcely
be any concern of yours, and the writer may have reasons for keeping back the information.   Rest assured
that whenever a public announcement of a new book
is expedient, it will certainly be made in print.

There are persons so rude as to question a literary
woman (even on a slight acquaintance) as to the re-
muneration she receives for her writings—in plain
terms, "How much did you get for that? and how

much are you to have for this? And how much do you make in the course of a year? And how much a page do you get? And how many pages can you write in a day?"

To any impertinent questions from a stranger-lady concerning the profits of your pen, reply concisely, that these things are secrets between yourself and your publishers. If you kindly condescend to answer without evasion, these polite enquiries, you will probably hear such exclamations as, "Why, really—you must be coining money. I think I'll write books myself! There can't be a better trade," &c.

Ignorant people always suppose that popular writers are wonderfully well-paid—and must be making rapid fortunes—because they neither starve in garrets, nor wear rags—at least in America.

Never ask one writer what is her *real* opinion of a cotemporary author. She may be unwilling to entrust it to you, as she can have no guarantee that you will not whisper it round till it gets into print. If she voluntarily expresses her own opinion of another writer, and it *is* unfavourable, be honourable enough not to repeat it; but guard it sedulously from betrayal, and avoid mentioning it to any one.

When in company with literary women, make no allusions to "learned ladies," or "blue stockings," or express surprise that they should have any knowledge of housewifery, or needle-work, or dress; or that they are able to talk on "common things." It is rude and foolish, and shows that you really know nothing about them, either as a class or as individuals.

17

Never tell an authoress that "you are afraid of her"—or entreat her "not to put you into a book." Be assured there is no danger.

An authoress has seldom leisure to entertain morning visiters; so much of her time being professionally occupied either in writing, or in reading what will prepare her for writing. She should apprize all her friends of the hours in which she is usually engaged; and then none who are really her friends and well-wishers, will encroach upon her convenience for any purpose of their own; unless under extraordinary circumstances. To tell her that you were "just passing by," or "just in the neighbourhood," and "just thought you would stop in," is a very selfish, or at least a very inconsiderate excuse. Is she to suppose that you do not consider her conversation worthy of a visit made on purpose?

Recollect that to a woman who gets her living by her pen, "time is money," as it is to an artist. Therefore, encroaching on her time is lessening her income. And yet how often is this done (either heedlessly or selfishly) by persons professing to be her friends, and who are habitually in the practice of interrupting her in her writing hours, which should always be in the morning, if possible. They think it sufficient to say, like Paul Pry, "I hope I don't intrude"—knowing all the time that they do, and pretending to believe her when civility obliges her to tell them they do not. Even if the visit is not a long one, it is still an interruption. In one minute it may break a chain of ideas which cannot be reunited, dispel

thoughts that can never be recalled, disturb the con
struction of a sentence, and obliterate a recollection
that will not return.   And to all this the literary lady
must submit, because her so-called friend "chanced to
be out that morning shopping"—or "happened to be
visiting in that part of the town"—and therefore has
called on *her* by way of "killing two birds with one
stone."   Very likely, the visiter will say to the unfortunate visited, "I know it is inconvenient to you to see
your friends in the morning, but I never feel like going
out in the afternoon.   As soon as dinner is over I must
have my nap ; and by the time that is finished, it is too
late for any thing else."

In consequence of these ill-timed visits, the printer
may have to send in vain for " copy" that is not yet
ready ; and an article written expressly for a magazine may arrive too late for the next month, and be
therefore deferred a month later, which may subject
her not only to inconvenience, but to actual pecuniary
loss—loss of money.   Or, at least, the interruption
may compel her to the painful effort of trying to
finish it even by sitting up late at night, and straining
her weary eyes by lamp-light.   Yet this she must
endure because it suits an idle and thoughtless *friend*
to make her a long and inopportune visit.   The children of the pen and the pencil might say to these
intruders, like the frogs in the pond when the boys
were pelting them with stones—" This may be sport
to you, but it is death to us."

If, when admitted into her study, you should find
her writing-table in what appears to you like great

confusion, recollect that there is really no wit in a
remark too common on such occasions,—" Why, you
look quite *littery*,"—a poor play on the words *literary*
and *litter*. In all probability, she knows precisely
where to lay her hand upon every paper on the table:
having in reality placed them exactly to suit her convenience. Though their arrangement may be quite
unintelligible to the uninitiated, there is no doubt
method (her own method, at least) in their apparent
disorder. It is not likely she may have time to put
her writing table in nice-looking order every day. To
have it done by servants is out of the question, as *they*
would make "confusion worse confounded;" being of
course unable to comprehend how *such a table* should
be arranged.

If you chance to find an authoress occupied with
her needle, express no astonishment, and refrain from
exclaiming, "What! can *you* sew?" or, "I never
supposed a literary lady could even hem a handkerchief!"

This is a false, and if expressed in words, an insulting
idea. A large number of literary females are excellent needle-women, and good housewives; and there
is no reason why they should not be. The same
vigour of character and activity of intellect which
renders a woman a *good* writer, will also enable her to
acquire with a quickness, almost intuitive, a competent
knowledge of household affairs, and of the art of needle-
work. And she will find, upon making the attempt,
that, with a little time and a little perseverance, she
may become as notable a personage (both in theory

and practice) as if she had never read a book, or written a page.

The Dora of David Copperfield is an admirable illustration of the fact that a silly, illiterate woman may be the worst of housewives. Dickens has unquestionably painted this character exactly from life. But that he always does. He must have known a Dora. And who has not?

If you find your literary friend in dèshabille, and she apologizes for it—(she had best *not* apologize)—tell her not that "authoresses are privileged persons, and are never expected to pay any attention to dress." Now, literary slatterns are not more frequent than slatterns who are not literary. It is true that women of enlarged minds, and really good taste, do not think it necessary to follow closely all the changes and follies of fashion, and to wear things that are inconvenient, uncomfortable, and unbecoming, merely because milliners, dress-makers, &c. have pronounced them "the last new style."

It is ill-manners to refer in any way to the profession of the person to whom you are talking, unless that person is an intimate friend, and you are alone with her ; and unless she herself begins the subject. Still worse, to allude to their profession as if you supposed it rendered them different from the rest of the world, and marked them with peculiarities from which other people are exempt.

It is true that authorlings and poetizers are apt to affect eccentricity. Real authors, and even real poets, (by real we mean good ones,) have generally a large portion of common sense to balance their genius, and are therefore seldom guilty of the queernesses unjustly imputed to the whole fraternity.

When in company with a literary lady with whom you are not on very confidential terms, it is bad taste to talk to her exclusively of books, and to endeavour to draw out her opinion of authors with whom she is personally acquainted—and whom she will, of course, be unwilling to criticise, (at least in miscellaneous society,) lest her remarks should be invidiously or imprudently repeated, and even get into print. "Any thing new in the literary world?" is a question by which some people always commence conversation with an author. Why should it be supposed that they always "carry the shop along with them," or that they take no interest or pleasure in things not connected with books. On the contrary, they are glad to be allowed the privilege of unbending like other people. And a good writer is almost always a good talker, and fully capable of conversing well on various subjects. Try her.

It was beautifully said of Jane Taylor, the charming author of a popular and never-tiring little book of "Original Poems for Children," that "you only knew that the stream of literature had passed over her mind by the fertility it left behind it."

We have witnessed, when two distinguished lady-writers chanced to be at the same party, an unmannerly disposition to "pit them against each other"—placing them side by side, or *vis-a-vis*, and saying something about, "When Greek meets Greek," &c.,

and absolutely collecting a circle round them, to be amused or edified by the expected dialogue. This is rude and foolish.

It is not treating a talented woman with due consideration, to be active in introducing to her the silliest and flattest people in the room, because the said flats have been worked up into a desire of seeing, face to face, " a live authoress"—though in all probability they have not read one of her works.

That notorious lion-hunter, the Countess of Cork, was so candid as to say to certain celebrated writers, " I'll sit by *you* because you are famous." To a very charming American lady whom she was persuading to come to her party, she frankly added, " My dear, you really must not refuse me. Don't you know you are my decoy-duck."

There are mothers (called pattern-mothers) who uphold the theory that every thing in the world must bend to the advantage (real or supposed) of children, that is, of their own children—and who have continually on their lips the saying, " a mother's first duty is to her children." So it is, and it is her duty not to render them vain, impertinent, conceited, and obtrusive, by allowing them to suppose that they must on all occasions be brought forward; and that their mother's visiters have nothing to do but to improve and amuse *them*. Therefore a literary lady often receives a more than hint from such a mother to talk only on edifying subjects when the dear little creatures are present; and then the conversation is required to take a Penny-Magazine tone, exclusively—

the darlings being, most probably, restless and impatient all the time, the girls sitting uneasily on their
chairs and looking tired, and the boys suddenly bolting out of the room to get back to their sports.   It is
true the children will be less impatient if the visiter
will t ⌣able herself to " tell them stories" all the time;
but ⌣ is rude to ask her to do so.

When directing a letter to "a woman of letters," it
is not considered polite to insert the word "Authoress"
after her name.   And yet we have seen this done by
persons who ought to know better.   If you are unac-
quainted with the number and street of her residence,
direct to the care of her publisher; whose place you
may always find, by referring to the title-page of one
of her last works, and by seeing his advertisements in
the newspapers.   The booksellers always know where
their authors are to be found.   So do the printers—
for their boys convey the proof-sheets.

Observe that the term "learned lädy" is not correctly applied to a female, unless she has successfully
cultivated what is understood to be the learning of
colleges—for instance, the dead languages, &c.   Unfortunately, the term is now seldom used but in deri-
sion, and to denote a woman whose studies have been
entirely of the masculine order.   You may speak of a
well-informed, well-read, talented, intellectual, accomplished lady; but call her not *learned*, unless she is
well-versed in the Greek and Latin classics, and able
to discuss them from their original language.   Even
then, spare her the appellation of *learned*, if gentlemen are present.   In the dark ages, when not every

lady could read and write, the few that *were* entitled to the "benefit of clergy," frequently "drank deep in tasting the Pierian spring," and proceeded to study the learned languages with great success; for instance, Lady Jane Grey and Queen Elizabeth.

In desiring the autograph of a literary lady, do not expect her to write in your album "a piece of poetry." Be satisfied with her signature only. There is a spice of meanness in requesting from her, as a gift, any portion of her stock in trade. As well might you ask Mr. Stewart, or Mr. Levy, to present you with an embroidered collar, or a pair of gloves. For the same reason, never request an artist to "draw something" in your album. It is only amateur poets, and amateur artists, that can afford to write and draw in albums. Those who make a living by their profession, have no time to spare for gratuitous performances; and it is as wrong to ask them, as it is to invite public singers to "favour the company with a song" at private parties, where they are invited as guests. It is, however, not unusual for professional musicians to kindly and politely gratify the company by inviting themselves to sing; saying, "Perhaps you would like to hear my last song." And sometimes, if quite "in the vein," a real poet, when modestly asked for merely his signature, will voluntarily add a few lines of verse. But do not expect it.

There are pretty little books of fine paper, handsomely bound, that are used for the purpose of containing signature autographs; one on each page. A lady owning such a book, can send it to any distinguished person of whose hand-writing she wishes to possess a specimen.

When the name at the bottom of a letter is shown to you as an autograph, it is rude to take the letter into your own hand, and read the whole, or even to glance your eye over it. It is not intended that you shall see any thing but the signature.

We will now address a few words to beginners in the art of writing, with reference to their intercourse with women of well-established literary reputation If these ladies of decided standing in the republic of letters have sufficient leisure, they will generally be very kind in assisting with their counsel a young aspirant, who shows any evidence of talent for the profession. Unluckily, too many novices in the art, mistake a mere desire to get into print, for that rarest of gifts—genius. And without genius, there is no possibility of gaining by the pen, either fame, or fortune.

Long manuscripts are frequently sent for the revisal "at leisure" of a person who has little or no leisure. Yet in the intervals of toiling for herself, she is expected to toil for some one else; probably for a stranger whom she does not know, in whom she can take no interest, and who has evidently "no writing in her soul." If, however, the modest request is kindly complied with, in all probability the corrections will only give offence, and may perhaps be crossed out before the manuscript is offered to the publisher, who very likely may reject it for want of these very corrections. We have known such incidents.

The least talented of the numerous females pretending to authorship, are generally the most conceited and the most obtrusive. They are frequently very great annoyances to women "well-up the ladder," who are expected, in many instances, not only to revise the manuscript, but immediately to find a purchaser for it—a purchaser of high rank among publishers—one who will bring it out handsomely, ensure it an immense circulation, pay promptly, and pay as much as is given to the standard authors. And besides being desired to "get it published," the reviser of the manuscript will, perhaps, be requested to correct the proofs; that is, if the literary novice should chance to know what proof-sheets are.

The work thus arrogantly thrust upon the time and attention of a deservedly-popular writer may be a book of "sweet poetry," on weak, worn-out, common-place subjects, done into feeble, halting, ill-rhyming verses, such as few read, and none remember. Or the aspirant after fame, may have chosen the easier path of prose, and produced a fiction without fancy, a novel without novelty, "a thrilling tale" that thrills nobody, a picture of fashionable life after no fashion that ever existed, or "a pathetic story of domestic life," neither pathetic nor domestic.

Yet if a practised and successful author ventures to pronounce an *unfavourable* verdict on such productions, because the writer desired her *candid* opinion, she will probably light up a flame of resentment, that may never be extinguished, and make an enemy for life; the objections being imputed to "sheer envy," and to a malignant design of "extinguishing a rising star."

A sufficient introduction to a publisher is to send him the manuscript, accompanied by a note requesting his opinion as soon as convenient. If he approves it, and believes it will be profitable, there is no doubt of his being willing to print the work. And if he thinks he shall make nothing by it, it is equally certain that he will decline the offer. It is too much to expect that he will be so regardless of his own interest as to publish a book, the sale of which will not remunerate him for the cost of paper and printing.

Ladies who live in the same house with an authoress, nave opportunities enough of seeing her in the parlour, and at table; therefore they may dispense with visiting her in her own room. Spare her all interruptions of applying for the loan of books, paper, pens, ink, &c. Do not expect that, because she writes, she must necessarily keep a free circulating library, or a gratuitous stationer's shop. Supply yourself with all such conveniences from the regular sources. Buy them, and pay for them, instead of troubling one who has not time to be troubled. Above all, refrain from the meanness of asking her to lend you any book written by herself. If she volunteers the loan, then receive it thankfully; and take care to return it speedily, and in good condition. It is *her* interest, and the interest of her publishers, that a large number of copies shall

be *sold;* not lent, or given away. Many persons erroneously suppose that an author has always on hand
an unlimited number of her own books; or that the
publisher will kindly give her as many as she can
want for herself and friends. This is by no means
the case. It is usual, when the first edition comes out,
for the publisher to send the author half a dozen
copies of the book, or a dozen, if it is a small one.
After that, if she wants any more, she is expected to
to buy them of the bookseller. Therefore, she has
none to *give away*, except to members of her own
family, or to friends whose circumstances will not
permit them to expend money in books, and who
have an ardent love for reading without the means
of gratifying it. We have known ladies, possessing
diamonds and India shawls, and living in splendid
houses, ask the author for the loan of a cookery-book,
with the avowed purpose of " copying out the best
receipts."

Apropos to cookery-books:—If you have faithfully
followed a receipt, and the result is not quite satisfactory, there is nothing amiss in your acquainting the
writer with that fact, provided it *is* a fact. On the
contrary, you may do her a kindness, by enabling her
to detect an error in the directions, and to rectify that
error in a future edition.

Women often assert that the receipt was not a good
one, and that upon trial it proved a failure, when, on
investigation, you will find that, from false economy,
some of the ingredients were left out; or the relative
proportions diminished in quantity—too much of the

cheapest articles being put in, and not enough of the more costly. Or else, that sufficient time and pains were not bestowed on the mixing and preparing; or that the thing was not sufficiently cooked.

By-the-bye, remember that a receipt for cookery, is not to be called a *recipe*. The word *recipe* belongs to pharmacy, and is only used with reference to medical prescriptions. The cook uses *receipts*, the apothecary *recipes*.

Whatever article you may wish to borrow from an inmate of the same house, apply first to persons whose time is of comparatively small importance to them, before you disturb and interrupt a literary lady. Do not trouble her for the loan of umbrellas, overshoes, hoods, calashes, &c., or send to her for small change.

We once lived in a house where coal-fires were scarce, and wood-fires plenty. Our own fire-arrangement was wood in a Franklin stove, and no other person in the house was the fortunate owner of a pair of bellows. Liking always to be comfortable, we had bought a pair for ourselves.

Ten times a day we were disturbed by a knock at the door, from a coloured girl who came "a-borrowing" this implement to revive the fire of some other room. She called it by a pleasing variety of names—running through all the vowels. Sometimes she wanted the bellow*sas;* sometimes the bellow*ses;* or the bellow*sis,* the bellow*sos,* or the bellow*sus.* These frequent interruptions, with others that were similar, became a real grievance. We thought it would cost us less to present the bellows to the house, and buy another pair for ourselves. We did so—but very soon the first pair was somehow missing, and our own was again in requisition.

Since that winter we have burnt anthracite, and therefore have no bellows*as* to lend.

CHAPTER XXI.

SUGGESTIONS TO INEXPERIENCED AUTHORS.

THERE is some economy and much convenience in buying your paper by the ream, (twenty quires,) having first tried a sample. The surface of the paper should be smooth, and somewhat glossy; particularly if you write with metallic pens. That which is soft and spongy, though a little lower in price, wears out the pen so fast that what is saved in paper is lost in pens; also, there is no possibility of writing on it with ease and expedition. You will find it best to use paper ruled in lines. If you write a large hand, take fools-cap; if a small hand, use letter-paper size. But note-paper is too small, when you are writing for the press.

Before you commence your manuscript, take a quire, and prepare each sheet by splitting it all down the folded side, with a sharp paper-cutter, thus divid-ing it into half-sheets. You can do this better on a flat table than on the slope of a desk. Keep your left hand pressing down hard on the quire, while you are cutting it with your right.

The best paper-cutters are those of real ivory. A handle is of no advantage to them, but rather the con-trary. They should be thin, plain, and perfectly straight, except being rounded off at the two ends. Ivory paper-knives of this form are generally used by the book-binders, an evidence that they are convenient and expeditious. Those of bone or horn are scarcely worth buying, though but half the price; the edges soon becoming blunt, and therefore useless. Wooden paper-knives are good for nothing. Paper-knives of mother of pearl, and other ornamental substances, are of little utility, being rarely sharp enough, (even when new,) and in a short time becoming quite dull. Also, they break very easily. Avoid cutting a sheet of paper, or the leaves of a book, with scissors; it is comparatively a slow and awkward process; and cannot, even with great care, be effected as smoothly and evenly as with a cutter of ivory.

Before you split or divide the sheet, press the paper-knife all along the fold, so as to flatten the crease, and make it cut evenly and easily. Having split your whole sheets into leaves or half-sheets, take each half-sheet separately, and fold over an inch or more all along the left-hand edge; so as to leave a margin or space for sewing the manuscript when finished. Do this with the paper-knife. Lay a pile of these half-sheets beside you when you sit down to write, and take them as you want them.

Write only on one side of the paper. If written on both sides, it will cause trouble and inconvenience to the printers, by obliging them to turn over at the end of every page. This rule, however, may be dispensed with, when a manuscript is so short that it may be comprised in one sheet, and is to be trans-

18

mitted by mail. This may be the more easily managed, by drawing with a pencil or pen a straight perpendicular line down the middle of each page, so as to divide it into columns. When it is finished, enclose it in an envelope, direct, and seal it, and put on a post-office stamp. If the manuscript occupies two or three sheets, put two or three stamps side by side. There are large envelopes that will hold foolscap paper, properly folded.

Do not use *blue* ink; for if any part of your manuscript should chance to get wet, there is a risk of the blue ink being effaced or obliterated by the damp, so as to render the writing illegible; and this has frequently happened.

Let your writing be large enough, and plain enough to be read with ease, and the compositor will be less likely to make mistakes. Printers, though accustomed to read all sorts of writing, are sometimes completely at a loss in deciphering a very bad hand. There is no excuse for a person in respectable life persisting in writing illegibly, as it is never too late to improve. You have only to take lessons of a good instructor, and apply yourself sedulously to acquiring a new hand, and you will succeed in doing so.

Do not, in writing for the press, affect the crow-quill calligraphy that is fashionable for album verses and complimentary billets. When your manuscript is finished, sew the leaves *evenly* together, with nothing more than a strong thread; or, if it is very thick, it may be sewed with a fine twine put into a large needle. A handsome cover, daintily fastened with a pretty ribbon, is of no account in a printing-office, where the first thing that is done with a manuscript is to remove the cover, and cut the leaves loose from the fastening. The printers will gladly dispense with covers, ribbons, and fairy-like penmanship, in favour of a plain legible hand, pages regularly numbered, and leaves written on one side only.

In commencing a manuscript, write the title or caption in large letters, at some distance from the top of the first page; and if you are not anonymous, put your name a little below the title. Then begin the *first* line of the first paragraph, several inches distant from the left-hand side, or margin. In this manner commence every paragraph. The length of the paragraphs may be regulated by the time when you think a pause longer than that of a period or full stop may be effective; or to give the reader an opportunity of resting for a minute; or to denote the commencement of another subject.

In writing a dialogue, begin every separate speech with a capital, and commence each speech on a new line, and at some distance from the left-hand margin. Also mark the beginning and end of every speech with double commas. If the names of the speakers are given at the *commencement* of every speech, write those names in *large* letters, putting a dot and a dash after them. All these arrangements are the same in writing as in printing.

If you are, unfortunately, not familiar with the rules of punctuation, refresh your memory by referring to them in a grammar-book. They must be strictly observed; otherwise your meaning will be un-intelligible. Always remember that every period or full stop, and every note of interrogation, or of admiration, must be followed by a capital letter, beginning the next word. Dashes, particularly in a dialogue, add much to the effect, if not used too lavishly.

Errors of orthography are rarely committed by any one who presumes to write for the press. It is scarcely possible for a person who reads much to spell incorrectly, as the appearance of the printed words becomes insensibly and indelibly fixed in the mind. Still it may be well to write with a dictionary on your table, in case you should have any doubt as to the proper spelling and meaning of a word with which you may not be very familiar.

Keep also a grammar on your table. Grammatical errors are annoying to the reader, and disgraceful to the writer, unless it is well known that she has not had the advantage of an education, even at a common school. Then she is to be pitied. But it is never too late to study grammar, and she had best do so before she ventures to write for the public. If she writes ungrammatically, how must she talk! In a work of fiction it is shocking to have lords and ladies, or the noble and dignified hero, and the elegant and refined heroine, conversing in "bad grammar," because the author knew no better. Yet such books we have seen. There are, luckily, not many of them. But there should be none.

Every morning, previous to commencing your task, revise carefully all that you have written on the preceeding day, and correct and alter whatever you may deem susceptible of improvement. Some authors revise every page as soon as they have written it. But, unless you are much pressed for time, it is best to do this next morning, when your perceptions are fresh and clear. In crossing or blotting out, do it effectually, so that the original words may not appear through, and remain still legible. If you find that you have omitted a word, or if you wish to change one word for another, interline it; inserting the new word just above the line to which it belongs, and placing this mark $\wedge$ below. Lay aside each page as you finish it, Be particular in numbering every page; and it is best to do this before you begin, placing the number near the top of the right-hand corner. Let not your lines be too close, or there will not be space enough for legible interlining.

If the publisher lives in your own town, it will be sufficient to roll up the manuscript in clean white paper, twisted at each end, and wafered in the middle. But however short the distance, write on the outside of the paper the full direction of the publishing office; that, in case of its being dropped in the street, any person finding it may know exactly where to take it.

In putting up a large manuscript, in a packet for transmission to a distant place, use strong nankeen paper for the cover, and secure it with wafers, or paste, if it is to go a voyage in a steamer, as a wax seal may be melted by the heat of the fire. If it will reach its destination in a few hours, you may seal it with wax, having tied red tape about. Do not use twine, as that may cut the paper. Newspapers are generally put up in a brownish paper cover, pasted at the side and bottom, with one end left open.

Postage is now so cheap, that manuscripts had best always be transmitted by mail; putting a sufficient number of stamps on the outside, all close to each other.

Few women can write well enough for publication, without going twice over the subject; first in what is called the rough copy, and then making a fair copy with all the original errors corrected, and all proper alterations inserted. If you have time, make *two* fair copies; one for the printer, and one to keep for yourself, in case the other should be accidentally destroyed or lost—retaining it till after the work is actually in print. Much postage is wasted, and much annoyance is given to the editors of periodicals, by applications for the restoration of unpublished verses, and other "Rejected Addresses," consisting, perhaps, of a sheet of poetry, or a few pages of prose, of which it would have been very easy to have made another copy for the author's keeping.

In writing articles for Annuals, let it be remembered that the printing of these books is always completed some months before they are published or announced for sale. Therefore, all contributions should be sent to the publisher before February, or March at farthest. For a magazine, they should be transmitted at least two months in advance. For a weekly paper, two weeks ahead.

Those who write for periodicals should remember

that it is the custom to address all letters on compensations, copies of work, &c. to the publisher; and not to the editor, who seldom has any concern in the pecuniary affairs, his business being solely to receive, and read the manuscripts, to accept or reject them, and to arrange them for the press. It is not usual for the compensation to be paid till after the book is published. Some publishers send to every contributor one copy of the work. Others do not present a copy when the article is very short—for instance, a few stanzas of verse. Prose obtains a higher price than poetry, of which there is always a superabundance in the market. Much poetry is published without any pay at all; the writers being contented with seeing their effusions in print. No *good* author has any occasion to write gratuitously. A "merely passable" or "just tolerable" writer of poetry or fiction, should give up the inventive line, and try something else—something for which genius is not indispensable; and from which, by patience and industry, a sort of living may be wrought out.

In composing poetry, a common, but unpardonable fault is that of introducing a lame or halting line—a line with one syllable too many, or too few. And if the author does not understand that it is an intolerable blemish, and sends it uncorrected to the press, she is unworthy of being called a poetess. We are inclined to believe that no person devoid of an ear for music, can write poetry deserving of the name. The ideas may be good, but the lines will have no melody, and will move harshly and ruggedly, very much like rough prose.

Some writers seem to think that blank verse is nothing but prose with a capital at the beginning of each line; never having learnt or remembered that though the lines do not rhyme, they must all comprise ten syllables, (syllables, not words,) otherwise the effect when read, will, to even a tolerable ear, be absolutely painful. We saw a play, (the first attempt of a since distinguished dramatist,) the dialogue of which was unintelligible to the audience, and nearly impracticable to the actors, who found it absolutely beyond their skill to enunciate; or rather beneath it. We afterward heard the manager of the Chestnut-street Theatre explain, that the difficulty, both with the speakers and the hearers, was the execrable blank verse in which the play was written; some of the lines containing but seven or eight syllables, (instead of ten,) and some twelve or fourteen. A very few English authors write irregular blank verse; but we are sorry to say that a great many Americans do not seem to understand the process, simple as it is, of confining themselves to ten syllables only,—neither more nor less.   Can they have read Shakspeare?

There is no blank verse in French poetry. That language seems incapable of it.

If you are writing for a periodical, and are desirous of ascertaining before-hand how many pages your manuscript will make when printed, take, at random, any printed page of the work, and copy it in your usual hand, and on a sheet of the same paper you intend using throughout. You will thus, by comparison, be able to judge with tolerable accuracy, how much of your writing will make a page when printed.

Keep a memorandum-book for the express purpose of setting down whatever relates to your literary affairs. Insert the day when you commenced a manuscript, the day when you finished it, and the day on which it went to the publisher. Also, the whole number of its pages. When you see it in print, put down the number of its printed pages. In this book, set down, *immediately on receiving them,* whatever sums are paid to you for your writings.

If you are a writer of fiction, have a large book for memorandums, of any amusing or remarkable things you may chance to hear, and which you may turn to account afterward. If you write truth only, keep a book for the reception of useful or interesting facts. A written book of names, alphabetically arranged, (surnames and christian names,) will be of great advantage in selecting appellations for your characters. Do not give elegant names to your common people; or to your patrician characters names that are coarse and vulgar. A fault in Dickens is that nearly all his names are rugged, uncouth, and ill-sounding, and seldom characteristic. Why should a very excellent and generous brother and sister be called Tom Pinch and Ruth Pinch. What did they pinch?

There is a proof-reader in every printing-office, but after he has done, the proofs are generally sent to the author for farther revisal.

In correcting proof-sheets, first see that they are quite dry. Draw your pen through any word you

desire to change, and then write the new word on the
margin, placing it even with the line of the rejected
word.   When you alter the punctuation, converting a
comma into a semicolon, or a period into a note of
admiration, make a slight mark on the margin of that
line, that the printer may not overlook it.   If you
have occasion to change a whole sentence, cross it
out, and put the new sentence on the margin at the
bottom of the page.

If the printer's boy can wait, you had best correct
the proofs while he stays.

CHAPTER XXII.

CHILDREN.

Miss Edgworth says that the education of a child begins at three months old. It is true that both bad and good habits may seem to commence at this early age; but we do not believe that in so slight a soil they take a very deep root, or that what is called a cross baby is sure to grow up an ill-tempered adult. Infants, when they are not really sick, frequently cry from some incidental annoyance, and not from a fretful disposition. If they feel comfortably they will usually be good-humoured and pleasant. Much of their comfort is sacrificed to the vanity of the mother in dressing them fashionably and expensively. We knew a baby that was very good in the morning, but very cross in the afternoon, or when dressed for show. And no wonder, for in her show-costume she was tortured with necklace, sleeve-loops, and bracelets of fine branchy, or rather briary coral, scratching and irritating her delicate skin, and leaving the print in red marks. On our representing this to the mother as the probable cause of the baby's fretfulness, the thorny ornaments were left off, and the child became amiable. Gold chains are also very irritating to the neck and arms of an infant. Coral beads of a smooth round form, strung evenly on a simple thread of silk, without any intermingling of gold chain, are, perhaps, the most comfortable necklaces for children, and are also very becoming; but as they are not expensive, they are of course not fashionable.

Fortunately, the days of worked caps are over. Young ladies are no longer expected to cover pieces of cambric with elaborate cotton embroidery for the babies of their married friends, and the tender heads of the babies are no longer chafed with rough needle-work rubbing incessantly upon them, or heated with a silk lining to the cambric already thickened all over with close, heavy patterns. We wish also that mothers, generally, were less proud of seeing their babies with "luxuriant heads of hair," which if it has no natural tendency to curl, disfigures the child and gives it a wild, ungenteel look. If it does curl, it still heats the head and neck, and is said to draw away much strength from the system. The most healthy infants we have seen, had very little hair, or it was judiciously kept closely cut. To curl children's hair in papers is barbarous. They pay dearly for the glory of appearing in ringlets during the day, if they are made to pass their nights lying upon a mass of hard, rough bobs, about as pleasant as if they had their heads in a bag of hickory-nuts. But then the mother has the gratification of hearing their curls admired!

Among other sufferings inflicted on babies is that of sending them out in bleak winter days with brimless hats, that, so far from screening their faces from the

cold wind, do not even afford the slightest shade to
their eyes, which are winking and watering all the
time from the glare of the sun and snow. We have
seen false curls pinned to these babies' hats, and dan-
gling in their eyes.

Another detestable practice is that of making the
waists of children's frocks ridiculously long and painfully tight; particularly over the chest and body,
which are thus pressed flat, to the utter ruin of the
figure, and the risk of producing incurable diseases—
such as consumption of the lungs, and projection of the
spine; to say nothing of the various complaints connected with the stomach, which is thus squeezed into
half its natural compass. Also, the sleeve-holes are
so small and tight as to push up the shoulders. Then
the hips are pressed downward far below their proper
place, and the legs are consequently in danger of
becoming short and bandy. Is it possible this vile
fashion can continue much longer!—and are "the
rising generation" really to grow up with high
shoulders, round backs, flat chests, bodies that seem
longer than their legs, and hips almost where their
knees ought to be.

Also, these limbs must suffer from cold in winter
with no other covering than cotton stockings, the
skirts of the dress scarcely reaching to the knees—the
little boys disfigured with the ugliest of all garments,
short knee-breeches.

Add to all the rest of these abominations, tight
boots with peaked toes, and can we wonder that children, even beyond the period of infancy, should, at

times, be cross, irritable, and unamiable. How can they be otherwise, when they seldom feel comfortably? Then, if the parents can afford it, (or whether or not,) the unhappy children are bedizened with all manner of expensive finery, and interdicted from romping, lest they should injure it. But, what matter if the children suffer—the mother's vanity *must* be gratified, and she *must* have the delight of seeing that her boys and girls are as fashionably dressed as the little Thomsons and Wilsons and Jacksons.

We look back with regret to the days when little girls, as well as boys, wore their hair closely cropped; convenient and cool, and showing to advantage the form of the head, till they were twelve or thirteen— and they wore only washable dresses, descending far below the knees, and with pantalets down to their ancles. In summer their frocks, had short wide sleeves, and were *not* close up to the throat. The bodies were of a natural length, the outside gathered full upon a moderately tight lining. If there is no lining to a full frock-body it will puff out at the back and front, and give the waist a look of deformity before and behind. Then the little girls went out in close cottage-bonnets of straw in summer, and beaver in winter—shading and screening their faces—and were kept warm when out of doors with long wide cloaks or coats of cloth or merino, instead of the fantastic short things now worn, with open sleeves and open fronts. Then, when at home, how innocent and childlike they looked in their long-sleeved convenient bib-aprons!—so much better than the short silk ones now worn,

trimmed and bordered and ribboned, and rendered so
fine that the children are expected to be as careful
of injuring their showy aprons as of soiling their
showy frocks.

Formerly, children learned to play various amusing
games, such as "Hot buttered beans," "Blind-man's
buff," &c. Now their play is chiefly running and
squeeling, and chasing each other about, without any
definite object, except that of making a noise. Then,
at a juvenile party, the amusement was chiefly in the
varieties of these entertaining games. Now it is
dancing—for as many as can find places to dance—
and nothing at all for those who cannot, but to grow
tired and sleepy. In former times, children's parties
commenced at two o'clock in the afternoon in winter,
and at four in summer. They played till they were
summoned to a large and well-supplied tea-table, and
were sent for to come home by eight o'clock, being
then quite tired enough to go to bed and sleep
soundly, and waken with pleasant recollections of
yesterday. If the party was very large, the elder
children sat round the room, and tea, &c. was handed
to them, while the little ones were accommodated at a
table where the hostess presided. The children of
that time really enjoyed these parties, and so would
those of the present time, if they could have such.
The juvenile-party dress was then but a simple white
muslin frock with a ribbon sash. We have since seen
little girls at a summer party stedfastly refuse straw-
berries and cream, in obedience to the interdiction of
their mothers; who had enjoined them to do so, lest

they should stain or otherwise injure their elegant silk dresses.

Fortunately, it is no longer fashionable for mothers to take their children with them on morning visits. On these occasions small children rarely behave well. They soon grow tired, and restless, and begin teazing to go somewhere else. Their presence is (or ought to be) a restraint on conversation, as much may be said during a visit that is not well for them to hear. They comprehend certain things far more easily than is supposed. Great mischief has ensued from allowing children to sit and listen; and there is no dependence on their discretion or secrecy.

It is not well to put a small child "through its facings," by trying to make it exhibit any of its little feats before strangers. They are generally very reluctant to make this exhibition. Sometimes they are bashful, sometimes perverse; but if the mother persists in her attempt to show them off, it will probably prove a complete failure, and end in a cry, or that outbreak usually called a tantrum. By-the-bye, there is no better way of stopping a tantrum than quietly to divert the child's attention to something else.

Beware of trusting an infant, too confidingly, to an European nurse; and when she carries out the baby, it would be well if an older sister or the mother herself could go along. Instead of carrying it to one of the public squares, or to some other place where there is air and shade, she may take it into dirty alleys, on a visit to some of her own relations, perhaps newly arrived in an emigrant ship, with the filth and diseases of a steerage passage still about them. This we know to have been done, and the child has in consequence taken a disgusting disease. Or, believing it a merito- rious act, an Irish nurse may secretly carry the infant to a priest, and have it baptized in the Catholic church, herself standing godmother. Of this there have been numerous instances. Young children fre- quently acquire, from being too much with ignorant and vulgar nurses, bad habits of talking that are exceedingly difficult to eradicate—so lasting are early impressions. We have heard an Irish brogue from infantine lips; and the letter H sadly misused by the American nursling of a low Englishwoman. Above all, do not permit your own children to play with the children of their nurse. No good ever accrues from it.

Children should not be brought to table till they are able to feed themselves, first with a spoon, and next with a fork. And not then, unless they can be depended on to keep quiet, and not talk. The chat- tering of children all dinner-time is a great annoyance to grown people. The shrill voice of a child can be distinguished annoyingly amid those of a whole com- pany. They should be made to understand that if they talk at table, they are to be immediately taken away to finish their dinner in the nursery. On no consideration should they be admitted to table when there is a dinner-party. The foolish custom of having all the children dressed for the purpose, and brought in with the dessert, is now obsolete. **It never was very** prevalent, except in England.

19

We have seen children so well and so early trained that they could be trusted to come to table every day without the least fear of their misbehaving by talking or otherwise. They sat quietly, asked for nothing, took contentedly whatever was put on their plates, made no attempt at helping themselves, and neither greased nor slopped the table-cloth; and when done, wiped their mouths and hands on their napkins, before they quitted their chairs, which they did at a sign from their mother; going out without noise, and neither leaving the door open nor slamming it hard. It is very easy to accustom children to these observances. Also, they may be taught very early, how to behave to visiters. For instance; not to pass between them and the fire, not to hang on the back of a lady's chair; or to squeeze close to her; or to get on her lap; or to finger her dress; or to search her reticule, or her pocket; or to ask a stranger for pennies or sixpences; or to tell her that she is not pretty; or to enquire "why she wears such an ugly bonnet?"

We have known a fine little boy, not three years old, who, on the entrance of a friend of his mother's, would haul up a chair for her, and invite her to a seat near the fire, place a footstool at her feet, ask her to let him take her bonnet, and invite her to stay to dinner, to stay all day, and to "stay for ever," adding, "I try to be polite."

There are very little girls who, if their mother is from home, can do the honours in her place; seat the visiter on the sofa, and press her to stay till their mother comes in; and if the lady declines doing so, they will ask her at least to stay awhile, and rest herself, and have a glass of cool water; and while she stays, they will do their best to entertain her. Such children always grow up with polished manners, if not removed from the influence that made them so in early life.

Children should be early taught not to repeat the conversation of grown persons, and never to tell the servants any thing they have heard in the parlour. When they come home from school, they ought not to be encouraged in telling school-tales. If they dine out, never question them concerning what they had for dinner. Forbid their relating any circumstances concerning the domestic economy of the house at which they have been entertained.

If a child purloins cakes or sweetmeats, punish him by giving him none the next time they are on table.

At four years of age, a beginning should be made in teaching them to read, by hearing them the alphabet every day till they have learned it perfectly; and afterwards the first spelling-tables. With a quarter of an hour's daily instruction, a child of common capacity will, in six months, be able to spell in two or three syllables, and to read short easy stories with the syllables divided. At the end of the year, if her lessons are regular, and not so long as to tire her, she will, in all probability, take pleasure in reading to herself, when her lessons are over. Were they taught *out of story-books only*, there are few children that at the age of six years would find any difficulty in reading fluently. If *very* intelligent, they often can read well at five. When they can once read, encourage them in the love of books; but do not set them at any other branch of education till they are eight. Then, their hands being strong enough to guide the pen firmly, they may commence writing copies. They should be supplied with slates and pencils at three years old. If they have any dormant talent for drawing, this will call it out. Little girls may begin to sew at four or five, but only as an amusement, not as a task. The best and most satisfactory dolls for young children are those of linen or rag, made very substantially. Much money is wasted in toys that afford them no amusement whatever; and toys that, being merely to look at, they grow tired of immediately, and delight in breaking to pieces.

Never give an infant a book to play with. He will most assuredly tear it; that being the only amusement it can afford him. It is possible at a very early age to teach a tractable female child such a respect for books that she will never attempt to injure them. When they are old enough to take pleasure in looking at the pictures, it is easy to accustom them to be always satisfied with the books being shown to them in the hands of grown persons. Do not buy those books that have absurd and revolting prints of people with gigantic heads and diminutive bodies. Children always dislike them, and so they ought.

Rejoice when a little girl shews a fondness for reading, and by all means encourage it. Keep her well supplied with good and entertaining books, and

you will have little trouble with her. Do not need-
lessly interrupt, and call her off—but let her read in
peace. It will do her more good than any thing else,
and lay the foundation of an intelligent mind. A
taste for reading, if not formed in early childhood,
may perhaps never come at all. And then what a
solace it is in bodily illness! How patiently a reading child, whose mind is stored with "pleasant memories," can bear pain, and submit to the confinement
of a sick-bed. We have known more than one
instance of the illness of a reading child taking a turn
for the better, from the time she was indulged with an
amusing and interesting book.

There is no place in which children appear to
greater disadvantage or are less ungovernable than at
hotels or boarding-houses. We are always sorry when
the circumstances of parents oblige them permanently
to live thus in public, with their young families, who
are consequently brought up in a manner which
cannot but have an unfavourable effect in forming the
characters of the future men and women. By way of
variety, and that they may not always be confined up-
stairs, the children are encouraged, or at least permitted by their mothers, to spend much of their time in
the drawing-room, regardless of the annoyance which
their noise and romping never fails to inflict upon the
legitimate occupants of that apartment. The parents,
loving their children too much to be incommoded
themselves by any thing that their offspring can say
or do, seem not aware that they can possibly interrupt or trouble the rest of the company. Or else,

conscious of their own inability to control them, they are afraid to check the children lest they should turn restive, rebel, or break out into a tantrum. "Any thing for the sake of peace," is a very foolish maxim where juveniles are concerned. By being firm once or twice, and dismissing them from the room when they deserve it, you may have peace ever after. The noisiest and most inconvenient time to have children in a public parlour is in the interval between their tea and their bed-time. Some children have no bed-time. And when they are tired of scampering and shouting, they lie about sleeping on the sofas, and cry if they are finally wakened, to go up with their mother when she retires for the night.

Still worse is the practice that prevails in some hotels and boarding-houses, of the mothers sending the nurse-maids with the babies, to sit in the drawing-room among the ladies; who are thus liable to have a vulgar and obtrusive servant-girl, most probably "from the old country," boldly taking her seat in the midst of them, or conspicuously occupying one of the front-windows; either keeping up a perpetual under-current of fulsome, foolish talk to the baby, or listening eagerly to the conversation around her, and, perhaps, repeating it invidiously as soon as she gets an opportunity. If one lady sends her nurse-maid to sit in the drawing-room with the child, all the other mothers of babies immediately follow suit, and the drawing-room becomes a mere nursery.

Every hotel should have a commodious and airy parlour set apart entirely for the children and nurses.

The proprietors could easily afford to keep one good room for that purpose, if they would expend a little less on the finery of the parlours, &c. We have heard of an embroidered piano-cover, in a great hotel, costing fourteen hundred dollars, and the children pulling it down and dragging it about the floor. With a piano-cover of the usual cost, and other things less ostentatious, a children's parlour might well have been afforded in this very establishment.

At a hotel, if the children come to the ladies' table, they are always in danger of eating food that is highly improper for them, and they very soon learn to help themselves to much more than they want, and to eat voraciously, in their desire to "have something of every thing." There is always a table purposely for those children whose parents pay half-price for them; and at which the housekeeper presides. However good this table may be, and though the pies and puddings may be excellent, the mothers are frequently dissatisfied with the absence of ice-cream, blanc-mange, charlotte-russe, &c., though certainly, were they in houses of their own, they would not have such things every day. Therefore, though it is "not in the bond," the mothers carry away from the table saucers of these delicacies, and the children learn to expect a daily supply of them from the ladies' dining-room. This, we must say, is a mean practice. We have, however, known some mothers, who, really being "honourable women," sent every day to a confectioner's to *buy* ice-cream for their children.

There is danger at a hotel of little boys loitering

about the bar or office, encouraged by unthinking young men, who give them "tastes of drink," and even amuse themselves by teaching them to smoke segars.

And no children, either boys or girls, can live at a public house without hearing and seeing much that it is best they should not know. The English travellers deprecate the American practice of bringing up young people in hotels or boarding-houses. And they are right.

When a lady, having with her a young child, and no nurse-maid, stops for a day at a hotel, she can avoid the inconvenience of taking the child with her to table, and incommoding herself and all who sit near her. She has only to intrust the little traveller to a chambermaid up-stairs; directing the girl how to take care of it, and promising her a gratuity for her trouble. She will rarely have cause to regret such an arrangement. It will spare the annoyance and mortification of having the child make a noise at table, and perhaps compelling the mother to go away with it.

CHAPTER XXIII.

DECORUM IN CHURCH.

WE wish it were less customary to go to church in gay and costly habiliments, converting its sacred precincts into a place for the display of finery, and of rivalry to your equally bedizened neighbours. In many Catholic countries,* a peculiar costume is universally adopted for visiting a place of worship—a very plain gown of entire black, with a long, black cloak, and a black hood finished with a veil that shades the face. This dress is kept for the purpose of wearing at church. We highly approve the custom, and wish that something similar could be introduced into the United States—particularly on the solemn occasions of taking the communion, or being confirmed as a christian member. We have known young ladies to have elegant dresses made on purpose, and to get their hair dressed by a barber when preparing for confirmation.

In a Sacred Melody of Moore's, St. Jerome tells us—

> "Yet worldly is that heart at best,
>   Which beats beneath a broider'd veil;
> And she who comes in glittering vest
>   To mourn her frailty—still is frail."

---

* The author is a Protestant.

Endeavour always to be in your pew before the service commences, and do not hurry out of it, hastily, the moment the benediction is finished; or begin visibly to prepare for departure as soon as it commences. Stay quietly till the mass of the crowd has gone.

If you go into a strange church, or rather into a church where you are a stranger, wait in the vestibule till you see the sexton; and then request him to show you to a vacant seat, or rather to one which he believes will be that day unoccupied—for instance, if the family owning it is out of town. This is far better than to wander about the aisles alone, or to intrude yourself into a pew where you may cause inconvenience to its owners. If you see that a pew is full, you know, of course, that you cannot obtain a seat in it without dislodging somebody.

Yet we have seen many a lady, on entering a church in which she was a stranger, walk boldly up the middle aisle to one of the best pews near the pulpit, and pertinaciously stand there, looking steadfastly at its rightful occupants, till one of them quitted his own seat, and gave it up to her, seeking for himself another place wherever he could find one. Those who go to strange churches should be contented with seats near the door; or at the lower end of the side-aisles; or up in the gallery.

If a family invites you to go to church with them, or to come thither, and have a seat in their pew, do not take the liberty of asking a friend of your own to accompany you; and above all, do not bring a child with you.

Should you (having a pew of your own) ask another lady to go with you, call for her in due time; and she ought to be quite ready. Place her in a corner-seat, (it being the most comfortable,) and see that she is accommodated with a foot-stool; and be assiduous in finling the places for her in the prayer-book, or hymn-book.

In American churches there is much civility to strangers. We have often seen, when a person of respectable appearance was in quest of a seat, the doors of half a dozen pews kindly opened to admit him, and, as soon as he entered, a prayer-book offered to him open at the proper place.

No good can result from taking children to church when they are too young to read, or to understand. They are always eager to go, because they like to go everywhere; but when once seated in the pew, they soon become tired and restless, and frequently there is no way to keep them quiet, but to let them go to sleep in the lap of the mother or elder sister. And then they are apt to cry whenever they waken. If there are two little boys, they are prone to get to playing, or what is far worse, quarrelling. And then if they make a noise, some elder member of the family is subjected to the mortification of conveying them out of church—perhaps by desire of the minister audibly expressed from the pulpit. We know clergymen who do not permit their children to be taken to church till they can read—convinced that if their first recollections of a place of worship are rather painful than pleasant, they are the less likely to grow up with a due regard for religion—that is, for religion of the heart—the spirit, and not merely the letter.

We are sorry to see young ladies, on their way to church, laughing and talking loudly, and flirting with the beaux that are gallanting them thither. It is too probable that these beaux will occupy a large share of their thoughts during the hours of worship. Nay, there are some so irreverent, and so regardless of the sanctity of the place, as to indulge in frequent whispers to those near them, or to their friends in the adjoining pews.

A lady of high fashion and fortune, formerly a resident of Philadelphia, was noted for the scandalous lightness and levity of her behaviour in church— laughing and talking, in more than whispers, nearly all the time, to the idle young men whom she always brought with her, and who, to do them justice, sometimes seemed rather ashamed of her conduct. Her pew was directly in front of the pulpit. One Sunday morning, Bishop White gave her a severe and merited rebuke, by stopping in his sermon, fixing his eyes sadly upon her, and bowing to her, as an intimation that till she had ceased he could not go on. We are sorry to add that the reproof had no other effect than to excite her anger, and caused her immediately to go out of church, highly exasperated. That lady went to live in Europe, and has not yet become a good woman, but greatly the contrary.

"The Lord is in his holy temple; let all the earth keep silence before him," was the solemn and impressive inscription over the altar of St. Augustine's church in Philadelphia.

In visiting a church of a different denomination from your own, comply, as far as you can, with all the ceremonies observed by the congregation, particularly if you are in a foreign country. Even if some of these observances are not the least in conformity with your own opinions and feelings, remember that you are there as a guest, and have no right to offend or give displeasure to your hosts by evincing a marked disapprobation of their mode of worship. If you find it very irksome to refrain, (which it should not be,) you need not go a second time. Every religious sect believes its own faith to be the best; but God only knows which really is. Christ has said, "By their fruits ye shall know them."

CHAPTER XXIV.

EVENING PARTIES.

HAVING made out a list of the persons you intend to invite, proceed to write the notes; or have them written in a neat, handsome hand, by an experienced calligrapher. Fashion, in its various changes, sometimes decrees that these notes, and their envelopes, shall be perfectly plain, (though always of the finest paper,) and that the wax seals shall of course be very small. At other times, the mode is to write on embossed note paper, with bordered envelopes, secured by fancy wafers, transparent, medallion, gold or silver. If the seals are gold or silver, the edges or borders of the paper should be also gilt or silvered. Sometimes, for a very large or splendid party, the notes are engraved and printed on cards. Consult the Directory, to obtain the *exact* address of those to whom you send them.

These invitations may be transmitted by one of the City post-offices; first putting a stamp on each. Let the stamps be such as will leave nothing additional to be paid by the receiver. If they go through the United States Post-Office, the carrier will require another cent for each, beside the stamp. In Philadelphïa, Blood's Dispatch Post may be trusted, as to punctuality, (if faithfully put into the letter-box at the proper time;) and there is no cost but that of the penny stamp which you put on yourself.

Another way is to send round the notes by a reliable servant-man of your own; or to engage, for this purpose, one of the public waiters that are hired to attend at parties. The notes are usually sent either eight, seven, or six days before the party—if it is to be very large, ten days or two weeks. In the notes, always specify not only the day of the week, but also the day of the month, when the party is to take place. It is very customary now to designate the hour of assembling, and then the company are expected to be punctual to that time. People, *really genteel*, do not go ridiculously late. When a ball is intended, let the word "Dancing" be introduced in small letters, at the lower left-hand corner of the note.

For a bridal party, subsequent to a wedding, the words now used are thus—.

MR. AND MRS. S. M. MORLAND,
At Home, on Thursday evening, Sept. 22, 1853.

Their residence must be given beneath, in a corner, and in smaller letters.

Oblong slices of plumb-cake, iced all over, are now sent round in very pretty white card-board boxes, exactly fitting each slice, covered on the inside with lace-paper, and an engraved card of the bride and groom laid on the top cf the cake. These boxes (to be had at the fancy stationers,) are of various prices; some of them are very elegant and costly.

At wedding-parties, it is usual for the bride and bridesmaids to appear in exactly the same dresses they wore at the marriage; all of them ranged in their respective stations before the company begin to arrive.

When the marriage-guests are not too numerous, it is customary to have all the company shown into the largest parlour, when they first arrive; the folding-doors being closed between. Meanwhile, the bride and groom, bridesmaids and groomsmen, with the heads of the family, arrange themselves in a line or a semi-circle; the most important personages in the centre, with the clergyman in front of them. When all is ready, the doors are thrown open, the guests advance, and the ceremony begins. When it is over, and the bride is receiving the compliments of her friends, we hope the silliest woman present will not go up and ask her the foolish question, "If she does not feel already like an old married woman?"

A crowd at a wedding is now obsolete. We once heard of a marriage in a great family, where the company was so numerous that all the doors were blocked up, and quite inaccessible; and the bride could only make her entrance by being taken round outside, and lifted through a back window—the groom jumping in after her.

Dancing at weddings is old-fashioned. A band of music playing in the hall is of no use, as on such occasions no one listens to it, and some complain of the noise. We think a marriage in church is not as fine a spectacle as may be imagined. The effect is lost in the size of the building, and broken up by the intervention of the aisles and pews; the wedding guests seated in the latter, and the former occupied by people out of the street, coming in to see the show. And this they will do, if not forcibly excluded; particularly idle boys, and nurse-maids with children, all trying to get as near the altar as possible.

If the bride and groom are to set out on a journey immediately after the ceremony, it is best for her to be married in a handsome travelling-dress—new for the occasion, of course. This is often done now. She can reserve the usual wedding costume for her first party after returning home.

In preparing for a party, it is well (especially if you have had but little experience yourself,) to send for one of the *best* public waiters, and consult with him on the newest style of " doing these things." A respectable coloured man will be found the most efficient for this purpose. He can also give you an idea of the probable expense. We do not, of course, allude to magnificent entertainments, such as are celebrated in the newspapers, and become a nine days' wonder; and are cited as costing, not hundreds, but thousands of dollars.

In case the required waiter should be pre-engaged, it is well to send for, and consult him, a week or two before your party.

We knew a lady who, some years ago, sent for Carroll, (a very excellent mulatto man, well known in

20

Philadelphia,) to officiate at a projected party. Carroll, in very polite terms, expressed that he was
engaged for that identical evening to attend at a ball.
"Then," said the lady, "you must try to furnish me
with some one else, in your place. Where is Bogle?"
"I know Bogle can't come," answered Carroll; "he
is bespoke that night for a wedding." "Shepherd,
then?" said the lady; "see if you cannot send me
Shepherd." "As to Shepherd," replied Carroll, "he
is sick in his bed, and like to keep so." "Where is
Solomon King, then?" pursued the lady; "Solomon
King will do very well." "Indeed, ma'am," answered
Carroll, "I don't think Solomon King will suit you
now, any how; he's taken very much to drink, and
besides he's dead!"

Apropos to the talk of coloured people.—We were
told by a southern lady, that one of her girls being
dressed for an entertainment given by a neighbour to
the servants, came to her, and said: "Mistress, Becky
has come for me to go with her; and she says *her* mistress has gave her two grand words to say at the
party.—Now, I want you to give *me* two words that
shall beat Becky's; for I know you are a heap smarter
than *her* mistress."

"Tell me the words given by Becky's mistress,'
said my informant.

"Yes, ma'am.—One is *Desdemona*, and one is
Cataplasm!"

No doubt, Becky, in some way, contrived to say
them both.

In engaging your presiding genius, it is well to

desire him to come on the morning of the party; he will be found of great advantage in assisting with the final preparations. He will attend to the silver, and china, and glass; and see that the lamps are all in order, and that the fires, coal-grates, furnaces, &c., are in proper trim for evening. He will bring with him (at whatever hour you indicate,) his " young men," as he calls them; (if coloured youths, they are too genteel to answer to the name of boys;) and these are his apprentices that he has in training for the profession.

One of these men should be stationed in the vestibule, or just within the front door. On that evening, (if not at other times,) let this door be furnished with a lamp, placed on a shelf or bracket in the fan-light, to illumine the steps, and shine down upon the pavement, where the ladies cross it on alighting from the carriages. If the evening proves rainy, let another man attend with an umbrella, to assist in sheltering them on their way into the house. The ladies should all wear over-shoes, to guard their thin slippers from the damp, in their transit from the coach to the vestibule.

At the top, or on the landing-place, of the first staircase, let another man be posted, to show the female guests to their dressing-room; while still another waiter stays near the gentlemen's room till the company have done arriving.

In the apartment prepared as a fixing-room for the ladies two or more women should be all the evening in attendance; both rooms being well warmed, well lighted, and furnished with all that may be requisite for giving the last touches to head, feet, and figure, previous to entering the drawing-room. When ready to go down, the ladies meet their gentlemen in the passage between the respective dressing-rooms; the beaux being there already, waiting for the belles, who must not detain them long—men being very impatient on these, and all other occasions.

If any lady is without an escort, and has no acquaintances at hand to take her under their wing, she should send for the master of the house to meet her near the door, and give her his arm into the drawing-room. He will then lead her to the hostess, and to a seat. Let her then bow, as a sign that she releases him from farther attendance, and leaves him at liberty to divide his civilities among his other guests.

In the ladies' room, (beside two toilet glasses with their branches lighted,) let a Psyche or Cheval glass be also there. Likewise, a hand-mirror on each toilet to enable the ladies to see the back of their heads; with an ample supply of pins, combs, brushes, hair pins, &c.; and a work-box containing needles, thread, thimble, and scissors, to repair accidents to articles of dress. Let there be bottles of fine eau de cologne, and camphor and hartshorn, in case of faintings. Among the furniture, have a sofa and several foot-stools, for the ladies to sit on if they wish to change their shoes.

The women attending must take charge of the hoods, cloaks, shawls, over-shoes, &c.; rolling up together the things that belong to each lady, and putting each bundle in some place they can easily remember when wanted at the breaking up of the assembly.

It is now the custom for the lady of the house (and those of her own family,) to be drest rather plainly, showing no desire to eclipse any of her guests, on this her own night. But her attire, though simple, should be handsome, becoming, and in good taste. Her business is, without any bustle or apparent officiousness, quietly and almost imperceptibly to try and render the evening as pleasant as possible to all her guests; introducing those who, though not yet acquainted, ought to be; and finding seats for ladies who are not young enough to continue standing.

The custom that formerly prevailed in the absurd days of crowds and jams, when dense masses were squeezed into small apartments, of removing every seat and every piece of furniture from the room, is now obsolete. A hard squeeze is no longer a high boast. Genteel people no longer go to parties on the stair-case, or in the passages. The ladies are not now so compressed that nothing of them is seen but their heads; the sleeves, skirts, &c., undergoing a continual demolition down below. We knew of a lady, who, at a late hour, went to a crowded party in a real blonde dress, which was rubbed entirely off her before she reached the centre of the room, and it was hanging about her satin skirt in shreds, like transparent rags dissolving into " air—thin air !" For this blonde she had given two hundred dollars; and she was obliged to go home and exchange its tatters for a costume that was likely to last out the evening.

In houses where space is not abundant, it is now customary to have several *moderate* parties in the course of the season, instead of inviting all your "dear five hundred friends" on the self-same night.

When the hour of assembling is designated in the notes of invitation, (as it always should be,) the guests, of course, will take care to arrive as nearly as possible about that hour. At large parties, tea is usually omitted—it being supposed that every one has already taken that beverage at home, previous to commencing the business of the toilette. Many truly hospitable ladies still continue the custom, thinking that it makes a pleasant beginning to the evening, and exhilerates the ladies after the fatigue of dressing and arriving. So it does. For a large company, a table with tea, coffee, and cakes, may be set in the ladies-room, women being in attendance to supply the guests with those refreshments before they go down. Pitchers of ice-water and glasses should also be kept in this room.

If there is no tea, the refreshments begin with lemonade, macaroons, kisses, &c., sent round soon after the majority of the company has come. If there *is* tea, ice-water should be presented after it, to all; otherwise, there will be much inconvenience by numerous ladies despatching the servants, separately, to bring them some.

After a little time allotted to conversation, music is generally introduced by one of the ladies of the family, if she plays well; otherwise, she invites a competent friend to commence. A lady who can do nothing "without her notes," or who cannot read music, and play at sight, is scarcely enough of a musician to perform in a large company—for this incapacity is an evidence that she has not a good ear, or rather a good memory for melody—or that her musical talent wants more cultivation. A large party is no time or place for practising, or for risking *attempts* at new things, or for vainly trying to remember old ones.

Some young ladies rarely sit down to a piano in any house but their own, without complaining that the instrument is out of tune. "It is a way they have." We have known a fair amateur to whom this complaint was habitual, and never omitted; even when we knew that, to provide against it, the piano had really been tuned that very day.

The tuning of a harp immediately before playing is sometimes a very tedious business. Would it not be well for the harpist to come a little earlier than the rest, and tune it herself previous to their arrival? And let her deem *that* tuning sufficient for a while, and not repeat the operation more than once again in the course of the evening, especially in the midst of her first piece. However delicate may be her own ear, or exquisitely fastidious her own taste, she may be assured that few of her audience would detect any deficiency, if she only went quietly on, and did not herself imply that deficiency.

Unless a gentleman is himself familiar with the air, let him not, on "mounting guard beside the piano," volunteer to turn over the pages for the lady who is playing. He will certainly turn them over too soon or too late, and therefore annoy and confuse her. Still worse, let him not attempt to accompany her with his voice, unless he is an excellent musician, or accustomed to singing with her.

For the hearers to crowd closely round the instru ment, is smothering to the vocalist. Let them keep at a proper distance, and she will sing the better, and they will hear the better. It is so rude to talk during a song, that it is never done in company; but a little low conversation is sometimes tolerated in the adjoin- ing room, during the performance of one of those inter- minable pieces of instrumental music, whose chief merit lies in its difficulty, and which (at least to the ears of the uninitiated,) is rather a bore than a pleasure. We have read a French novel, in which the only child of a farmer has just come home from a provincial boarding- school, and the seigneur, or lord of the manor, has volunteered a visit to these his respected tenants. The mother, amidst all the bustle of preparing a great dinner for the occasion, comes in to remind Annette that if the seigneur should ask her to play for him, she is to curtsey very low, and thank him for the honour. "And then, Annette," adds the good old dame, "be sure to play that tune which your father and I hate so much !"

By the bye, it is very old fashioned to return thanks to a lady for her singing, or to tell her she is very kind to oblige the company so often. If she is con- scious of really singing well, and sees that she delights her hearers, she will not feel sensible of fatigue—at

least till the agreeable excitement of conscious success
is over.

It is ill-mannered, when a lady has just finished a
song, for another lady to exclaim in her hearing—
"Mary Jones sings that delightfully!"—or—"How
charmingly Susan Smith gives us that ballad!" Let
the glories of Mary Jones and Susan Smith rest, for
that evening, within the limits of their own circle.

Do not ask any lady for a song that has already
been sung on this very evening by another person.

People who have no idea of music sometimes make
strange blunders in their requests. We know of a
female who, at a large party, hearing a young lady
accompany her voice on the national instrument of
Spain, became very urgent to have the Battle of Prague
performed on the guitar.

It is sometimes fashionable, when the company is
not too large for what is called "a sitting party," to
vary the amusements of the evening by introducing
some of the numerous plays or games which are always
the delight of fine children, and which, by way of
variety, frequently afford much diversion to adults. It
is not necessary that all these plays should become "a
keen encounter of the wits," or that all the players
should be persons of talent. But it is certainly desirable that the majority of the company should have
some tact, and some quickness of parts; that they
should have read some books, and mixed somewhat
with the world—otherwise, they will not be clever even
at playing plays. Those who are incapable of understanding, or entering into the spirit of a play, would

do well to excuse themselves from joining in it, and prefer sitting by as spectators. Many young ladies can play nothing beyond " How do you like it?" and are not great at that—saying, when the question is put to them—" Me! I am sure I don't know how I like it—can't you pass me by?" You may as well take her at her word, pass her by, and proceed on to her next neighbour; for if she *does* concoct an answer, it will probably, if the word is "*brush*," be liked "to sweep the hearth with;" or if "*Hat*" is the word, it will be liked " *of Beaver*"—or something equally palpable.

Such plays as *The Lawyer*, and *The Secret Word*, are very entertaining in good hands, but complete failures when attempted by the dull or illiterate. The amusing game of Proverbs had best be given up for that evening, if, on trial, it is found that few of the ladies have any knowledge of those true, though homely aphorisms, that have been aptly called " the concentrated wisdom of nations."

We know a very ingenious gentleman who, in playing the Secret Word, contrives to introduce that word in some very short and very humorous anecdote.

A family, on one side of European origin, made a visit to the transatlantic continent, where they found, still living in a certain great city, a relative connected with an ancient branch of nobility. This rendered them more genteel than ever—and when, covered with glory, they returned to this poor republic of ours, the names of nobles, and even of princes, with whom they had associated, were " familiar in their mouths as

househo.d words." At a party where these personages
were so engaged in talking, that they forgot to keep
the run of the plays; a new game was commenced by
a young gentleman slipping out of the room, and then
returning with a very lugubrious visage, and announ-
cing, in a melancholy tone, the death of a certain
monarch, whom all the company were immediately to
unite in lamenting loudly, on pain of paying forfeits
unless they steadily persisted in their dismal faces.
On the sad intelligence being proclaimed—"The king
of Bohemia is dead!"—one of our travelled ladies
mistaking it for a solemn truth, turned to her daughter
with—"Ah! Caroline! did you hear that? The
dear good king of Bohemia, who was so kind to us
whenever we attended his court!" "Oh! mamma!"
replied Caroline, putting her handkerchief to her
eyes—"the news is really heart-breaking. He paid
us so much attention all the time we were in ——, in
his dominions. It will be long before we cease grieving
for the king of Bohemia."

The gentleman who brought this deplorable news
also had recourse to *his* handkerchief, and slipped out
into the hall to indulge his mirth; and several others
slipped out after him for the same purpose. No one,
however, undeceived these ladies, and for several days
at their morning calls they continued to mourn for the
king of Bohemia.

Conundrums * afford infinite diversion at a small

* Miss Leslie's American Girl's Book (published by C. S. Francis,)
contains a great variety of amusing plays, ways to redeem forfeits,
&c., with an unusual number of conundrums.

party, provided the company, like Billy Black's cat, "almost always gives up." Long guessing occupies too much time; a commodity of which we Americans seldom have any to spare.

Early in the Mexican war, a premium was awarded in Philadelphia for a very clever conundrum, alluding to a certain "Bold Dragoon" at Palo Alto. "In what manner did Captain May cheat the Mexicans?" "He charged them with a troop of horse which they never got?"

Our confectioners, in making up the *bon bons* called "*secrets*," instead of enfolding with the sugar-plumb a printed slip containing a contemptible distich, would do well to have good conundrums printed, (with the answer,) and enclosed in the ornamented papers. They would certainly be more popular than the old-fashioned mottoes—such, for instance, as

> "My heart, like a candle of four to the pound,
> Consumes all the day, and no comfort is found."

Yet the above is one of the least bad. Most of these mottoes are so flat as to be not even ridiculous.

At a dancing party, the ladies of the house decline joining in it, out of politeness to their guests, till towards the latter part of the evening, when the company begins to thin off, and the dancers are fatigued.

We admire a charming girl, who, in her own house, being asked to dance by an agreeable man, has the self-denial to say to him—"Being at home, and desirous that my friends shall share as much as possible in the enjoyments of the evening, I would rather refrain from dancing myself. Let me present you to Miss Lindley, or to Miss Darwood; you will find either of these young ladies a delightful partner."

These amiable refusals we have heard from our amiable and unselfish young friends, and such, we hope, are heard often in what is *truly* "the best society."

Ladies who are strangers in the place, are, by courtesy, entitled to particular attention from those who know them.

We have sometimes seen, at a private ball, the least attractive woman dancing every set, (though acquitting herself very ill,) while handsome and agreeable ladies were sitting still. The mystery was solved on finding that the lady of the house carried her ultra benevolence so very far, as to make a business of procuring partners all the time for this unlovely and unprepossessing female, lest she should feel neglected. Now a certain portion of this officiousness is highly praiseworthy, but too much of it is a great annoyance to the victimized gentlemen — especially to those who, as a backwoodsman would say, are certainly " some pumpkins."

Even the most humane man, whatever may be the kindness of his heart, would rather not exhibit himself on the floor with a partner *ni jeune ni jolie*, who is ill-drest, looks badly, moves ungracefully, can neither keep time to the music nor understand the figure, and in fact has " no dancing in her soul." If, with all the rest, she is dull and stupid, it is cruel for any kind friend to inflict her on a gentleman as a partner. Yet such things we have seen.

On one occasion we threw away a great deal of good pity on a youth, whom we thought had been inveigled into quadrilling with a lady who made the worst figure we ever saw in a ball-room. We afterwards learned that he had actually solicited the introduction; and we saw that he devoted himself to her all the remainder of the evening. She was a rich heiress.

Self-knowledge is a rare acquirement. But when a lady *does* suspect herself to be deficient in all the essential qualifications of a ball-room, she should give up dancing entirely, and be magnanimous enough always to excuse herself positively, when asked to dance; especially if verging on "a certain age." Let all "trippings on the light fantastic toe" be left to the young and gay.

A deformed woman dancing is "a sorry sight." She should never consent to any such exhibition of her unhappy figure. She will only be asked out of mere compassion, or from some interested and unworthy motive. We are asked—"Why should not such a lady dance, if it gives her pleasure?" We answer—"It should *not* give her pleasure."

When a lady is so unfortunate as to have a crooked or misshapen person, it is well for her to conceal it as much as possible, by wearing a shawl, a large cape, a mantilla, a long sacque, (not a polka jacket;) and on no account a tight-bodied pelisse; or still worse, a spencer—than which last, nothing is more trying to the form of the waist, except a riding-habit.

We saw Frederika Bremer at an evening assemblage, and she was so judiciously attired, that her personal defects did not prevent her from looking really well. Over a rich black satin dress, she wore a long loose sacque of black lace, lined with grey silk. From beneath the short sleeves of her sacque, came down long wide sleeves of white lace, confined with bracelets round her fair and delicate little hands. Her throat was covered closely with a handsome collar of French embroidered muslin, and her beautiful and becoming cap was of white lace, white flowers, and white satin ribbon — her light hair being simply parted on her broad and intellectual forehead. With her lively blue eyes, and the bright and pleasant expression of her countenance, no one seemed to notice the faults of her nose, mouth, and complexion—and those of her figure were so well concealed as to be scarcely apparent. And then her lady-like ease, and the total absence of all affectation, rendered her graceful and prepossessing. True it is, that with a good heart and a good mind no woman can be ugly; at least, they soon cease to be so considered, even if nature has been unkind to them in feature, figure, and complexion. An intelligent eye, and a good humoured mouth, are excellent substitutes for the want of regular beauty. Physiognomists say that the eye denotes the mind, and the mouth indicates the heart.

Now as a deformed lady may render herself very agreeable as a good conversationist, we repeat that she has no occasion to exhibit the defects of her person by treading the mazes of a cotillion, or above all, in going down a country dance, should those "never-ending, still beginning" performances come again into fashion. Young men say that an ugly, misshapen female, who waltzes, or joins in a polka, or redowa, or mazurka, deserves the penitentiary.

We deprecate the practice of keeping the small children of the family up all the evening, running and scampering in every one's way, or sleeping about on the chairs and sofas, and crying when wakened up to be carried to bed. Would it not be much better to have them sent to bed at their usual time? We knew two well-trained little boys, who submitted obediently to go to bed at their customary hour, on the night of their mother's party, of which they had seen nothing but the decorations of the parlours. They told their parents next morning, that still they had a great deal of pleasure, for after the carriages began to arrive, they had lain awake and "heard every ring."

At a large party, or at a wedding, there is generally a supper table; lemonade and cakes having been sent round during the evening. The host and hostess should see that *all* the ladies are conducted thither, and that none are neglected, particularly those that are timid, and stand back. It is the business of the host to attend to those himself, or to send the waiters to them.

If the party is so large that all the ladies cannot go to the table at once, let the matrons be conducted thither first, and the young ladies afterwards. If there is a crowd, it is not unusual to have a cord (a handsome one, of course,) stretched across the door of the supper-room, and guarded by a servant, who explains that no more are to pass till after that cord is taken down. Meanwhile, the younger part of the company amuse themselves in the adjacent rooms. No lady should take the liberty of meddling with the flowers that ornament the table, or of secreting " good things" to carry home to her children.

Apropos to flowers.—The stiff, hard bouquets are now obsolete, where the flowers (stripped of their natural green leaves,) were tied *en masse* on a wooden skewer, against a flat back-ground of cedar sprays. The more elegant arrangement is revived of arranging them in a full round cluster, with a fair portion of their real leaves ; the largest and finest flowers in the centre, (large white ones particularly); those of middle size next; and the light, long, and branchy sprays and tendrils at the extremities, the smallest near the bottom of the bouquet, which is not so large and massy as formerly, but more graceful and select. The bouquet may be carried on the young lady's arm, suspended to a long and handsome white ribbon tied in a bow—a *coloured* ribbon will disturb the effect of the flowers. There should be nothing to interfere with their various and beautiful tints.

At a ball, let no *coloured* chalks or crayons be used for the floor. They will rub off on the white shoes of the ladies, and spoil them.

When, instead of *setting* a supper-table, refreshments are handed round to the ladies, the fashion has long since gone by of a gentleman walking beside each

21

waiter, and "assisting the ladies." It is now found
that if the articles are properly arranged, and of the
proper sort, the ladies can much more conveniently
help themselves, and with less risk of staining or
greasing their dresses. Unless the gentleman was "a
thorough-going party-man," and stereotyped as such,
he often committed rather vexatious blunders, particularly if he was not *au-courant* to the new improvements, and accustomed to being "at good men's
feasts;" or rather, at *women's good feasts*. One evening at a party, we saw an "ingenuous youth," whose
experience in that line must have been rather limited,
officiously undertake the portioning out to the ladies
of a composition hitherto quite new to himself. This
was "a trifle," being the contents of a very large glass
bowl, filled with macaroons, &c., dissolved in wine, &c.,
with profuse layers of custard, sweetmeats, &c., and
covered in at the top with a dome of whipt cream
heaped high and thick over the whole. The pea-green
youth assisted the ladies to nothing but saucers of
froth from the top, thinking that was the right way.
At last, the mulatto man, whose superior tact must
have been all this time in a state of suffering, explained
to the novice in trifles, that a portion of all the various
contents of the glass bowl should be allotted to each
saucer. "That!" said the surprised doer of honours,
"I thought all that was only the grounds!" The
coloured man relieved him by taking the silver server
round a second time to all the ladies, who had hitherto
missed the sediment of the syllabub.

At a summer evening party, the refreshments are

of a much lighter description than at a winter entertainment; consisting chiefly of ice-creams, watèr-ices, fresh fruit, lady-cake, and almond sponge-cake. Also strawberry or raspberry charlottes, which are made by arranging in glass bowls slices of cake cut in even and regular forms, and spread thickly over with the fruit mashed to a jam with white sugar—the bowls being heaped with whipt cream.

The dresses of the ladies are of clear muslin, or some other light material, and without any elaborate trimming. The hair is simply arranged—curls being inconvenient in warm weather; and the only head ornaments are ribbons, or *real* flowers.

At summer evening-parties the veranda is always put into requisition, being cooler than any part of the house.

At summer dinner-parties, let the dessert be served in another and cooler apartment; the company quitting the dining-room as soon as they have done with the meats, &c. The beauties of the dessert appear to greater advantage, when seen all at one view on a fresh table.

We will introduce a minute account of a very fashionable English dinner-party, obtained from a friend who was one of the guests. It may afford some hints for the routine of an elegant entertainment, *à l'Anglais*, in our own country.

The guests were twenty-four in number, and they began to assemble at half past seven, punctually. They were received in the library, where the host and hostess were standing ready to receive them, introducing those who were strangers to each other. When all had arrived, the butler entered, and going up to the lady of the house, told her in a low voice that "dinner was served." The hostess then arranged those that were not previously acquainted, and the gentlemen conducted the ladies to the dining-room; the principal stranger taking the mistress of the house, and the master giving his arm to the chief of the female guests. In England, these arrangements are made according to the rank of the ladies—that of the gentlemen is not considered. A duchess takes precedence of a marchioness, a viscountess of a countess, a baroness of a baron*et*'s lady, &c.,—for a baron is above a baronet. Going into the dining-room, the compay passed by the butler and eight footmen, all of whom were stationed in two rows. The butler was drest entirely in black—the footmen in their livery. According to a new fashion, they may now wear long gaiters. White kid gloves are indispensable to the footmen.

The table was set for twenty-six—and standing on it were elegant gilt candelabras. *All* the lights were wax candles. Chandeliers were suspended from the ceiling. In the middle of the table was a magnificent plateau, or centre ornament of gold; flowers surmounted the summit; and the circular stages below were covered with confectionery elegantly arranged. On each side of the plateau, and above and below, were tall china fruit-baskets. In the centre of each basket were immense pine-apples of hot-house growth, with their fresh green leaves. Below the pine-apples were large

bunches of purple and white hot-house grapes, beautifully disposed, with leaves and tendrils hanging over
the sides of the baskets.   Down each side of the whole
long table, were placed large, round, saucer-shaped
fruit-dishes, heaped up with peaches, nectarines, pears,
plumbs, ripe gooseberries, cherries, currants, strawber-
ries, &c.   All the fruits not in season were supplied
from hot-houses.   And alternating with the fruit were
all the *entremêts* in covered dishes, placed on long slips
of damask the whole length of the table.   All the
plate was superb.   The dinner-set was of French china,
gilt, and painted with roses.   At every plate was a
caraffe of water, with a tumbler turned down over it,
and several wine-glasses.   The napkins were large.
The side-board held only the show-silver and the wine.
The side-tables were covered with elegant damask
cloths.   On these were ranged, laid along in numerous
rows, the knives, forks, and spoons to be used at
dinner.   The dessert-spoons were in the form of hollow
leaves, the stems being the handles.   They were beautifully engraved in tasteful patterns.   The fruit-knives
had silver blades and pearl handles.   There were two
soups (white and brown,) standing on a side-table.
Each servant handed the things in his white kid
gloves, and with a damask napkin under his thumb.
They offered (mentioning its name in a low voice,) a
plate of each soup to each guest.   After the soup,
Hock and Moselle wine were offered to each guest,
that they might choose either.   A dish of fish was
then placed at each end of the table—one was salmon,
the other turbot   These dishes were immediately

taken off to be helped by the servants, both sorts of fish being offered to each person. Then the appropriate sauce for the fish—also cucumbers to eat with the salmon. No castors were on the large table, but they were handed round by the servants. Directly after the fish came the *entrémets*, or French dishes. The wine following the fish was Madeira and Sherry.

Afterwards, a saddle or haunch of Welsh mutton was placed at the master's end of the table, and at the lady's end a boiled turkey. These dishes being removed to the side-tables, very thin slices of each were handed round. The poultry was not dissected— nothing being helped but the breast. Ham and tongue was then supplied to those who took poultry; and currant-jelly to the eaters of mutton. Next came the vegetables, handed round on dishes divided into four compartments, each division containing a different sort of vegetable.

Next, two dishes of game were put on—one before the master of the house, and the other before the mistress. The game (which was perfectly well-done,) was helped by them, and sent round with the appropriate sauce. Then, placed along the table, were the sweet things—charlottes, jellies, frozen fruit, &c. A lobster salad, drest and cut up large, was put on with the sweets. On a side-table were stilton and cream cheese, to be eaten with the salad. After this, port wine—the champagne being early in the dinner. Next the sweets were handed round. With the sweets were frozen fruits—fruits cut up, and frozen with isinglass-jelly, (red, in moulds.)

Next, a dessert plate was given to each guest, and on it a ground glass plate, about the size of a saucer. Between these plates was a crochet-worked white doyly, of the size of the under-plate; the crochet-work done with thread, so as to resemble lace. These doylies were laid under the ground-glass plate, to deaden the noise of their collision. Then was brought from the side-table a ground-glass plate of ice-cream, or water-ice, which you took in exchange for that before you. The water-ice was frozen in moulds, in the form of fruit, and suitably coloured. The baskets containing the fruit were then removed to the side-tables, where the servants had silver scissors, with which they clipped off small bunches of the grapes, and the green tops of the pine-apples, and a portion of the flesh of the fruit. The middle part was then pared and sliced. On each dessert-plate was placed a slice of pine-apple, and small bunches of white and blue grapes. After the grapes and pine-apples were thus handed round, the dishes of the other fruits were then offered successively to every guest. After the ground-glass and doylies, there was no farther change of plates.

After sitting a while over the fruit, the lady of the house gives the signal, by looking and bowing to the ladies on each side, and the ladies at this signal prepare to retire. The gentlemen all rise, and remain standing while the ladies depart—the master of the house holding the door open. The servants then all retire, except the butler, who remains to wait on the gentlemen, while they linger awhile (not more than a quarter of an hour,) over the fruit and wine.

CHAPTER XXIV.

MISCELLANIES.

It may be well to caution our young friends against certain bad practices, easily contracted, but sometimes difficult to relinquish. The following are things not to be done:—Biting your nails. Slipping a ring up and down your finger. Sitting cross-kneed, and jogging your feet. Drumming on the table with your knuckles; or, still worse, tinking on a piano with *your fore-finger only*. Humming a tune before strangers. Singing as you go up and down stairs. Putting your arm round the neck of another young girl, or promenading the room with arms encircling waists. Holding the hand of a friend all the time she sits beside you; or kissing and fondling her before company. Sitting too closely.

Slapping a gentleman with your handkerchief, or tapping him with your fan. Allowing him to take a ring off your finger, to look at it. Permitting him to unclasp your bracelet, or, still worse, to inspect your brooch. When these ornaments are to be shown to another person, always take them off for the purpose. Pulling at your own ringlets, or your own ear-rings— or fingering your neck ribbon. Suffering a gentleman to touch your curls. Reading with a gentleman off the same book or newspaper. Looking over the shoulder of any person who is reading or writing Taking up a *written* paper from the table, and examining it.

To listen at door-cracks, and peep through keyholes, is vulgar and contemptible. So it is to ask children questions concerning their parents, though such things are still done.

If you mean that you were angry, do not say you were "mad."—"It made me so mad"—"I was quite mad at her," are phrases not to be used by people considering themselves genteel. Anger and madness are not the same, or should not be; though it is true that ungoverned rage, is, sometimes, carried so far as to seem like insanity.

Enter into no freaks of fashion that are silly, unmeaning, and unlady-like; even if they *have* been introduced by a belle, and followed by other belles. Commit no absurdity because a public singer or dancer has done so in her ignorance of good behaviour. During the Jenny Lind fever, there were young ladies who affected to skuttle into a drawing-room all of a sudden, somewhat as the fair Swede came skuttling in upon the concert stage, because in reality she knew not how to make her entrance gracefully. Other demoiselles twined and waved about, with body, head, and eyes, never a moment quiet. This squirming (as it was called) originated in a very bad imitation of Fanny Elssler's dancing motions. At one time there were girls at parties, who stood on one foot, and with the other kicked up their dresses behind, while talking to gentlemen. This fashion began with a celebrated beauty who "dared do any thing." Luckily, these "whims and oddities" are always of short duration, and are never adopted by young ladies of good taste and refinement.

Do not nod your head, or beat time with fan or foot while listening to music.

Never at a party consent to accompany another lady in a duet, unless you are accustomed to singing with her. Still worse—do not volunteer to "assist" her in a song that is not a duet. Each voice will interrupt and spoil the other. A lady who sings by ear only, cannot accompany one that sings by note.

One of the most horrible sounds imaginable is that produced by several fine voices all singing different songs. This cats' concert (as school-girls call it) results in a shocking and yet ludicrous discord, equally frightful and laughable. And yet all the performers are singing individually well. Try it.

Raising a window-sash, in cold weather, without first ascertaining if the rest of the company are, like yourself, too warm. Leaving the parlour door open in winter—a perpetual occurrence at hotels and boarding-houses.

Talking so loudly that you can be heard all over the room. Or so low that you cannot be heard at all, even by those who are conversing with you. This last fault is the worst. To talk with one who has a habit of muttering unintelligibly, is like trying to read a letter illegibly written.

Using too often the word "madam" or "ma'am," which in fact, is now nearly obselete in familiar conversation. In the old French tragedies the lovers addressed their mistresses as "madam." But then the stage Alexander wore a powdered wig, and a laced coat, knee-breeches, and a long-skirted waistcoat; and Roxana figured in a hoop-petticoat, a brocade gown, a flowered apron, and a towering gauze cap. The frequent use of "sir" is also out of fashion. "Yes, ma'am," "No, ma'am," "Yes, sir," "No, sir," no longer sounds well, except from children to their elders. If you have not distinctly heard what another lady has just said to you, do not denote it by saying, "Ma'am?" but remark to her, "Excuse me, I did not exactly hear you!"

Never, in a public parlour, place yourself in a position where you can secretly hear conversation that is not intended for you—for instance in a corner behind a pillar. If you hear yourself talked of, it is mean to stay and listen. It is a true adage that "Listeners seldom hear any good of themselves."

However smart and witty you may be considered, do not exercise your wit in rallying and bantering your friends. If you do so, their friendship will soon be worn out, or converted into positive enmity. A jest that carries a sting with it can never give a pleasant sensation to the object. The bite of a musquito is a very little thing, but it leaves pain and inflammation behind it, and the more it is rubbed the longer it rankles in the blood. No one likes to have their foibles or mishaps turned into ridicule—before other persons especially. And few can cordially join in a laugh that is raised against themselves.

The slightest jest on the personal defects of those you are conversing with, is an enormity of rudeness and vulgarity. It is, in fact, a sneer at the Creator that made them so. No human creature is accountable for being too small, or too large; for an ill-formed figure, or for ill-shaped limbs; for irregular features, or a bad complexion.

Still worse, to rally any person (especially a woman) on her age, or to ask indirect questions with a view of discovering what her age really is. If we continue to live, we must continue to grow old. We must either advance in age, or we must die. Where then is the shame of surviving our youth? And when youth departs, beauty goes along with it. At least as much beauty as depends on complexion, hair, and teeth. In arriving at middle age, (or a little beyond it,) a lady must compound for the loss of either face or figure. About that period she generally becomes thinner, or fatter. If thin, her features shrink, and her skin shrivels and fades; even though she retains a slender and perhaps a girlish form. If she grows fat, her skin may continue smooth, and her complexion fine, and her neck and arms may be rounder and handsomer than in girlhood; but then symmetry of shape will cease—and she must reconcile herself to the change as best she can. But a woman with a good mind, a good heart, and a good temper, can never at any age grow ugly—for an intelligent and pleasant expression is in itself beauty, and the best sort of beauty.

Sad indeed is the condition of women in the decline of life when "No lights of age adorn them." When, having neglected in the spring and summer to lay up any stores for the winter that is sure to come, they find themselves left in the season of desolation with nothing to fall back upon—no pleasant recollections of the acquisition of knowledge or the performance of good deeds, and nothing to talk about but the idle gossip of the day—striving painfully to look younger than they really are; still haunting balls and parties, and enduring all the discomforts of crowded watering-places, long after all pleasure in such scenes must have passed away. But then they must linger in public because they are miserable at home, having no resources within themselves, and few enduring friends to enliven them with their society.

The woman that knows how to grow old gracefully, will adapt her dress to her figure and her age, and wear colours that suit her present complexion. If her neck and arms are thin, she will not expose them under any circumstances. If her hair is grey, she will not decorate it with flowers and flimsy ribbons. If her cheeks are hollow, she will not make her face look still longer and thinner by shadowing it with long ringlets; and setting her head-dress far back—but she will give it as much softness as she can, by a light cap-border tied under her chin. She will not squeeze herself out of all human shape by affecting a long tight *corsage;* and she will wear no dresses glaring with huge flowers, or loaded with gaudy trimmings. She will allude to her age as a thing of course; she will speak without hesitation of former times, though the recollection proves her to be really old. She will be kind and indulgent to the young; and the young will respect and love her, and gladly assemble near her chair, and be amused and unconsciously instructed. As long as she lives and retains her faculties she will endeavour to improve, and to become still a wiser and a better woman; never excusing herself by indolently and obstinately averring that "she is too old to learn," or that she cannot give up her old-fashioned habits. If she finds that those habits are unwarrantable, or that they are annoying to her friends, she ought to relinquish them. No one with a mind unimpaired, and a heart still fresh, is too old to learn.

This book is addressed chiefly to the young; but we shall be much gratified by finding that even old ladies have found in it some advantageous suggestions on points that had hitherto escaped their notice.

THE END.

American Women: Images and Realities

An Arno Press Collection

[Adams, Charles F., editor]. **Correspondence between John Adams and Mercy Warren Relating to Her "History of the American Revolution," July-August, 1807.** With a new appendix of specimen pages from the **"History."** 1878.

[Arling], Emanie Sachs. **"The Terrible Siren": Victoria Woodhull, (1838-1927).** 1928.

Beard, Mary Ritter. **Woman's Work in Municipalities.** 1915.

Blanc, Madame [Marie Therese de Solms]. **The Condition of Woman in the United States.** 1895.

Bradford, Gamaliel. **Wives.** 1925.

Branagan, Thomas. **The Excellency of the Female Character Vindicated.** 1808.

Breckinridge, Sophonisba P. **Women in the Twentieth Century.** 1933.

Campbell, Helen. **Women Wage-Earners.** 1893.

Coolidge, Mary Roberts. **Why Women Are So.** 1912.

Dall, Caroline H. **The College, the Market, and the Court.** 1867.

[D'Arusmont], Frances Wright. **Life, Letters and Lectures: 1834, 1844.** 1972.

Davis, Almond H. **The Female Preacher, or Memoir of Salome Lincoln.** 1843.

Ellington, George. **The Women of New York.** 1869.

Farnham, Eliza W[oodson]. **Life in Prairie Land.** 1846.

Gage, Matilda Joslyn. **Woman, Church and State.** [1900].

Gilman, Charlotte Perkins. **The Living of Charlotte Perkins Gilman.** 1935.

Groves, Ernest R. **The American Woman.** 1944.

Hale, [Sarah J .] **Manners; or, Happy Homes and Good Society All the Year Round.** 1868.

Higginson, Thomas Wentworth. **Women and the Alphabet.** 1900.

Howe, Julia Ward, editor. **Sex and Education.** 1874.

La Follette, Suzanne. **Concerning Women.** 1926.

Leslie, Eliza . **Miss Leslie's Behaviour Book: A Guide and Manual for Ladies.** 1859.

Livermore, Mary A. **My Story of the War.** 1889.

Logan, Mrs. John A. (Mary S.) **The Part Taken By Women in American History.** 1912.

McGuire, Judith W. (A Lady of Virginia). **Diary of a Southern Refugee, During the War.** 1867.

Mann, Herman . **The Female Review: Life of Deborah Sampson.** 1866.

Meyer, Annie Nathan, editor.**Woman's Work in America.** 1891.

Myerson, Abraham. **The Nervous Housewife.** 1927.

Parsons, Elsie Clews. **The Old-Fashioned Woman.** 1913.

Porter, Sarah Harvey. **The Life and Times of Anne Royall.** 1909.

Pruette, Lorine. **Women and Leisure: A Study of Social Waste.** 1924.

Salmon, Lucy Maynard. **Domestic Service.** 1897.

Sanger, William W. **The History of Prostitution.** 1859.

Smith, Julia E. **Abby Smith and Her Cows.** 1877.

Spencer, Anna Garlin. **Woman's Share in Social Culture.** 1913.

Sprague, William Forrest. **Women and the West.** 1940.

Stanton, Elizabeth Cady. **The Woman's Bible** Parts I and II. 1895/1898.

Stewart, Mrs. Eliza Daniel . **Memories of the Crusade.** 1889.

Todd, John. **Woman's Rights.** 1867. [Dodge, Mary A .] (Gail Hamilton, pseud.) **Woman's Wrongs.** 1868.

Van Rensselaer, Mrs. John King. **The Goede Vrouw of Mana-ha-ta.** 1898.

Velazquez, Loreta Janeta. **The Woman in Battle.** 1876.

Vietor, Agnes C., editor. **A Woman's Quest: The Life of Marie E. Zakrzewska, M.D.** 1924.

Woodbury , Helen L. Sum n er. **Equal Suffrage.** 1909.

Young, Ann Eliza. **Wife No. 19.** 1875.